The New Woman in Alabama

The New Woman in Alabama

Social Reforms and Suffrage, 1890–1920

Mary Martha Thomas

THE UNIVERSITY OF ALABAMA PRESS

Tuscaloosa

The University of Alabama Press
Tuscaloosa, Alabama 35487-0380
uapress.ua.edu

Hardcover edition published 1992.
Paperback edition published 2020.
eBook edition published 2020.

Designed by Paula C. Dennis

Paperback ISBN: 978-0-8173-6010-8
E-ISBN: 978-0-8173-9353-3

A previous edition of this book has been cataloged by the Library of Congress.
ISBN: 978-0-8173-0564-2 (cloth)

CONTENTS

PREFACE

riginally my interest in Alabama women of the Progressive period centered on the suffrage drive. Scholars have investigated and written extensively on the national movement, but little has been written on the South and even less on the Alabama movement. As a result the existing knowledge is skewed toward national figures and northeastern activism. I felt that new information from Alabama and the South would complement our understanding of the overall movement.

As my research progressed, I became aware that virtually all suffrage histories treat the drive as an institutional reform entirely within the context of political history. My aim became to write a comprehensive history of the suffrage drive in Alabama that would reflect women's lives and the larger society in which they lived. I wanted, in short, to write the history of the suffrage movement within a feminist framework.

Moreover, as I investigated the activities of Alabama women, I became increasingly aware that suffrage was only one among many issues that interested the women of the state. They were also concerned with the abolition of child labor, the problems of poverty in an industrial community, the creation of reform schools for juvenile offenders, the improvement of the public schools, and a host of other reforms tackled by both black and white women.

Hence, as the work evolved, I found myself investigating the activities of the Alabama Woman's Christian Temperance Union, the Alabama Federation of Women's Clubs, and the Alabama Federation of Colored Women's Clubs as well as the Alabama Equal Suffrage Association. In the end I wrote the story of middle-class women, both black and white, as they moved from their private world of the home to the public world of politics and reform. These women did not fit the role of the mythical Southern Lady who was confined to the private world of the home and the hearth. They were active, articulate, gutsy women who defied convention and played an important role in the history of the state. They are also a group of women for whom I have the greatest admiration.

In the course of my research and writing, I have become indebted to librarians, archivists, colleagues, friends, and family. The original research was funded in part by generous grants from Jacksonville State University's newly established Faculty Research Program. The unsung heroes and heroines of most research projects are the librarians and archivists who assist scholars in their research. I wish especially to commend the staffs of the Alabama Department of Archives and History, the Birmingham Public Library, Tuskegee University, Jacksonville State University, The University of Alabama, Auburn University, the University of North Carolina, the Library of Congress, and the Schlesinger Library of Radcliffe College. I am especially indebted to Anne Johnson of Jacksonville State University, Wayne Flynt of Auburn University, and Betty Brandon of the University of South Alabama, who reviewed the manuscript and offered positive suggestions. No author could have asked for a better publisher than Malcolm M. MacDonald and the staff at The University of Alabama Press.

The New Woman in Alabama

1 INTRODUCTION

During the decade of the 1890s, the women of Alabama created a large number of clubs and organizations that took them out of the home and provided them with a role in the public sphere. These women began to erase the line between the public and private world as they tried to ameliorate the problems posed by rapid industrialization. Martha L. Spencer, as president of the Alabama Woman's Christian Temperance Union (WCTU), asked who was responsible for addressing the problems of poverty in an urban industrial community, while Elizabeth Johnston Evans Johnston of the Alabama Federation of Women's Clubs (AFWC) undertook to eradicate juvenile delinquency and to improve the treatment of juvenile offenders. Kate Hutcheson Morrissette, another member of the AFWC, led the drive to decrease illiteracy and reform the public school system, and Margaret Murray Washington worked in the black community to improve homes and schools in order to bring about the advancement of all African Americans. Nellie Kimball Murdock, as chair of the Alabama Child Labor Committee, spearheaded the movement to abolish child labor, while Pattie Ruffner Jacobs created the Alabama Equal Suffrage Association (AESA) to fight for the right of women to vote so that these other problems would be resolved. These middle-class white and black women, seeking validation for their roles as homemakers and mothers, demanded a hearing in the political arena for issues that affected them and their families. These women were the New Women of the New South.

Such women were the products of the vast changes under way in American society in the 1890s due to increased industrialization and growing urbanization. During the nineteenth century the separate spheres ideology had been dominant, but by the end of the decade these beliefs were breaking down. According to this ideology, women were restricted to the private sphere of the home and the hearth, whereas men's sphere was the public world of business and politics. Women participated in society only through their subordinate position as wives and mothers. But by the 1890s under the impact of social and economic changes, the division between the public and private worlds of men and women was beginning to disappear with the result that middle-class white and black women experienced a dramatic expansion of opportunities that took their domestic concerns and values into the public arena. Working-class women also experienced greater autonomy in their lives as employees and participants in the new commercialized leisure of modern urban life. The lives of rural black and white women, however, were still shaped far more by the struggle for survival than by any dramatic increase in options associated with the New Woman.

During the Progressive period of reform from the 1890s to the 1920s, leaders nationwide began to confront the problems raised by rapid industrialization. American women shaped the new order with a profusion of new voluntary associations, institutions, and social movements. The collective power of women reached its apex in a massive push for social reforms and woman suffrage. While male Progressive leaders talked about efficiency, regulation, scientific management, and experts, female Progressives directed their attention toward humanitarian and social reforms—concern for child labor, long hours and low pay in factories, and unhealthy conditions in city neighborhoods. What had long been women's province through voluntary associations and charitable benevolence was increasingly defined as a proper scope for public policy. By pioneering in the creation of new public spaces—voluntary associations located between the public world of politics and work and the private intimacy of family—these women made possible a new vision of active citizenship.

This vision developed within the context of southern progressivism, which can be divided into two distinct categories. One group of reformers, which was largely male, was primarily concerned with the imposition of social controls and state regulation in areas such as commerce, agriculture, race relations, and antimonopolism. A second class of progressive campaigns was dominated by the theme of social justice.[1] These drives were led primarily by women who were strongly committed to decrease human suffering in their communities. Seeing the consequences of industrialization for ordinary people, they became increasingly convinced of the need for social services and developed creative responses to the plight of the disadvantaged. The child labor campaigns brought women into common cause with other reformers, giving them valuable experience in organizing for reform purposes. As a result of these campaigns, women pushed for other needs of children, such as the creation of juvenile courts, the establishment of reform schools, and the improvement of the public schools. Women also participated in organized charity movements, which by the end of the first decade of the twentieth century began to put greater stress on casework, surveys, and organization. These reform movements unfolded more or less simultaneously during the first decades of the twentieth century, with many women participating in several of them.

Middle-class women throughout the nation were able to be active in this wide range of reforms because their lives in urban areas changed dramatically. Technological advances began to free women from some of the hardest toil associated with housekeeping. Such improvements as central heating, electricity, indoor plumbing, and kitchen appliances lightened their chores, as did the availability of store-bought goods and food—commercially baked bread and ready-to-wear clothing. The family was completing a long-term shift from a unit of production to one of consumption. In the agricultural economy of the early nineteenth century, the family had been a unit of production in which almost all family needs were produced at home. But after the advent of industrialization at the end of the century, the family became a unit of consumption where the father was paid a salary that bought the family necessities. The national birth rate declined steadily throughout the nineteenth century, and by 1900 women were having an average of 3.5 children, half the level in 1800.

Since middle-class women were devoting less time to housekeeping and child rearing, they were able to be more active beyond the walls of their homes. One of the most striking characteristics of American society by the 1890s was the proliferation of women's organizations. The key to understanding this development can be found in the way that women extended the values they prized in the family and domestic sphere to the broader body politic—a change that historians have identified as Municipal Housekeeping. Women now clearly meant to utilize their domestic housekeeping skills in an attack on the worst abuses of an urban, industrial society, since the household now included the marketplace and city hall. Women's special mission in public was to purify, uplift, control, and reform society. This stance proved a powerful tool during the reform activism of the Progressive period, especially in efforts to make the cities more livable environments.

Middle-class women, black and white, had institutional or organizational bodies with which to influence public policy. Although they were excluded from positions of political power, women compensated by activity in their various organizations. Beginning with the temperance societies, then followed by the women's club movement, women strove to fuse politics with their domestic ideals. Such an ideology also fostered the creation and development of suffrage associations. It was due to the efforts of women that governments increasingly took responsibility for improving the social welfare of citizens. By the early twentieth century, women's activities made clear the fundamental erosion of the old separation of the public and private spheres. Women's sphere was visibly expanded as a result of these single-sex associations, which were used by women to penetrate public affairs. Women moved steadily from the domestic sphere into the public sphere, changing both in the process.

The New Women of Alabama followed in the footsteps of women

nationwide. Women of the state established a wide variety of organizations and clubs during the 1880s and 1890s. The first of these was a series
of local temperance unions that joined together in 1884 at Tuscaloosa
to create the Alabama Woman's Christian Temperance Union. Women
were attracted to temperance because alcohol was seen as a basic factor
in the disruption and corruption of family life. The WCTU was closely
associated with the Protestant churches, which made it a respectable
organization with which to be associated. The Alabama WCTU worked
not only for prohibition, but also for several other issues, such as the abolition of child labor, the improvement of conditions in jails and prisons,
and the establishment of homes for abandoned women and children. By
the turn of the century, unions, which had been established first in small
towns and rural areas, had spread to the large cities. Both black and
white women supported the temperance cause. The WCTU educated
many home-bound, rural, and small-town women to a sense of social
responsibility. The organization provided a training ground for female
leaders to become speakers and writers, many of whom later moved on
to other reform causes, including woman suffrage.[2]

The largest women's organization in the state was the Alabama Federation of Women's Clubs, which was created in 1895 by literary clubs
from five towns. These clubs began in the cities and spread to the smaller
communities; by the turn of the century, virtually every community
had one or more women's clubs. Club women were interested in a wide
variety of civic and community issues. They worked for the elimination
of child labor. They supported an eight-hour day and a minimum wage
for women, a mother's compensation act, and the concept of equal pay
for equal work. They sought to improve the educational system of the
state by making school attendance compulsory, by attacking illiteracy,
by placing women on school boards, and by introducing kindergartens,
manual training, and domestic science into the school system. They
worked to secure a women's dormitory at the University of Alabama.
They were instrumental in establishing industrial reform schools for
both boys and girls. They became the municipal housekeepers of the
Progressive Era who wanted to transform the state by creating a new
understanding of what responsible government should provide.[3]

Excluded from the white women's clubs, black women established their own clubs as early as 1890. Several of these early clubs then united and created the Alabama Federation of Colored Women's Clubs in 1899. These women established a settlement school for women and children, created a reform school for black boys, visited the jails and prisons, and formed mothers' clubs. They were able to initiate long-lasting educational and social service programs for poor and uneducated blacks. In addition to these interests, black women always placed a strong emphasis on pride of race, on the defense of the black community and home, and on race advancement. Black women demonstrated that they had the motivations and skills to contribute to the improvement of conditions within the black community. The club motto was Lifting as We Climb.[4]

Woman suffrage was also an item on the progressive agenda. The southern suffrage movement falls into two broad periods. The first is the decade of the 1890s during which suffrage leaders hoped women might be given the vote to help maintain white supremacy. These hopes were not fulfilled when southern legislatures rejected the idea of women voting, and as a result, the suffrage associations ceased to exist by the early years of the twentieth century. For nearly a decade, suffrage activity lay dormant in the South. The second period began about 1910 when new associations were created and lasted until suffrage was won in 1920. In this period the Progressive movement with its many reforms fueled the suffrage movement and shaped the strategy of the suffragists.[5]

In Alabama the suffrage drive followed the pattern of other southern states. The first period dated from 1892 until the turn of the century. During this time suffrage leaders created small and relatively weak organizations with encouragement from the National American Woman Suffrage Association (NAWSA). Since southern legislatures were searching for methods to disfranchise the blacks, NAWSA hoped to use the votes of white women to achieve that end. The Alabama Constitutional Convention of 1901 actually considered enfranchising women, but the proposal found little support. Despite this racist approach to suffrage, black women also supported the movement, primarily through their women's clubs. They had no separate suffrage organizations.[6]

With the second period in Alabama, from 1910 to 1917, strong and active organizations were created in Selma in 1910, Birmingham in 1911, and subsequently in other communities. These groups then formed a state organization that affiliated with NAWSA in 1912. The reform impulse of a child labor conference in Birmingham in 1911 motivated this phase of the suffrage drive. At that time women reformers realized that they would never be able to regulate child labor until they had the vote. The major goal of this period was to persuade the state legislature of 1915 to enfranchise women by an amendment to the state constitution. Despite the organizational ability of women such as Pattie Ruffner Jacobs, the proposal was defeated. After this defeat, the Alabama Equal Suffrage Association experienced a brief period of growth, which was cut short by the entry of the United States into World War I in 1917. The suffrage associations virtually suspended their work until the war was over in November 1918.

In addition to the two surges of activity typical of the South, Alabama can be said to have had a third period during the spring and summer of 1919, when the legislature considered the Nineteenth Amendment, which had by then been passed by Congress. NAWSA classed Alabama as a "hopeless" state, but the state leaders waged a strong battle anyway. By this time the opposition had organized and both groups lobbied the legislators. The argument turned on the race issue and the threat of federal control of the state's elections. Despite the efforts of the suffrage leaders, Alabama rejected the Nineteenth Amendment.[7]

The white women reformers and suffrage leaders came largely from Birmingham because it was here that the social dislocations that accompanied industrialization existed. Birmingham, as a city of the New South with its iron and steel industry, its railroads, and its rapidly expanding population, experienced the problems of urban poverty and social injustice more acutely than other less industrialized areas did. Black women reformers were centered largely in Tuskegee, where most educated, middle-class black women lived and worked at Booker T. Washington's newly established institute. It was from here that black women spearheaded the drive to uplift their race. Despite the similarity of interests of black and white women, these two groups never worked together but were always segregated, with each tackling the problems of its own race. Even by the 1920s, when women of both races began to work together in interracial committees in other states, there is little evidence that such cooperation took place in Alabama. The typical woman reformer, both black and white, was a married woman with children, not a single woman like Jane Addams, who personified the movement on the national level. These women usually did not confine their activities to just one reform, but instead worked in a variety of areas. The same women who were members of the WCTU were also active in the women's clubs and sometimes in the suffrage drive as well. Black women tended to have only one organization, their women's clubs, which tackled reform programs in all areas.

During this period Alabama women learned the art of politics. They perfected the technique of lobbying their legislators, filling the gallery with advocates for the various measures they were supporting. At first women were hesitant to push their programs and would not dare to testify before a legislative committee. For example, in 1899 when Elizabeth Johnston Evans Johnston wanted the state to provide money for a boys' industrial school, she had no idea how to approach the legislature; the only action she took was to speak privately with the governor. And in 1901 when club women adopted as their goal the improvement of the schools, they only wrote letters or sent petitions to the legislators, efforts which were either ignored or lost. But by 1915 women had become bolder and summoned up their courage to deal with the legislators directly. During this session women of the WCTU were on hand to lobby for prohibition; the Alabama Child Labor Committee and the Alabama Federation of Women's Clubs supported a stronger child labor law; club women also supported substantial improvements in the educational system; and the Alabama Equal Suffrage Association was pushing for an amendment to the state constitution to allow women to vote. Women from one group or another were in the capitol building in Montgomery lobbying for their favorite causes and filling the halls and gallery. At first male legislators did not know how to respond to women who were so aggressive about their causes and who engaged in activities thought unsuitable for a lady, but the men, too, learned to cope with this new influence in state politics.

Male and female Progressive leaders had different political agendas. Male Progressives pushed legislation that dealt with industry, agriculture, and commerce, whereas women fought for issues that affected the home and the family. The Alabama legislature usually could find time and money for commercial or agricultural projects, but they expressed little interest in education, abolition of child labor, pensions for widowed mothers, or pure food or sanitation laws until the issues were brought to their attention by women. When the state finally created a child welfare committee in 1919, one club woman commented, "Cow, cotton, corn, and cabbage have had millions spent for their protection, the child's welfare is now going to be considered." Even though they had been excluded from positions of political power, women made their influence felt through their various organizations.

By 1920 Alabama women reformers had reason to be proud of their accomplishments and to be optimistic about the future. With the enactment of the federal amendments providing for prohibition and woman suffrage, the two major reforms for which women organized and worked had been achieved. Organized women had also been successful in securing protective legislation for child labor, educational reforms, prison reforms, and other social welfare measures. The work of these Progressive women was proof that women could be leaders and innovators in society. As a result of these new experiences, traditional gender roles were eroded as women experienced changes in life-style and expectations. At all economic levels women were breaking out of the confines of the home and entering the public arena. Expanding their sphere, they had gone forth from the home to deal with the issues of the day. No longer bound by the ideology of the Southern Lady, these women were ready, able, and willing to participate in public affairs.

2 TEMPERANCE UNIONS, 1882–1915

*T*he first large national organization that Alabama women joined was the Woman's Christian Temperance Union, which was established in Tuscaloosa in 1884. The WCTU was built upon the structure of the Protestant churches, which enabled women to move easily from their earlier work in missionary societies to the temperance unions. However, it took courage for Alabama women to join these early organizations because they were required to take part in activities outside the home and in effect to become social reformers. Even though the WCTU was regarded as a relatively "safe" reform organization because it did not seriously challenge the status quo or the doctrine of the two spheres, women such as Mary T. Jefferies, Martha L. Spencer, and Julia S. Tutwiler were regarded as "advanced" because they supported its goals. But the WCTU enabled these women and others to engage in respectable reforms and at the same time to educate themselves and the public. Through these organizations, Alabama women were socialized and trained for public life—an opportunity that had never existed before. Combining self-help and social mission, they created an avenue to civic affairs, or what the national WCTU president Frances Willard called "the home going forth into the world." The temperance societies, in short, opened new opportunities for southern women and allowed them to have experiences outside the home and church that they had never had before.

The creation of the WCTU, as well as the women's clubs, was made possible by several changes in the position and role of women nationwide. First, American society by the 1870s and 1880s had a large enough body of middle- and upper middle-class women to support such a movement, and these women in turn had sufficient leisure to permit them to devote themselves to organizational work. By the last decades of the century, a clear line had been drawn between the proper sphere of work for poor women and for their middle- and upper-class sisters. Until industrialization, virtually all women contributed to the economic well-being of their families. They were an integral part of the economic production of the family. But after the advent of industrialization, poor women worked in the new factories and middle- and upper-class women were expected to remain at home and care for the family and do the domestic duties. Being able to support a wife in relative leisure became a significant mark of a man's financial success. Thus it was only in the late nineteenth century that child care and homemaking became a full-time job for urban middle-class women.

Moreover, the national birth rate was falling. The average number of children born to a white woman fell from 7.04 in 1800 to 4.24 in 1880 and to 3.56 in 1900. Since women were having fewer children, less time was absorbed by pregnancy and the care of infants and young children, which increased women's leisure time. Falling fertility rates were most pronounced in native-born middle-class white families, especially as women's education levels rose.[1] Black fertility did not decline appreciably until the 1880s.

Increased education was another factor that promoted the growth of women's organizations. There was a marked increase in the number of women exposed to at least a common school education, as well as an increase in the number of college educated women. Hence, an educated clientele existed for a mass movement. These factors, combined with the urbanization and industrialization of the late nineteenth century, all contributed to creating social and economic patterns that made a mass movement of women possible.[2]

The Woman's Christian Temperance Union, formed in 1873 in Chicago, was first led by Annie Wittenmyer. The organization achieved national prominence under the leadership of Frances Willard, who was the president from 1879 until her death in 1898. Temperance became the issue that attracted tens of thousands of women to women's and reformist causes. Compared to those associated with other women's organizations, women joined the WCTU in far greater numbers. In 1892 the WCTU had well over 200,000 dues-paying members, while 20,000 women were affiliated with the General Federation of Women's Clubs, and the National American Woman Suffrage Association had only about 13,000 members. The WCTU was the largest organization of women that had existed until that time; the size and influence of other women's groups were not comparable. Why did women flock to the temperance cause in such impressive numbers? The answer requires an explanation of how women perceived temperance.[3]

Temperance was seen as a woman's issue because drink presented a threat to the home. Serious drinking was considered a male prerogative and the saloon was a male institution. Women saw the saloon as a pervasive and pernicious influence on their lives. A drunken husband could easily be a wife beater, a child abuser, and an irresponsible provider for his family. Since women had few legal rights, a husband could drink up not only his pay, but anything his wife might earn as well. As late as 1900 in thirty-seven states, a woman possessed no rights to her children and all her possessions were her husband's property.

Temperance was also congenial with the dominant sexual ideology, the doctrine of the two spheres. Men functioned in the world of politics and commerce; women presided over the spiritual and physical maintenance of home and family. Woman, as the protector of the home and nurturer of children, had a compelling duty to save these sacred trusts from external threats. Willard used the phrase "Home Protection" as a description of the activities of the WCTU. It was a masterstroke of public relations, which made it easy for both men and women to accept the activities of the union. Women who joined identified specific grievances from which women suffered and tried to do something about them. They did not argue, at least at first, for women's rights as such. They were believers in "true womanhood," but they did eventually push for widening spheres. The WCTU consciously used the doctrine of domesticity to move women into public life.[4] Historian Anne Scott has written that the WCTU "did more to subvert the traditional role of women, or to implant in its southern members a sort of unself-conscious radicalism which would have turned the conservative southern male speechless if he had taken the trouble to listen to what the ladies were saying."[5]

Another factor that no doubt contributed to the ease with which women flocked to the WCTU was the presence of an already existing network through which women could function in the temperance cause. The missionary societies and the churches of the several Protestant denominations provided already functioning female networks that could easily be converted into WCTU chapters. The WCTU was church-oriented and almost all of its members were churchgoing. In its early days, the WCTU was primarily an evangelical movement devoted to moral persuasion. But under Willard's leadership, legislative goals became more important. Eventually the WCTU supported suffrage and attacked a multitude of social problems. The spectrum of the organization's concerns significantly widened, reflecting the growing conviction that drunkenness was a result of environment as well as a cause of misery. By the late 1880s the WCTU promoted prison reform, special facilities for women offenders, the eight-hour working day, facilities for dependent and neglected children, the kindergarten movement, child care for working mothers, federal aid to education, and vocational training for women. In its early years the WCTU viewed drink as a main cause of poverty. It was drawn into wider concerns because of its initial commitment to fighting alcohol abuse, but by the late 1880s the WCTU was beginning to see poverty as the cause rather than the result of drinking.[6]

Unions were created in Alabama as a result of the southern trip of Frances Willard in 1881. Until then the South was relatively unorganized; it lagged nearly a decade behind the rest of the country. One southern woman observed that the "prejudices of the Southern people are all against women doing anything in public, and especially opposed to the Woman's Temperance Crusade. Particularly is this true of our ministers. They quote St. Paul, and tell us we are wonderfully out of our places." Yet on her southern trip, Willard was well received. Few people who heard her had ever listened to a woman speak in public before. The *Montgomery Advertiser and Mail* reported, "Her manner is easy, her language chaste," and added that her address "was one continued flow of eloquence and learning, and engaged the most attention from first to last."[7]

When the women of Gadsden created the first union in 1882, they felt that the saloon, which "was destroying their homes and bringing so much sorrow into their families," should be banished from their midst.[8] This new society immediately caught the imagination of other women in the state because additional unions were shortly organized in Tuscaloosa, Attalla, Collinsville, Ft. Payne, and Talladega. The WCTU began in small towns and spread slowly to the cities; Montgomery, for example, did not have a union until 1906, when prohibition had become a political issue.[9] Prohibition always found more support in the small towns and rural areas than in the cities. The more exclusive women's clubs, on the other hand, were first created in the cities and spread slowly to the smaller towns.

These Alabama unions assembled delegates in Tuscaloosa in January 1884 to establish a state union, which then affiliated with the national WCTU. The purpose as stated at the first convention was to create a "union of the moral and Christian women of all communities and churches, for the purpose of educating the young, forming a better public sentiment, reforming the drinking classes and removing the dram-shops from our state by law." A pledge of total abstinence and dues of fifty cents were required by the constitution adopted at this meeting. The members pledged themselves to support prohibitory measures to abolish the liquor traffic and to engage in active effort to organize new unions throughout the state. The number of auxiliaries grew rapidly. At the second meeting of the state convention held in Selma in November 1884, twenty-four auxiliaries with a membership of 550 were reported.[10]

This rapid growth did not continue, however. The organization struggled to organize unions and maintain members during the late

1880s and 1890s, even under the capable leadership of Ellen Clarkson Bryce of Tuscaloosa and Martha L. Spencer of Birmingham. The state union seldom sent delegates to the national conventions and the corresponding secretary wrote discouraging annual reports. The women of the state were fearful that the national WCTU was too "advanced" for them. Even at the organizational meeting in 1884, some of the women wanted to call their organization simply the Woman's Home Union and to take as their motto "The home is the woman's sphere." The national organizer who had been sent to create an Alabama union had to assure the convention that each state could manage its own work and that state WCTUs were not required to adopt what were regarded as the advanced views of the national organization.[11]

Since the idea of women speaking in public was not widely accepted, Alabama women were a little afraid of women lecturers coming among them. But after the national WCTU sent several to the state, the women of the state came to the conclusion that "a woman may speak out in public without seeming to be out of her sphere." In 1894 the corresponding secretary stated that the "work done in the state has not been what she could desire, because the women have not been allowed to take active part in church work, consequently [are] not trained in public work."[12] For many southern women the WCTU was their first activity outside the home, but even this work was seen as inappropriate by many.

The organization began to grow when prohibition became the major political issue of the day after the turn of the century. In 1903 the WCTU began publication of a newspaper, the *Alabama White Ribbon,* which was a regular medium of communication between unions and ensured better and more systematic work. In 1904 there were thirty-four auxiliaries with a membership of 619, but this number dramatically increased until by 1915, when statewide prohibition was adopted, there were over one hundred unions with a total membership of nearly 1,200.[13]

Men were allowed to become honorary members if they paid the annual dues of fifty cents, but they could not vote, hold office, or participate in debates. The exclusion of men was most important for the development of the women themselves. Because males were banned from voting membership, they never became competitors for leadership roles.

No other existing organization provided women with a similar forum. The suffrage movement was led by women, but it could scarcely be called a mass organization. Women had developed their own missionary societies, but they did not exercise complete control over the Woman's Board of Missions until much later. As a result, the WCTU became the major outlet for the women's movement in the late nineteenth century.[14]

The Alabama WCTU embarked on an ambitious program as early as the first convention in 1884. The major thrust of the work was educational. The union aimed to teach the detrimental effects of alcohol and the principles of temperance to the Sunday schools, the public schools, and the general public. It encouraged observing Temperance Day, distributing literature, holding medal and essay contests, signing temperance pledges, and attending rallies and speeches. It proposed that the churches use unfermented wine at communion services. It opposed the use of alcohol as a medicine and sought to educate the public to the dangers of patent medicines. It also tried to educate the public concerning the danger of tobacco, opium, and other narcotics. By 1915 the WCTU had broadened its work to include opposition to child labor, establishment of industrial training programs for both boys and girls, and creation of juvenile courts. WCTU members visited the inmates in the jails and prisons, bringing them the temperance gospel and working for better conditions and treatment. They worked to secure the employment of policewomen and for the establishment of a women's reformatory. Their Travelers' Aid workers offered protection to traveling women and children. They established homes where friendless women and children could find refuge. They tried to rescue "fallen" women. They carried their temperance message to black people, the foreign-born, railroad employees, and lumbermen. They encouraged their members to wear their white ribbons, the badge of the WCTU, and to "Agitate! Educate! Organize!" These activities made the WCTU the major reform organization in the state. In 1900 Mary T. Jefferies of Birmingham, who was state president, observed, "The W.C.T.U. is favorably looked upon by the thinking people of the state, its influence being often solicited for movements which are for the betterment of conditions."[15]

This wide and varied program was similar to the breathtaking sweep of the concerns of the national union. Frances Willard's motto was Do Everything. The WCTU of the 1870s had concerned itself primarily with temperance and temperance-related issues. But by the 1880s and 1890s it added most of the social problems of the day to the list of issues it embraced. Do Everything also moved the WCTU into legislative halls where it lobbied for institutional change, and in this sense Do Everything was a program of social reform. The union's attention to improving prisons and reformations, its work with and for indigent children, its concern for working women, and its attention to public health were all designed to find solutions to problems created by growing cities and a developing economy.[16]

Part of the union's appeal in the closing decades of the nineteenth century was the wide scope of its program. The WCTU offered some way for almost every woman to relate to the movement. It helped make possible the WCTU's impressive numerical growth and thereby its importance as a vehicle for the women's movement. Do Everything made the union strong and gave it depth. James B. Sellers, writing of the Alabama WCTU, saw its eclectic program as a lack of strength. He insisted, "The scattering of energy implied in this wide and varied program was undeniably a source of weakness. With a fine lack of discrimination the ladies took up arms against everything they considered untrue, unjust, and unchristian."[17] Other historians have been equally critical, but if numbers point to success, the national WCTU was more successful in the late nineteenth century when it tackled the nation's problems than later when it reverted to a single-minded temperance stance.

Do Everything was operationally possible because of the large measure of organizational local autonomy that the WCTU constitution provided from the beginning. Aside from a commitment to teetotaling temperance and a willingness to pay nominal national dues, each local union could decide for itself which aspects of the program it wished to pursue. The major proposal of the national union to which Alabamians objected was the WCTU's 1881 endorsement of woman suffrage. In fact, this endorsement was a major obstacle to organizing unions in the state. The corresponding secretary wrote in 1890: "You can not realize how that phase of W.C.T.U. meets us at every turn. It is the point of opposition when we solicit members or assistance." [18] The attitude of Alabama women to suffrage was made clear at the 1885 convention. Several men attended the convention, including a prominent newspaper editor who told the women that they needed to "demand the ballot, and with it they can destroy whisky, and by no other agency." The women were astounded by such a proposal because woman suffrage was viewed as highly radical. If a thunderbolt had fallen it could not have created a greater sensation. "The ladies at first grew indignant and uttered protestations." When they grew calmer, they thanked the editor for "his kindly and progressive suggestions, but in their opinion, they are not ready to ask any political favors." [19] The *Alabama White Ribbon* of December 1904 emphasized the point that even though the national WCTU supported woman suffrage, the Alabama WCTU did not. The paper maintained that the battle in the state was being waged for temperance, prison reform, mission work, charity, and Sunday school work. Later, votes for women ceased to be so shocking because by 1914 the Alabama WCTU endorsed suffrage.

The national WCTU organized "colored" unions in several southern states during the 1880s, after Reconstruction but before more stringent segregation laws were adopted in the 1890s. Because of this fortunate timing, the WCTU was never an exclusively all-white organization. Southern black and white women were never members of the same local, but black women created their own unions alongside white women. In the 1880s black and white southern local unions were affiliated with the same state and national bodies and were addressed by the same missionary speakers. Willard was heard by audiences of both races on her southern tour. Although this degree of oneness seems surprising, it must be remembered that only relatively radical and emancipated southern white women were affiliated with the union in the 1880s, when most southerners, male and female, still found participation in public affairs by women distasteful, if not shocking. However, the WCTU's racial policy became equivocal in the 1890s as growing Jim Crowism had its effects on the organization. The WCTU Department of Colored Work was allowed to lapse in 1890 because it was poorly supported financially; however, it was shortly revived.[20]

The white women of the Alabama WCTU created the Department of Colored Work in 1884 in order to work among the blacks. White temperance leaders felt that the African Americans, with their "crude religious ideas and limited educational facilities," were ready victims for the liquor men. White women saw whiskey as the greatest enemy of the blacks, a situation to which they felt whites could not be indifferent. In 1884 the president of the Alabama WCTU observed, "They [black men] are voters, they help form our laws, and if ignorance must use the ballot box, let it be in sober ignorance." Indeed, much of the prohibition argument centered on "the negro phase of the liquor question," in which prohibition was viewed as an effective means of controlling and eliminating the allegedly unreliable and menacing behavior of blacks.[21]

Despite this racist element in the prohibition movement, Alabama black women supported the temperance movement as well as white women did and usually for the same reasons. African-American women desired to protect their homes and families from drunken, abusive husbands who deprived their families of necessities by wasting money in the saloons. They created a "colored state union" as early as 1886 at a convention in Selma. At that time there were three unions that had a membership of 285, which by the next year had increased to six unions with 324 members. They created only four departments in which to carry out their work but they contributed $32.40 to the national WCTU in 1887, which was more than the white unions gave. The president, Mrs. C. C. Boothe, wrote that "we are with you in the battle against alcohol and I long to see the day when the colored mother, as well as the white mother, can shake hands and rejoice over glorious victories won for temperance." Helen M. Andrews, who worked with the students of Talladega College, said that temperance was the "only hope of the colored people" and that her students needed to learn the effects of alcohol and to let it alone.[22]

Despite this hopeful beginning, the Alabama No. 2 Unions, as the black unions were called, did not thrive. By 1890 they ceased to send in reports and neither the national nor the state WCTU knew where to get information. In 1896 the national superintendent for the Department of Colored Work, Lucy Thurman, attempted to organize black Alabama women again. She met with success in Montgomery and especially in Tuskegee, where she found "an army of men and women numbering 1000" who wanted to sow the seeds of "temperance and purity." Encouraged by this situation, later that year Frances Willard and Frances A. Griffin of Wetumpka (who worked for the national WCTU at this time, but later led the Alabama suffrage association) visited Tuskegee and were impressed with the leadership ability of Margaret Murray Washington, wife of Booker T. Washington. Willard and Griffin spoke at the meetings of mothers' clubs, which had been organized by Margaret Washington to teach African-American women the practical aspects of maintaining a home and family. They realized that Washington was the one to lead the temperance movement in Alabama among black women.[23]

Despite Washington's interest in temperance, she decided to use her energy and resources to organize the Alabama Federation of Colored Women's Clubs, which she did in 1899. Thurman said of Washington: "She is full of zeal for the work, but is a woman with many cares." In 1900 the Federated women adopted a resolution at their annual convention recommending the work of the WCTU and advising their members to start branch organizations in cities where temperance work had been neglected. Temperance work among black women then was carried on largely by the women's clubs. Separate unions for black women were few in number and limited in their activity. In 1903 Alabama No. 2 Union experienced a brief revival led by Mrs. J. R. England of Birmingham, but it did not turn out to be long lasting. Since there were relatively few middle-class black women to provide leadership for organizations, they had to spread their abilities and energies over a wide variety of projects. Black women chose to concentrate their efforts on their women's clubs, in which they literally tried to do everything.[24]

A major goal of the WCTU at both the national and state level was the promotion of temperance education in Sunday schools. This program received early support in Alabama when the Baptist State Convention of 1885 endorsed it. In March 1887 the first temperance lessons appeared in the quarterlies of the Southern Baptist church. The General Conference of the Methodist Church endorsed temperance lessons in 1880 and the Methodist Church, South, followed suit in 1886 with a recommendation that the Sunday School editor provide an occasional lesson on temperance. In 1885 the North Alabama Conference resolved "that we will teach temperance from the pulpit, in the Sunday-school, and from house to house until public opinion is properly educated." As a result some 50,700 boys and girls had education in temperance by 1887. The Presbyterian church was less inclined to adopt temperance lessons, but by 1893 it began to have occasional lessons.[25]

The WCTU was also interested in promoting temperance lessons in the public schools of the state. The union created loyal temperance legions, bands of hope, and kindergarten schools to reach those not in church schools. They also held declamation contests with medals for the winners, who spoke on the bad effects of intoxicating liquors. These were viewed as effective methods to bring temperance sentiment before the public and to sow the seeds of temperance in the minds of the young speakers. The goal was to have as many as a thousand of these contests in the state, which meant each county would have to hold fifteen. Both gold and silver medals were given as prizes for the best speeches. The titles of some of these young speakers' efforts were "The Two Glasses," "The Converted Rumseller," and "The Old Man's Story."[26]

In 1884 the Alabama WCTU began a campaign to petition the state legislature to require in the public schools scientific teaching on temperance and the evil effects of alcohol on the various organs of the body. The legislature ignored this petition as well as a similar one from the Selma union later in the same year. The next year the lawmakers did put physiology and hygiene on the list of subjects necessary for teacher certification. In 1889 Ellen Clarkson Bryce of Tuscaloosa read a paper on "scientific instruction" to the Alabama Educational Association, which endorsed the measure. Finally in 1891 the legislature was forced to act in response to pressure brought by the WCTU, the churches, and the educational association. At that time, it passed legislation adding instruction on the evil effects of alcohol on the body and mind. The WCTU regarded this action as significant because by 1908 there were in the state 260,000 white children and 127,500 black children being taught the dangers of intemperance.[27]

A large share of local union effort in the early years went into the campaign to banish wine from the communion table. A committee of the national union reported in 1876 that biblical scholarship showed that fermented wine was not condoned by scripture or necessary for the sacraments. The committee argued that the word *wine* was actually a mistranslation that referred to an unfermented grape juice in common use among Jews in the first century, and that the Bible taught total abstinence from alcohol except for medicinal use. The report was adopted by the convention, and the battle against communion wine began. It was most successful. Over the next few years grape juice replaced wine in almost all Methodist, Baptist, and Congregational churches and in some Presbyterian churches, although the change met with much more initial resistance from that denomination. Episcopal, Lutheran, and Catholic churches were unmoved. Some WCTU members even abstained from partaking in the rite of holy communion until their congregations fell into line.[28]

The Alabama union lost no time in tackling this issue. At the time the state WCTU was organized in 1884, Rosa Parker of Gadsden, corresponding secretary, reported that she had "circulated literature on unfermented wine for sacramental purposes" to several churches. Results began to show slowly. In 1886 the local unions in Collinsville and Fort Payne reported that they had distributed literature and had received some encouragement that the local churches would cease using wine. In 1887 Marietta Sibert, the superintendent of the unfermented wine committee, reported that she had written letters to churches across the state and had received assurances from several of them that they were willing to use pure grape juice. She also wrote a letter to the *Alabama Christian Advocate,* the official publication of the Methodist church, requesting that the editor support the use of "unfermented wine at the Lord's table." A resolution to that effect was introduced into the North Alabama Conference of the Methodist Church in 1887. It received the support of several lay people, but failed to pass because of the opposition of Bishop J. C. Keener.[29]

The Collinsville union met with success as a result of their efforts. The local Methodist and Baptist churches, as well as several in the county, adopted the practice of using grape juice. The president of the Collinsville union went so far as to prepare the juice for these churches, since the ministers did not have any other readily available source. However, in Uniontown the women met strong opposition to their program. The local clergy told them not to speak of this work of the WCTU. Despite their work, neither the Methodist conferences nor the Baptist State Convention ever adopted any rules on the subject. However, by 1910 the churches had practically abandoned the use of wine for communion without formal action.[30]

A logical extension of gospel temperance was to visit jails, almshouses, and prisons. Jail visiting, if only to hold a prayer meeting, had the effect of calling women's attention to serious evils in the prison system. Men, women, and children frequently occupied common and squalid prison quarters in the late nineteenth century. Prostitutes, elderly drunks, felons, and young children might share a single cell. Prison work was slowest to move beyond the gospel temperance syndrome in the South. Some southern unions found it difficult to find recruits for prison work because all the women who became superintendents soon found that their husbands disapproved of their visiting prisons.[31]

Prison work attracted the energies of the most prominent women's leader of the state, Julia S. Tutwiler. During most of the thirty-two years she was a member of the WCTU, she was the superintendent of the prison and jail department. Tutwiler was well known primarily as an educator, but she was involved in every reform in the state during her long life. She worked for prohibition in Livingston even before the Alabama WCTU was organized; she worked for prison reform; she supported the drive to abolish child labor; and she was active in the early suffrage drive. Born in Tuscaloosa in 1845, she was the daughter of Henry Tutwiler, who was an early leader in education in Alabama. Julia

JULIA S. TUTWILER WAS PRIMARILY AN EDUCATOR SERVING AS PRESIDENT OF ALABAMA NORMAL COLLEGE IN LIVINGSTON, BUT SHE ALSO WORKED FOR PRISON REFORM, THE ABOLITION OF CHILD LABOR, AND WOMAN SUFFRAGE. *FROM THE COLLECTIONS OF THE BIRMINGHAM PUBLIC LIBRARY.*

was tutored by her father as a child, then attended Vassar briefly, studied in Germany and France, and took courses at Washington and Lee University. She taught first at Tuscaloosa Female College and then at Green Springs School, which her father had established. In 1881 she was made principal of the Livingston Female Academy, which shortly became the Alabama Normal College. Tutwiler was made president, a position she held until her retirement in 1910. She died in 1916.[32]

In the course of her many years with the WCTU prison and jail department, Julia Tutwiler brought about many needed changes in the Alabama prison system. Alabama, like other southern states, used the convict lease system during this time. In 1893 Tutwiler described this system as "one that combines all the evils of slavery with none of its ameliorating features."[33] She was not successful in abolishing the system, but she worked to make life more tolerable for the inmates. She proposed the establishment of night schools for convicts and eventually pressured the legislature to provide funding in 1887. The night schools flourished at the state farm in Springer, at the Pratt mines, and at Coalburg. For several years she traveled by train from Livingston to Birmingham on Friday nights in order to be able to teach during the weekends at the prison camps located in the coal mines outside the city. Tutwiler wrote in 1888 when the school first opened: "I felt repaid for all trouble that Saturday night, when to the sound of our cabinet organ, our pupils in their garb of degradation filed into the clean, bright, comfortable school-room which we had prepared for them. The dull saddened faces, bearing the impress of crime and misery, and the hopeless look of those who feel that they have been forgotten by God and man, visibly brightened as they saw the care and thought extended to them."[34]

The Alabama Board of Prison Inspectors said that in all their years of management of convicts, nothing has been of so much help to them as the school Tutwiler created. The mining company was sufficiently impressed with the benefits that it promised to assume the pay of teachers and the construction of schoolhouses for both races. It was solely through Tutwiler's efforts that the legislature passed a bill in 1880 to provide heat for the jails of the state and to subject them to frequent sanitary inspection. She encouraged the state to provide separate facilities for women prisoners, which became a reality later. She served for many years as the Alabama secretary for the National Society of Charities and Corrections. At an 1893 meeting of the society in Chicago she reported on the major developments in the field of social work and reform in Alabama.[35]

In addition to Tutwiler, another important woman leader who was farsighted enough to try to deal with a major problem of the day was Martha L. Spencer. Who is responsible for relieving the problems of poverty in an urban industrial community? Spencer posed this question to the Birmingham City Council in 1905. She had come to the conclusion that "the men of our city and State are indifferent to this question of the care of the dependent and defective and most of them seem to consider all efforts of this class a kind of woman's 'fad,' instead of an important social obligation."[36] She believed that care of the poor was an important obligation of the state, but if it failed to act, then private organizations would have to provide the necessary services. This Spencer and the WCTU did.

In 1892 the WCTU established the Mercy Home for friendless women and children in Birmingham. The WCTU women had become aware of the homeless mothers and children who were becoming ever present on the streets of the city. Birmingham had experienced tremendous growth during the decade of the 1880s as a result of the recently established iron and steel industry. Birmingham was the Magic City for many of its residents, as speculators opened huge coal mines and built blast furnaces. In 1870 only twenty-two manufacturing establishments employing forty-four people existed in the county. By 1900 there were almost 500 manufacturing establishments employing 7,000 workers. The population of Birmingham increased from 3,000 in 1880 to 26,000 by 1890. But the Magic City proved to be a cruel deception for the many women and children who were not able to gain a foothold in the prosperity of the city.[37]

Several members of the WCTU conceived of the idea of the Mercy Home and set about to raise money for the project. The guiding spirit was the newly elected president, Martha L. Spencer, who served as president of the Board of Managers of the Mercy Home for fifty years, from 1892 until her death in 1942. Other active and prominent WCTU members were Mary T. Jefferies and Nellie K. Murdock, both of whom

THE BOARD OF MANAGERS OF THE MERCY HOME, ABOUT 1898–99. FIRST ROW FROM
LEFT TO RIGHT: MRS. A. B. WHEELER AND NELLIE KIMBALL MURDOCK; SECOND
ROW: MRS. G. L. THOMAS, MRS. T. N. HAMILTON, MARTHA L. SPENCER, MRS. JOHN
WHITE, AND MRS. L. F. STRATTON; THIRD ROW: MRS. WILLIAM REDD, MARY T.
JEFFERIES, MRS. A. N. BALLARD, MRS. A. L. BILLHEIMER, AND DR. DICIA BAKER.
FROM THE COLLECTIONS OF THE BIRMINGHAM PUBLIC LIBRARY.

were from Birmingham and worked in other organizations as well. (Later
Murdock devoted most of her efforts to the child labor movement and
the suffrage drive.) Twelve active members of the WCTU constituted
the board of managers, whose main duty was to raise money to operate the home. The city was divided into carefully selected districts and
women were appointed to solicit their districts for money or useful
articles for the home. The home opened on February 1, 1892, in a five-
room, poorly furnished house.[38]

The Mercy Home was a place of refuge for children and women of all
ages from the city and surrounding territory. To it came victims of tuberculosis who had no families, women who worked and could not care for
their children, children whose parents were in the hospital, pregnant
girls, transients awaiting transportation from the city, orphans, and de-

linquents. Spencer said in her annual report for 1894, "[T]he sick, the helpless and hopeless, the semi-invalid and the aged, all appeal to us, and to each we endeavor to reach out a helping hand." The home began with an annual budget of just under $700. In 1893 it admitted fifty-nine persons and had an average of thirteen people in residence. By 1920 it had a budget of nearly $18,000 and had an average of seventy-five residents during the year. Margaret C. Ramsey, the long-time matron, managed the home with the help of two or three assistants. The adult residents were expected to assist in the work and to care for the children.[39]

The women who were on the board of managers were closely involved with the operation of the home. They met monthly to review the applications of the people who were seeking admission. They knew the residents of the home and were personally acquainted with the circumstances of their lives. They rejoiced in the child successfully adopted or the young girl turned from "a life of shame." They grieved at each death or the failure of former residents whose lives did not lead to Christian morality. In addition to this highly personal attention bestowed upon the residents, the board was responsible for raising the money to operate the home.[40]

Even though the Mercy Home was operated under the auspices of the WCTU, the organization contributed little money to the operation of the home. The core of the Mercy Home's support was a group of private citizens who responded to the solicitations of the board with contributions of money and necessary goods. Merchants and industrialists donated ice, fish, bread, drugs, milk, and coal to the home. Housewives and schoolgirls gave clothes and mended garments. Physicians donated their services to the residents. The Water Works Company provided free water to the home and the Birmingham Telephone Company installed a phone at half the usual rate. The county and the city of Birmingham paid the home to care for indigents, which provided the institution with a small fixed income.[41]

Throughout depressions and wars the home remained open and was even able to expand its facilities. In April 1899 the home moved to larger quarters, and an isolation ward was added in 1905. After the turn of the century, the mission of the home changed. In 1906 it became

THE MERCY HOME AT ELEVENTH AVENUE, NORTH, AND TWENTY-SECOND STREET, 1909, AFTER IT BECAME A CHILDREN'S HOME. *FROM THE COLLECTIONS OF THE BIRMINGHAM PUBLIC LIBRARY.*

almost exclusively a children's home; in 1913 it opened the Mercy Home Industrial School, a state-supported institution owned by the board that offered industrial education for "the white girls in Alabama" between the ages of thirteen and eighteen. Here girls were taught housekeeping, laundry work, and sewing, along with the equivalent of an elementary education.[42]

By 1914, after the home had been operating for twenty-three years, Spencer began to consider some permanent solution to the problem of dependent children. She realized that the work the home did was a stop-gap measure. She asked, "Must we forever be caring for the waste of humanity? May we never get a plan that will more actively engage the causes instead of continually working with effects?" The solutions she proposed were better housing, more schools, industrial training, child labor laws, and juvenile courts.[43] By that time the state of Alabama was beginning to move in that direction. The legislature adopted laws to limit child labor, establish juvenile courts, create industrial training institutions, and provide better funding for its schools. But it was women like Martha Spencer who led the way and showed the state what its responsibilities were. These women were actually acting as social workers, although they would not have recognized themselves as such because the field was only in the process of being developed.

In addition to their long list of ongoing activities, the WCTU worked in the several campaigns waged to bring about statewide prohibition. During the early years of the twentieth century, the hottest political issue in the state was the drive to prohibit alcoholic beverages. It dominated the political life of the state and consumed the energies and attention of the governors and legislators at every regular session and sometimes at the special sessions also. The WCTU initially led the prohibition drive beginning in 1882 with the first union, but the women had met with limited success. However, they had raised the issue and laid groundwork with their stress on temperance education. But in 1904 the leadership of the prohibition drive was taken over by the men of the Anti-Saloon League. This organization was established in the state under the leadership first of the Rev. W. B. Crumpton and, after 1906, of the Rev. Brooks Lawrence with strong support from the evangelical

Protestant churches, Baptists, Methodists, Presbyterians, and Disciples of Christ.

Historians have given little consideration to the question of why and how the women lost the leadership role, but certainly one explanation lies in the difference in motivation of the two groups. Women supported prohibition in order to protect their homes and families from drunken, abusive husbands. Viewing temperance as a woman's issue, they also attacked the saloon as a symbol of male power and influence that if destroyed would give women more control over their lives. The male Anti-Saloon League naturally did not have these motives. To the league, prohibition was an instrument of social control with far-reaching class, gender, and racial implications. It was seen as a means to control undependable blacks and maintain white supremacy; it would ensure a sober and hard-working labor force and discourage the formation of labor unions. It also offered a means of moral reaffirmation of traditional values and the promise of cleaner politics.[44] But probably the most important reason for the transfer of the leadership role was that prohibition became a major political issue in the state, and once this occurred, men were bound to be in a leadership role because they dominated politics. Despite agreement between male and female Progressives on this issue, they were motivated by entirely different reasons.

With the creation of the Anti-Saloon League, the women of the WCTU were denied a decision-making role. The strategy and the timing of the campaigns, the decisions about which candidate to support, the coordination of the various groups, and the lobbying of the legislators were in the hands of the Anti-Saloon League and Brooks Lawrence. But despite this, women played an influential role in the campaigns. An important task of the women during this long battle was to work in the local campaigns getting out the vote of church members and Sunday schools, addressing letters, making posters, and generally doing the office work of a campaign. But beyond this the members of the WCTU developed a new strategy of flocking about the polls pressuring the voters to support prohibition. On election day they served temperance drinks and sandwiches while endeavoring to convince men that a vote against the saloon was a vote for the home. They pinned a white ribbon on every man who said he would support prohibition or, for that matter, on anyone who would accept one. Few men had the courage to refuse. Their effect on men as they entered the polling place is difficult to determine, but women exerted a kind of pressure never used before in Alabama politics. Dressed in white and carrying flowers, women filled the galleries of the house and senate chambers when a prohibition bill was being considered and made their presence felt. The male legislators and voters were not accustomed to seeing women in such public roles. Some felt intimidated by the women, but the presence of the WCTU provided a new and exciting element in the campaign, which may have been more significant than contemporaries realized.

The state of Alabama had experimented with several methods of controlling and regulating the liquor traffic. The oldest method was to charge high license fees, thus reducing the number of liquor dealers. Far from correcting the evils of the liquor traffic, the high license fees aggravated them. The counties came to depend upon the revenue from the licenses to operate the school system and, hence, gave the liquor dealers political power that was difficult to attack. In 1898 the state adopted the dispensary system, which was essentially a state-run liquor store. At first this system was supported by the temperance advocates, because it was widely believed that it would be better than the saloon. After dispensaries were established, however, the WCTU reevaluated them, deciding that they had set back the cause of temperance.[45]

By 1907 the temperance forces were sufficiently strong that they persuaded the legislature to adopt a statewide local option bill. According to the provisions of this act, each county rather than precinct or city would be the unit for local option elections. At the hearing of the bill, seventy-five women of the Montgomery WCTU were present to listen to the discussion. The legislature passed the measure and the newly elected governor, B. B. Comer, signed it in February 1907. Mrs. J. B. Chatfield, president of the newly organized Montgomery WCTU, was present at the capitol during the entire session. She commented, "It was a hard fight. The whiskey men did not give up until the last moment, but our men were brave and true."[46]

Elections were held in county after county with success for the prohibitionists. The total rolled up in landslide proportions. The most hotly contested election was in Birmingham. Jefferson County had the largest population in the state and held a strategic place in the movement for local option. The election was ordered for October 28, 1907, after 25 percent of the voters signed a petition requesting that it be held. The WCTU took the initiative in leading the women in the fight because they had had experience on the firing line. The organization issued a call to the women of the county and created a Women's Central Committee composed of twenty-five of the most prominent women. Mrs. W. C. Sibley was chairman of the central committee; her assistant was Mary T. Jefferies and Annie K. Weisel was the treasurer. They held meetings in every precinct and organized the women for campaign work by creating committees on prayer meetings, petitions, advertising, literature, and finance. The women visited Sunday schools, distributed thousands of pages of literature, and sent 6,000 personal letters to voters. The white ribbon was declared the official badge for the campaign. The prohibitionists had strong opposition from the business and industrial leaders of Birmingham, who opposed the measure for economic reasons. They too had a central committee and were hard at work.[47]

On election day thousands of mothers, daughters, college students, and schoolchildren turned out to parade in the streets of Birmingham. The parade that gathered at Capitol Park at 7:30 in the morning was more than a mile in length. They sang "Jefferson Is Going Dry" to the tune of "Bringing in the Sheaves" and carried banners with slogans that read Down with Booze, Save the Boys, Vote for the Home, Down with the Saloon, Save the Girls, and We Pray for You. Carriages and automobiles decorated with white ribbons moved through the streets with the parade. The city had never seen anything like it. At the four voting places, the women served lunches and coffee to the voters while they pleaded with the men to vote for the protection of their homes. They pinned white bows on coat lapels of converts while they sang "Jefferson's going dry, Jefferson's going dry/Pass along the watchword, Jefferson's going dry." This approach was so new that the male voters were not sure how to respond. One man said, "You may talk about a woman's influence, but I'll tell you that it would take a strong conviction to cast a vote against what the women are fighting for." Some claimed that the women were intimidating them and wore white badges to keep the women from electioneering them. Others threatened to carry the matter to the courts, but the women kept up their vigorous work until the polls closed.[48]

The official returns showed that the prohibitionists had carried the day by a majority of 1,750 votes. But the city of Birmingham had voted 55 percent against prohibition, while the suburbs and rural portions of the county voted 66 percent for it, overcoming the city vote and carrying the county with a 59 percent prohibition majority. On January 1, 1908, Birmingham became—against the will of a majority of its voters—legally dry. The keys to prohibitionist success had been the rural strength in the legislature and the county-unit plan, which included the suburban and rural voters of Jefferson County in the decisive election. Thanksgiving services were held at the churches celebrating the victory. The Rev. Brooks Lawrence gave the credit for the victory to the women.[49]

Successful local option elections gave new courage and boldness to the prohibition forces. They brought pressure upon Governor Comer to include a statewide prohibition law in his call for a special session in 1907. Before the extra session assembled, new local option victories and the surge of public opinion made it a foregone conclusion that the bill the temperance forces were demanding would be brought before the legislature. Strong opposition to this bill came from the citizens of Mobile, who were convinced that such a law would ruin the port traffic, because foreign ships would not come to a port where liquor could not be sold. They also believed that it would ruin the schools of the county because their revenue was derived largely from liquor licenses.[50]

The house adopted a statewide prohibition measure on November 12, and on November 19, when the senate was to consider it, women who both favored and opposed the measure descended upon the capitol. The presence of such a large number of women in the capitol caused one observer to call it "Ladies Day." The number was so great that it was necessary to throw open the senate doors, but even then not all could get inside the chamber. On this occasion a delegation of Mobile women who opposed the measure made the long trip to Montgomery to make their opposition known. Many of them were teachers who came to plead that the liquor money should not be taken away from the schools. The schools even declared a two-day holiday in order for the women to make the trip. They brought with them a petition signed by 5,000 women—women whose signatures had been hastily gathered in a four-hour period. One of these women who came was the daughter of Adm. Raphael Semmes, the hero of the Civil War. They visited every senator to make it clear what the loss of the liquor money would mean to the school system.[51]

The WCTU delegations from Birmingham, Selma, and Montgomery were also present in great numbers. They were wearing white ribbons on which was printed the slogan Prohibition for All Alabama. They arrived two hours before the session was to begin and occupied the front seats of the gallery. When the Mobile delegation came, they were forced to sit in the rear, a fact which they resented. They had hoped to pack the gallery chambers and applaud the wet speakers, but the WCTU heard of the plan and got to the gallery first. The senate adopted the statewide prohibition measure that would be effective on December 31, 1908. As soon as the vote was announced, there was wild cheering in the gallery and in the lobby. Flowers were strewn from the gallery onto the senators on the floor beneath. Many attempts were made to surround the lawmakers, but they were quickly repulsed. Meanwhile, women in the gallery hastily went into the rotunda and there they sang "Praise God from Whom All Blessings Flow." One report said the "calm dignity of the women of Alabama had given place to that which bordered on fanaticism. Some wept, others pleaded and still others uttered invectives against all those among the law-makers" who did not agree with them.[52]

The signing of this bill on November 23, 1907, was carefully staged by the friends of prohibition. The Reverend Lawrence, Speaker A. H. Charmichael, legislative leaders, and WCTU members gathered in a semicircle to watch the governor. For the ceremony Mrs. J. B. Mell, president of the Montgomery WCTU, handed the governor a gold pen. The governor signed his name and wiped the pen on a fresh linen handkerchief that the state president of the WCTU, Mrs. J. B. Chatfield, handed to him.[53] The participation of the women in this ceremony indicated the strong role that they had played in the campaign. Both Lawrence and Crumpton felt that the prohibition forces were indebted to the WCTU for victory.

As it turned out, the local option laws proved difficult to enforce and the courts questioned their constitutionality. The statewide prohibition act was still only a statute, which could be repealed. Both prohibition laws proved too loosely drawn to be enforced effectively, and soon, to the dismay of many citizens, liquor was readily available again in secret, illegal, totally unregulated saloons and locker clubs. In 1909 the Anti-Saloon League made the decision to work for a constitutional amendment prohibiting alcoholic beverages. Again they enlisted the support of the WCTU, the churches, and Sunday schools. Mary T. Jefferies represented the WCTU at the planning sessions. Governor Comer called a special session of the legislature to convene in July 1909 to consider an amendment. He frankly said that the statutory prohibition law was not enforceable, that open defiance of the law was manifest. The legislature adopted an amendment to the constitution prohibiting alcoholic beverages amid the same emotionalism that had been present two years earlier. Men and women crowded the galleries when the vote was taken. Using the pen with which he had signed the statutory prohibition bill earlier, Governor Comer affixed his signature to the constitutional amendment on August 18, 1909. Then turning to the women of the WCTU, he said: "You ladies must get behind this amendment and adopt it. The fight is not yet over. It is only started and we need your efforts." The ladies in turn gave evidence of their goodwill and cooperation; they presented to the chief executive a bouquet of roses with a card of scriptural quotations.[54]

Both sides geared up for the ratification election of the constitutional amendment on November 29, 1909. This time the antiprohibition interests—the liquor dealers and the business and industrial leaders —were better organized. They presented several arguments. First, they maintained that police forces of the state could invade the home if the amendment were ratified. They also felt it unwise to write into fundamental law legislation still in an experimental stage. The amendment would not ensure enforcement of the laws. The Safe and Sane Business-

PROHIBITION PARADES IN BIRMINGHAM SPONSORED BY THE WCTU, 1909.
THESE PARADES WERE HELD THE DAY BEFORE THE VOTE ON THE
CONSTITUTIONAL AMENDMENT. *FROM THE COLLECTIONS OF THE
BIRMINGHAM PUBLIC LIBRARY.*

men League claimed to have the names of 10,000 businessmen who were against the amendment. The pro-amendment forces were led by the Anti-Saloon League, the WCTU, and the churches. They saw the issue as the same as in the past—liquor or no liquor. They felt that the public sentiment was unmistakably against the liquor traffic. They saw the campaign as the last-ditch fight of the liquor forces. Chatfield said the battle was of "vital importance, for the saloons have robbed us of our husbands, sons, and daughters, destroying both body and souls." [55]

The campaign was bitter, hot, and expensive. The day preceding the vote was observed as Temperance Day in most of the churches. Prayer meetings held in the early afternoon were followed by parades of wearers of white ribbons. In Birmingham the parade was more than a mile long. When the votes were counted, the amendment was defeated by a 60 percent majority. It lost in all but six counties. The prohibitionists were stunned and deeply disappointed, but they had antagonized the voters by asking for too much too soon. They were trying to hurry voters into action that they were not yet ready to take. Although the drys had failed to write prohibition into the constitution, they still had the statewide prohibition laws on the statute books. [56]

However, the prohibitionists were not able to maintain the law. Under the governorship of Emmett O'Neal, the legislature repealed the prohibition law and reenacted the local option laws in February 1911. Counties and cities again voted and this time the wets won heavily in the urban areas. The campaigns in Mobile and Montgomery counties, where local optionists were recognized to be in an overwhelming majority, were never in question. Prohibitionists hardly attempted to fight back. Local optionists won landslide victories in both counties. Jefferson County was the scene of a real fight, but even here the prohibitionists were defeated and the county went wet. [57]

But the drys were not to be defeated; the leaders laid their plans to swing Alabama back into the ranks of prohibition states. By 1914 the prohibitionists had rallied their forces and, working effectively in rural Alabama, gained control of the 1915 legislature. They continued to work through the Baptist, Methodist, Presbyterian, and Disciples of Christ churches. The WCTU launched an extensive advertising campaign. Posters were displayed in conspicuous places and letters were sent to ministers asking them to influence their congregations in favor of statewide and national prohibition. The women cooperated with public schoolteachers in the temperance work. Some unions offered prizes to schoolboys and girls for the best essays on temperance. Temperance calendars were made and distributed. Other unions sent postcards to voters just before the election, but their most effective work was among the children.[58]

As soon as the legislature convened in January 1915, it took up the question of prohibition. A statewide prohibition act was adopted by both houses in a matter of days. Gov. Charles Henderson vetoed the measure, but the legislature passed it over his veto. The law was to become effective on July 1, 1915; the liquor establishments in the state were to be legally closed on that day. The prohibitionists rejoiced at their victory. Two years later, in 1917, the movement for national prohibition culminated when Congress adopted the Eighteenth Amendment and sent it to the states for ratification. Prohibition forces in Alabama had been agitating for national prohibition ever since their victory in 1915. They were now ready for action. On January 14, 1919, the legislature ratified the federal amendment by a joint resolution of both houses. The amendment became a part of the federal constitution later that month. The prohibitionists had finally reached their goal.[59]

The Alabama women who worked in the WCTU had a totally different experience from any they had ever had before. They had never participated in a national movement. They had not been part of the antislavery campaign or any of the other reformist causes of the 1830s and 1840s—prison reform, communitarianism, education for women, or even temperance, which had little impact on the prewar South. The WCTU introduced significant numbers of Alabama women to extra-domestic concerns; a wholly domestic class was socialized with astonishing rapidity. The union took as its starting point woman's position within the home; it catalogued the abuses she suffered there as it proposed necessary reforms to ameliorate her domestic situation. However, as the WCTU developed, its concerns went far beyond the family to include the quality of community life, even though its standards remained the family and the moral values women had developed within it. Alabama women who joined the union reached out beyond the home and began to deal with the problems of an industrial society. They became concerned with homeless women and children and established the Mercy Home, a remarkable and enduring institution. They worked for the creation of industrial schools for girls; they supported the creation of juvenile courts; they worked for prison reform; they gained political experience by working in the prohibition campaigns. They participated in and hosted national conventions of the WCTU. They learned how to hold meetings and campaign for a cause. The WCTU had much to do with putting southern women into the mainstream of American life. Belle Kearney, a suffrage leader from Mississippi, described the WCTU as "the generous liberator, the joyous iconoclast, the discoverer, the developer of Southern women." She felt that the organization changed southern attitudes and made a different world for southern girls.[60]

3 WHITE WOMEN'S CLUBS, 1890–1915

s the temperance unions were a product of the 1880s in Alabama, the women's club movement was a product of the 1890s. The early white women's clubs were primarily literary societies formed in various towns for cultural purposes, which united in 1895 to form the Alabama Federation of Women's Clubs (AFWC). Later the members turned to a wide variety of civic and community projects. Like the WCTU, women's clubs educated their middle- and upper-class members while providing an avenue to public affairs. Often less embattled and more exclusive than the WCTU, the clubs had the potential of appealing to a different range of members. However, in Alabama many of the same women belonged to both organizations. These women were often members of the South's emerging business and professional middle class, but present also were representatives of the prominent aristocratic families.

From its inception the AFWC tackled substantial statewide projects that benefited women and children. Elizabeth Johnston Evans Johnston of Birmingham saw the need for an industrial school for boys and determinedly sought methods of creating one. Lura Harris Craighead of Mobile, pursuing the ever-present interest of the women in public education, organized the Alabama School Improvement Association. Julia S. Tutwiler of Livingston demanded that the board of trustees of the University of Alabama open its doors to women, while the federation provided scholarships for needy female students. Lillian Milner Orr and Nellie Kimball Murdock spearheaded the long drive to abolish child labor.

The first women's clubs in the nation were established in the East in 1868. Jane Croly, a newspaper columnist and avid supporter of women in public affairs, organized Sorosis in New York City. The purpose of this club was to "render the female sex helpful to each other and actively benevolent in the world." The New England Woman's Club, organized at the same time, intended to serve as "an organized social center for united thought and action." Its founders were Caroline Severance, a veteran antebellum reformer, and the well-known author Julia Ward Howe. The motivating drive behind club formation was simply the desire to associate. Throughout the 1880s and 1890s, women's clubs proliferated. By the time the General Federation of Women's Clubs (GFWC) was established in 1890, there were almost 500 affiliate clubs and over 100,000 members. At the end of the century, women's clubs had 160,000 members; and by World War I, over a million. Throughout the decades, the women's club movement served a special purpose. It enabled white middle-class women to enter public life without abandoning domestic values and without adopting the aggressive stance associated with either the temperance crusade or the more highly politicized movement for woman suffrage.[1]

But women's clubs were a step toward politicization as well. The typical women's club of the 1880s began by holding weekly meetings for lectures, discussions, and book reports. These literary and cultural overtones provided club women with a substitute for the higher education now open to their daughters. The club was also an exclusionary society, defined as much by who was admitted and who was left out as by the novels or works of art that were discussed. By the turn of the century, however, the thrust of the clubs had shifted to civic affairs, a crucial change in direction. "I have an important piece of news to give you," the president-elect of the GFWC told the convention in 1904. "Dante is dead. He has been dead for several centuries, and I think it is time we dropped the study of his *Inferno* and turned our attention to our own." [2]

Women's clubs tackled local and noncontroversial projects. They raised funds for planting trees, establishing libraries, building hospitals, and creating playgrounds. They supported worthy projects, such as women's colleges, social settlements, and visiting nurses. They pressured local governments for clean drinking fountains and better school facilities. After women's clubs federated in 1890, delegates to biennial meetings took a stand on national issues in which women, the home, and the family had a stake. They passed resolutions in support of protective labor legislation for women, abolition of child labor, pure food and drug legislation, and finally in 1914, woman suffrage.

Beginning in the late 1880s and continuing through the 1890s, middle-class Alabama women created literary clubs. The first of these appears to have been the Mobile Reading Club, which began meeting as early as 1882 under the leadership of Lura Harris Craighead. In 1888 the Kettle-Drum club of Tuscaloosa and the Cadmean Circle in Birmingham held their first meetings. However, these did not have a formal organization and regular meetings. That honor belongs to the Thursday Literary Club of Selma, which was created in 1890 by Mary LaFayette Robbins. These were shortly followed by additional clubs in other towns—the New Century Club of Sheffield, the Progressive Culture Club of the Decaturs, the Helen Keller Library Association of Tuscumbia, the No Name Club of Montgomery, Studiosis and the Finde Siecle of Anniston, and the Highland Book Club of Talladega. [3]

By 1895 there was a sufficient number of literary clubs in the state to create a federation. Representatives from the literary clubs of Birmingham, Montgomery, Selma, Tuscaloosa, and Decatur met in Birmingham at the South Highland Presbyterian Church and established the Alabama Federation of Women's Clubs, which was one of the earliest federations in the nation. Beginning with a membership of approximately 130 women representing six clubs, the Alabama federation easily became the largest women's organization in the state. By 1915 it had grown to 153 clubs with an estimated membership of 4,250. The origi-

THE CLUB WOMEN SPONSORED TRAVELING LIBRARIES SUCH AS THIS BOOKMOBILE AT THE SAYRE COMMISSARY, ABOUT 1915. *FROM THE COLLECTIONS OF THE BIRMINGHAM PUBLIC LIBRARY.*

nal purpose of the AFWC was "To bring together for mutual help, for intellectual improvement and for social union the different literary clubs of the state." The first president of the organization, Mary LaFayette Robbins of Selma, said, "The dimensions of our sleeves plainly indicate that we are not here in the interest of dress reform. The truth is we are not reformers in any sense of the word, nor is it a part of our purpose to disturb in any way the public equilibrium. . . . The sole purpose of our coming together is mental culture." However, the women were less conservative and more progressive than they themselves realized. Even from the beginning, they said that the federation was formed also "for the advancement of women." Robbins was sufficiently aware of the position of women when she noted at the first meeting that "ministers frequently stated . . . that they would explain certain propositions for the benefit of the woman and the uninformed." Indeed, by 1915 these women were sufficiently informed that they became a powerful factor in the educational, civic, and social life of the state.[4]

The first women who embraced the club movement did so with a certain amount of fear and trepidation as they moved out of accustomed domestic roles. Here was a group of proper southern ladies who were concerned that they could not retain their former image and still be club women. Many were troubled about reconciling this new role with the traditional southern view of women as wholly domestic creatures. In 1896 at the first convention of the federation, Ella Gaines Parker Going of Birmingham said that the American woman had become a topic both at home and abroad and that the club movement was one of "the wonders of the age." But she saw the conservatism of the South as a safeguard against the danger of club life becoming a drain on women instead of an outlet for women. She said, "The home comes first. . . . All [other] things, no matter how important, are secondary. . . . [T]he conservative upbringing of the southern woman had caused her to shrink from any duty outside of her home." Yet she added that club life was leading her to take a broader view of her duty to society, recognizing that women needed to be involved in altruistic work that would improve the home and the community.[5]

This major concern of reconciling club life with domestic responsibilities was addressed by Mrs. George M. Cruikshank in 1897 in a paper entitled "Is Club Life at Variance with Home Life?" Cruikshank thought the topic would be of interest to men as well as to women because men doubted that women could unite in club work without shirking their home duties. Her answer to the question was that if women regulated their affairs properly, there should be no conflict between the two. She laid a heavy responsibility on women to do all things well and implied that nineteenth-century ladies could become superwomen. But she was clearly attracted to a life outside the home when she went on to say that the club "teaches women to talk about things, not persons" and that it brings women into "harmonious and congenial contact with many women" at the same time. Club life "broadens the mind and the heart."[6]

One of the greatest fears that these early women had was speaking in public. They had little experience in affairs outside the home and had seldom been called upon to address a group of people. Clara Louise Berry Wyker said, "Do you remember, how afraid we all were of the sound of our own voices and how hard and often we had to swallow to keep that sound going and how relieved we were at the conclusion of a debate." In 1906 a young delegate remarked that she did not know that women could speak out at a convention like men. She found it all very interesting and hoped she could come again.[7]

Despite the attractiveness of the outside world, these club women were fearful of being identified with what they saw as the objectionable New Woman. They did not see themselves as "advanced" or as supporters of woman's rights. Even the term *club woman* was subject to wide differences of interpretations. Wyker, president of AFWC, said in 1902:

> To many, it means the woman with masculine tendencies, such as
> staying out nights, wanting to vote, to go to war and emancipate her-
> self from doing what she has been brought up to do. Others define
> her as a restless woman who cannot be contented with minding her
> own business, but must needs gossip over the business of others with
> like-minded women. Far from having masculine tendencies, the club
> woman never goes to clubs at night, and is against war even for men. To
> the charge that she has a tendency to do what she has a mind to do, she
> must plead guilty. Education, art, music, domestic science and chari-

ties form the list of the dreadful things the Alabama club woman has a mind to study.[8]

The Alabama club woman preferred to think of herself as "a home-maker in the broadest sense, her labors not confined to brightening merely her own fireside circle, but reaching State-wide, to countless homes where wretchedness and poverty sit side by side with ignorance and crime. It is here the Alabama club woman realizes her highest and noblest work."[9] Club women were playing a wider role, but they continued to do so in the name of the home and family.

By 1907 the president of the federation, Mrs. Joseph McLester, commented on the changed role of women:

> Fifty years ago a convention like this composed exclusively of women would have been impossible. Vox populi forbade it. I smile to think what would have been the attitude of my grandfather and his compeers of the early nineteenth Century toward such an assemblage.
>
> At that period, when Paul's injunction 'Let your women keep silence among you,' was held in higher reverence than many of his other commands, a woman's life was bounded on the north by the nursery, on the east by her kitchen, on the south by her church, and on the west by a loom.
>
> But woman now may do what she can and this with the warmest possible approbation, encouragement and co-operation of husbands, brothers, and fathers. That women of Alabama have used this freedom of action nobly for the betterment of humanity, for the advancement of education, for the protection of children and for the promotion for all that tends to good citizenship, I believe you will admit.[10]

These Alabama women's clubs had begun as literary societies that studied art, music, drama, and literature, but by the early 1900s women had turned their interests to a wide variety of civic and community issues. They were concerned with child labor and worked for its elimination. They sought to improve the educational system by making school attendance compulsory, by attacking illiteracy, by placing women on school boards, and by introducing kindergartens, manual training, and domestic science into the school system. They worked to secure a women's dormitory at the University of Alabama and to provide scholarships for women. They were instrumental in establishing industrial reform schools for both boys and girls. They also supported the work of the WCTU; in fact, the same women often worked in both organizations.[11] They became, in short, the municipal housekeepers of the Progressive Era who wanted to transform the state by creating a new understanding of what responsible government should provide.[12]

However, their interest in reform did not extend to woman suffrage, which they viewed with horror. Political equality was an explosive issue because it challenged women's place in the home and demanded for them power and connection with the social order that was not based on the family and their subordination within it. The demand for the franchise appeared to forecast the demise of the family and the integration of women into the heretofore male-dominated world of politics, business, and the professions. The women's club movement had worked to improve society in the name of the home and family. This position avoided public criticism and thereby gained more supporters than suffrage did. As a result, these clubs attracted thousands of women who recognized their own subordinate status but were not willing to go so far as to demand suffrage to rectify injustice.[13]

A brief discussion of suffrage occurred in 1896 at the first convention of the Alabama Federation of Women's Clubs, but the consideration of such a radical issue was barely acknowledged. By 1906 the president, Mabel Wiley Hutton Goode, stated that the federation had been asked to support an amendment to the state constitution enfranchising women. The convention voted at that time to table the motion. Ten years later, in 1916, the legislative chair commented: "We women may not choose our lawmakers and may not ourselves attain that honor, but there is no power on earth that can prevent our telling them what we want and making things lively and interesting until we get it."[14] At last club women were beginning to understand political power. The AFWC, however, did not endorse the suffrage amendment until 1918.

One of the many social problems the women's clubs tackled was juvenile delinquency and the treatment of juvenile offenders. As mothers concerned with children and the family, they worked toward changing a child's environment to improve conditions created by industrialization and urbanization. Under the leadership of Elizabeth Johnston Evans Johnston (who was called "Johnsie" or sometimes "Lizzie"), club women persuaded the state in 1899 to establish an industrial school for boys at East Lake just outside of Birmingham. The legislature appropriated money for the project and the governor appointed a board of directors composed of members of the AFWC. Johnston served as president of the board from its inception until her death in 1934.[15]

Born in Greensboro, North Carolina, in 1851 and educated at Charlotte Female College, Elizabeth Johnston moved to Birmingham in 1887 with her husband, Robert Douglas Johnston, and eight children. Both she and her husband became active in civic and philanthropic affairs in the city. Elizabeth Johnston organized the Highland Book Club and served as its president for more than twenty-five years. She also taught Sunday school for ten years in the prison camp located at the Pratt coal mine outside of Birmingham. She was appalled that boys, some only fourteen years old, committed to prison for minor offenses were housed with hardened criminals, especially in the day of Alabama's convict lease system. She decided that she would establish a home for the training of boys in an environment that was conducive to good citizenship. She was convinced that the children needed to have moral and religious training—that they needed love, understanding, adequate housing, nourishing food, and a chance to learn a trade. She did not visualize a juvenile reformatory for young lawbreakers, but a school where untrained boys might be led into lives of usefulness. But as she tried to sell her ideas to others, she discovered that few were concerned with the inmates of the prisons. The general belief was that they had broken the law and deserved to be punished for their deeds.[16]

Since there were no men's service clubs nor organized social work, Johnston turned to the Alabama Federation of Women's Clubs for help. The AFWC created a reformatory committee, which Johnston chaired. She and other club women traveled over the state speaking to churches, private gatherings, and women's clubs. Johnston visited industrial schools in the North and East collecting information that would strengthen her arguments when she presented her plan to the state legislature. She was especially impressed with the Tennessee Industrial School located in Nashville. By this time she had collected some money. Her first gift came from a surprising source; one of the prisoners at the Pratt mine heard of her project and gave her $100. He was serving a life sentence, but he wanted to prevent other boys from being imprisoned. The Birmingham Chamber of Commerce donated $3,000 provided that the school would be located in Birmingham.[17]

Johnston and other women from the AFWC went to Montgomery to present their proposal to the 1899 session of the legislature. They were not sure just how to make a request of the legislature, but their task was doubtless made easier because the governor, Joseph F. Johnston, was Elizabeth's brother-in-law. They met with the leaders of the senate and house privately and presented their proposal. No woman had ever addressed the legislature at this time. Much to their surprise the legislature approved the charter, which called for a board composed of seven women from the Alabama Federation of Women's Clubs, and appropriated $3,000 for the school. What the state did was to charter a project of the women's clubs, make the women the board of trustees, and give them $3,000. This boys' industrial school was the only one in the nation that had a board composed exclusively of women. All in all, it was a substantial victory for the women's clubs.[18]

Johnston purchased 136 acres of land in East Lake near Birmingham with the money donated by the chamber of commerce. She bought the Roebuck farm, which later included the famous spring that fed East Lake. Because the $3,000 appropriated by the legislature was not adequate to provide for the school's needs, Johnston started another campaign to raise the necessary material by donations. Architects donated their services; lumber mills supplied the lumber needed for construction; carpenters, brick masons, plumbers, and other workmen donated their services. Johnston's efforts were rewarded when the school opened in June 1900 with "nine boys, a mule, a superintendent, and a tract of land at East Lake." The boys were sent from the police court in Birmingham by Judge N. B. Feagin, who was a strong supporter of the school and later was responsible for creating the first juvenile court in the state. By 1915 the school had sheltered 1,392 boys, and in that year it had 363 boys in residence. The boys were trained to be carpenters, printers, dairymen, machinists, plumbers, pipe fitters, tailors, and for other useful trades. All of the boys took academic courses and some were able to attend colleges or universities. The school always maintained an open-door system; there were no armed guards or boundary walls. An outstanding characteristic of the school was that it was part of the larger world. The boys frequently left the institution as members of the band or athletic teams. Johnston felt that the school fulfilled its mission and hundreds of boys were trained to be good and productive citizens.[19]

The legislature was never generous with its money. Johnston, other club women, and Superintendent David M. Weakley spent considerable time in Montgomery lobbying the legislators. If the appropriation bill did not pass, there would be nothing with which to feed and clothe the boys. As early as 1902 the trustees requested $15,000, but the legislature appropriated only $5,000. Lillian Milner Orr of Birmingham suggested that at the next session the AFWC send their prettiest and best-dressed women to Montgomery. The president, Clara Louise Berry Wyker, said, "Yes, they will look at the pretty women and then go and vote for the small appropriation." Yet Gov. B. B. Comer said in his inaugural address in 1907 that "The work accomplished by the ladies with what subscriptions they could get from the public and the meager help from the counties and the State has been wonderful." He strongly recommended that sufficient funds be provided for the school. He saw the importance of surrounding boys with the best possible influences at the beginning of their lives. In 1906 the legislature appropriated $50,000 for a schoolhouse, but did not appropriate any additional funds for building until the 1920s. The school did build a new cottage, but the money for its construction was obtained from the meager monthly allowance of $12.50 provided for each boy. In a survey of social problems in Alabama conducted by the Russell Sage Foundation in 1918, Hastings H. Hart recommended that the allowance for each boy at the school be increased to twenty dollars.[20]

The women who served on the board of trustees of the school were women of unusual ability who provided stability and consistent leader-

LURA HARRIS CRAIGHEAD WAS A LEADER IN THE AFWC WHO WORKED IN
THE CAMPAIGNS TO ABOLISH CHILD LABOR AND TO IMPROVE THE PUBLIC
SCHOOLS. SHE WAS ALSO THE AUTHOR OF THE *HISTORY OF THE ALABAMA
FEDERATION OF WOMEN'S CLUBS. ERIK OVERBEY COLLECTION/UNIVERSITY
OF SOUTH ALABAMA ARCHIVES.*

ship to the institution. As founder and organizer, Elizabeth Johnston
deserves most credit. For nearly forty years, she gave of her time and her
efforts to this project. Her actions were appreciated by many. In 1931
she was selected as the outstanding Woman of the Year and awarded

the *Birmingham News* Loving Cup. Later that same year, just before her eightieth birthday, the state legislature adopted a resolution thanking her for establishing the Alabama Boys' Industrial School. Lura Harris Craighead, one of the original members appointed by Governor Johnston in 1899, served as vice-president until her death in 1926. Craighead, the wife of the editor of the *Mobile Register,* was the organizer of the Shakespeare Club and Clara Schumann Club in Mobile and the president of the AFWC in 1899 when the industrial school was established. She continued to be an active member of the federation, writing the first volume of a history of the organization covering the years from 1895 to 1918. She was well known throughout the state as a result of her interest in educational and welfare activities. She was responsible for creating the Alabama School Improvement Association; she supported the drive to restrict child labor and served on the Alabama Child Labor Committee; she worked for the establishment of juvenile courts.[21]

Alberta Williams Bush was also a long-time board member, serving as the treasurer from the school's inception in 1899 until her death in 1930. Bush had the difficult task of trying to meet the school's expenses with what was always an inadequate amount of money. Under her leadership the board accumulated a special trust to be used in case of emergency for board, room, and the teachers' salaries when the state appropriation was insufficient. Bush had the honor of being the first woman appointed to serve on the Alabama Board of Education. She also organized the first District Nursing Association and served as president until the function was taken over by the Community Chest.[22]

As important as a boys' training school was to the Alabama Federation of Women's Clubs, education had been a prior concern. Interest in the education of children came naturally to these club women, who saw themselves primarily as mothers. Their efforts were directed toward improvement of the public schools of the state by providing better-trained teachers; establishing qualifications for the county superintendents; attacking illiteracy; supporting laws to allow local taxation; placing women on school boards; securing a dormitory for women at the University of Alabama; introducing kindergartens, manual training, and domestic science into the public school system; sponsoring libraries; and providing scholarships to help educate worthy and ambitious women.[23]

In the early 1900s these club women were in blissful ignorance about the condition of education in the state. Many of them assumed that Alabama stood first in everything as it does in the alphabetical list of states. They were profoundly shocked by the straightforward revelations of the 1912 report of the Russell Sage Foundation, which placed Alabama at the bottom of the list of states in support for public schools. This comparative study of the public schools in all of the states caused a wave of mortification to sweep over the state. At the time citizens demanded measures to improve the state's educational system. Yet these demands were not new; for more than a decade educational and civic leaders had been attempting to arouse interest in tackling the educational problems.

As early as 1898 the newly organized Alabama Federation of Women's Clubs recognized the educational needs of the state. Kate Hutcheson Morrissette of Montgomery, chair of the first committee on education, put the matter clearly before the organization. In 1898 Alabama ranked third in illiteracy among the states. Only South Carolina and Louisiana had more illiterate people, but both of these states had recently adopted constitutions with provisions favorable to the development of their public school systems. Illiteracy operates as a "bar to civil, moral, and religious progress," she maintained, and the current public school system was entirely inadequate to wipe out illiteracy. Morrissette encouraged the mothers of Alabama, the press, businessmen, commercial interests, and the clergy "to create a public sentiment strong enough to demand for the children of the state adequate educational facilities." She asked, "Does the State of Alabama dare face the future with this mass of ignorant citizenship when intelligence is the test of efficiency and efficiency is the test of leadership? I beg the womenhood of Alabama to ponder well this question." [24]

The status of the educational system in Alabama in 1900 was, as historian A. B. Moore said, "abysmal." At this time Alabamians did not have a genuine appreciation of the value of education. The political leaders of the state believed that a good school system could be built from the meager appropriations of the legislature. Even school leaders themselves took the view that the needs of the schools were not so much more funds as better use of funds. The school year was three or four months in duration, scheduled at times that suited the convenience of the parents. No schools were graded except a few in the towns, and each school determined its own course of study and selected the textbooks to be used. Teachers were poorly paid and lacked professional training. Because the superintendents were not professionally trained either, the teachers in the local schools were almost totally without supervision. Public education made some progress in the cities by the turn of the century, where the school terms were lengthened to five or six months, better buildings were provided, teaching was improved, and the scope of the work broadened. But the rural areas saw few changes.[25]

The state began to deal with the problems of the public school system in 1898. The state superintendent of education, John W. Abercrombie, was the first professionally trained person to hold the position. He undertook to direct the public education of the state in a systematic manner from Montgomery. He laid out a plan of action that included better training of teachers, state certification of teachers (as opposed to county certification), grading of schools, uniform texts, free schools for five months available to all, and compulsory school attendance. He also favored granting taxing powers to the counties for school purposes and establishing qualifications for the county superintendents. Abercrombie was able to identify the major problems of the schools and to propose remedies. His proposals for improving the schools found little support in the state legislature, but they did find a receptive audience in the club women.[26]

The Alabama Federation of Women's Clubs was enthusiastic about Abercrombie's program and in 1898 pledged its active support. "Education became the keynote for the Federation—the moral, intellectual, and industrial education for the young women and the children of the state." The women felt no need to apologize for taking a role in the effort to improve the schools. They firmly believed that in the "history of reform in education there is a chapter of women's endeavors." The women were convinced of the necessity of creating a sound system of common schools for the masses. In 1900 the chair of the education committee said, "Since it is true a state can rise no higher than the level of its average citizen, shall we spend our time and energy upon the higher development of a favored few while the great mass of the children of Alabama send forth a vain cry for deliverance from ignorance?" Here was a group of well-educated, interested citizens who, even though they could not vote, had a vested interest in the welfare of children. They could and did build support for the policies of the state superintendent. Abercrombie later said, "The Federation has done much toward bringing the people to a realization of the state's duty in this respect." [27]

The Alabama Educational Association, which supported Abercrombie's proposals, recognized the club women as useful allies. In 1899 the association invited the committee on education of the AFWC to speak at its annual meeting. Mrs. A. T. Goodwyn and Clara Louise Berry Wyker addressed the teachers. Goodwyn made a series of recommendations dealing with the most pressing educational deficiencies that had been proposed by Abercrombie and supported by the AFWC. These recommendations laid out a course of action that the women were to follow for the next decade and a half. But the women had little idea about how to implement this ambitious program. In 1900 and 1901 club women had not yet learned how effective organized women could be in campaigning for their goals and in lobbying the legislators. At first they only wrote petitions and sent letters, which got buried in other business and were not seriously considered. It was not until later that they went to the legislative sessions in person to press their views on the legislators. However, these goals remained fairly constant for the next fifteen years and eventually the legislature acted upon most of them. [28]

The issue of local taxation for school purposes was a major issue all during this period. Educators had hoped that the constitution of 1901 would invest the school districts with the power to levy taxes, but the convention actually lowered the limit on the state's taxing power. The failure of the Constitution Convention of 1901 to support education was disappointing. The delegates to this convention missed a rare opportunity to promote free public education. The chair of the education committee of the AFWC, Morrissette, said, "Alabama is one of the few states in the union which does not allow for local taxation, a principle which is the basis of all school systems."[29] Educational leaders strongly believed that the schools could never rank with other states until provision was made for local taxation.[30]

Another ever-present issue that educational leaders dealt with was the problem of qualified and full-time county superintendents. The men who were elected to this position were not educators but were farmers, lawyers, or businessmen who had little or no idea how to oversee the county teachers. The certification of teachers was in the hands of superintendents who were deficient in even the rudiments of education.[31] The AFWC early recognized the problem and adopted a series of resolutions indicating that superintendents should know the principles and methods of teaching and should have actually been teachers. The federation gave continued publicity to the issue and encouraged all local clubs to support the issue. Superintendent I. W. Hill expressed the opinion that "our club women can very greatly assist in remedying this condition." But it was not until 1911 and later in 1915 that the state legislature passed acts enlarging the duties and powers of the superintendents and requiring each to maintain an office at the county seat.[32]

An important work of the AFWC was the creation of school improvement associations in 1905. These associations had their origin at a dinner given by Lura Harris Craighead, a past president of the AFWC. One of the dinner guests was the state superintendent of education, I. W. Hill. In discussing what the federated club women could do to help the state department of education with its plans, Hill suggested that possibly some work that was being carried on in other states might appeal to Alabama club women. What Hill had in mind was the organizing of school improvement or parent-teacher associations for the purpose of interesting communities in the betterment of their schools and bringing together the school and home. This suggestion of going directly to the people met with the enthusiastic approval of the women present. Consequently Craighead proposed that the AFWC take on as a new project the creation of local school improvement associations throughout the state.[33]

In this new endeavor the women were entirely successful. The first year communities created only twenty-nine associations, but the number jumped to 130 by 1907. The following year 300 associations were actually counted, but they were being created so rapidly the federation could not gain an accurate figure. One member estimated the number to be near 500. The major work of the associations was first to arouse the interest of the people in their schools and second to build, repair, equip, and maintain the local school buildings. The state by law was allowed to spend its money only for teachers' salaries and supervision, not on buildings or equipment. Hence, it was up to the local school districts to equip and maintain the buildings. At first the amount of money raised was small, but in 1910 the school improvement association raised $47,775 and the following year $42,778.[34] The AFWC offered an annual prize of $100 to the association that improved its school the most. In 1910 the prize was won by Fairhope, which voted bonds for a new school building, donated a site valued at $1,500, erected outbuildings, installed gas heat in the schoolhouse, purchased new desks, and raised an additional $1,300 for full payment on the building itself.[35]

The club women wrote and distributed pamphlets describing the purpose of the associations and how each community could organize one. They spoke to parents and teachers about the associations; they addressed the teachers' institutes when and wherever they met; and they spoke to conventions of the Alabama Teachers' Association and the University Summer Schools. In short, the women used their organization and skills to create school improvement associations in every town and county in the state and thus to support the ambitious plans of the department of education for the betterment of the schools.[36]

Superintendent Hill praised the work of the AFWC in creating the local school improvement associations. He said that he had appealed to various organizations to assist him, but had found none more responsive than the women's clubs. He said, "This organization came to my assistance with a strong committee which undertook the herculean task of organizing the counties and districts of the state into school improvement associations." The work was so successful that it became necessary for the department to employ a full-time worker for the project. Hill was able to secure funds from the Peabody Board to employ an experienced teacher to aid the committee in doing its work.[37]

The work of the AFWC was so successful that in 1907 a separate organization, the Alabama School Improvement Association, was created from the numerous local associations. This statewide organization was formed at the Conference for School Improvement called by the AFWC in Montgomery in December. The decision to create a separate organization was a wise one. It indicated the growth of the associations and made it possible for persons not connected with the women's clubs to work in the state organization. The chair of the AFWC committee said of this move, "Born of the spirit of helpfulness, fostered by woman's untiring energy and woman's genius for looking carefully after details, this infant has suddenly rounded out onto such proportions that the state, recognizing a power for good, quietly says, 'Now he is mine.'" She went on to say, "The organization of the State Association does not mean that the work no longer belongs to the Alabama Federation of Women's Clubs. The State organization is in its infancy and needs the fostering care of its mother."[38] The club women performed a service for state education in supporting the associations and publicizing their purposes until they could establish their own organization. Even though the AFWC was no longer directly involved, the members continued to work with the local associations on an individual basis.

The superintendents of education were lavish in their praise of the club women's work with the school improvement associations. Not only did the associations improve the material condition of the schools, but they brought the parents and the teachers together and created a base of support for the public school system that did not exist before. Superintendent Henry J. Willingham said, "The public schools of this state have reason to be grateful to the Federation of Alabama Clubs [sic] for the splendid results to which they have already contributed so much in improving conditions in the rural schools." A later superintendent, William F. Feagin, said, "No tales of yesterday and no romance of today can eclipse in wonder the improvements that they have wrought in local school conditions."[39]

By 1915 the improved leadership of the superintendents along with the work of the AFWC and other interested citizens began to pay off. The legislature of that year enacted a substantial number of education reforms for which these groups had long been working. The lawmakers adopted an amendment to the constitution authorizing the counties to levy a special school tax, thus culminating a long drive. They created a county board of education with authority to select a full-time qualified county superintendent. Another new law provided for higher standards for the certification of teachers. The legislature approved a compulsory attendance law providing that all children between the ages of eight and fifteen years should attend school at least eighty days a year and created an illiteracy commission to tackle that serious problem.[40] This 1915 session was one at which women were constantly present because the legislature considered not only these education issues, but it was at this time that it adopted statewide prohibition and a new child labor law and rejected the demand of women to vote.

Much to the surprise of the AFWC, the legislators also quickly and without much fanfare passed a law making women eligible for service on school boards. In 1903 the federation adopted a resolution that supported the fitness of women to serve on school boards, boards of education, and boards of trustees of state institutions. The AFWC felt that if women were on the boards they would have an opportunity for greater service to the schools, and the children of the state and the schools would also benefit by their presence. The motion was made by Mrs. K. M. Jarvis of Selma, a member of the Dallas County school board, the first woman to serve in that position in the state. The chair of the legislative committee, Dixie Bibb Graves, commented that "the bill for which we had least hope—women on school boards—passed so quickly as almost to startle us!"[41]

The success of the drive to improve the educational system was so marked that the impression was given that Alabama would surely rise in the ranks of the states. But what some people failed to understand was that education was improving in all of the states. Even though Alabama brought about much-needed improvements, the Russell Sage Foundation study of the state social agencies authorized by Gov. Charles Henderson showed that the rank of the state remained nearly the same. This report, which was published in 1918, showed that Alabama spent less on higher education than any state except Arkansas. The expenditure for the public schools in proportion to property values was lower than any state except Oklahoma. The average rural school term was still five months. The average annual salary of teachers was 79 percent of the U.S. average and 83 percent of the average for the region, less than the amount the state received from the hire of a convict.[42]

In addition to their interest in the public schools, the club women were also deeply concerned with the education of women. Women were limited in their choices for education because few institutions admitted them. Alabama Normal School at Livingston and the Alabama Girls' Industrial School at Montevallo were the only two state colleges for women. Both owed their existence to Julia S. Tutwiler, pioneer educator and philanthropist. Tutwiler was first made coprincipal of the Livingston Female Academy in 1881 when it was a private school. The next year the state legislature appropriated $2,500 for the academy and mandated the addition of a normal school. Tutwiler remarked, "This was the first and only gift which the women of the state had up to that time received from state or federal treasury." In 1883 the name was changed to the Alabama Normal College and Tutwiler was made president. From a small academy, she made it a respectable normal college in which the legislature saw fit to invest increasing sums of money. Tutwiler was ahead of her time in developing a program of teacher education that is recognized as standard today. She joined basic general education, which she called "culture," with professional study in order to develop good teachers. She served as president until her retirement in 1910.[43]

Tutwiler became an advocate for women's vocational education. She believed that the state had an obligation "to provide literary and vocational education for women at the college level." She expressed this view in a paper, "The Technical Education of Women," which a man read for her before the Alabama Education Association in 1880. (At that time it was not viewed as proper for a woman to speak in public.) The article was published in a national magazine, *Education,* in 1882. Tutwiler said that some of the "anxious, aimless spinsters" should be given a technical education; the "vast unused capital of womanly intellect" that was going to waste should be educated. Such advocacy made Tutwiler one of the first educators to champion the cause of vocational education for women. It was largely through her efforts that the legislature established Alabama Girls' Industrial School for the white women of the state in 1892. Tutwiler had hoped that the industrial school would be located on land adjacent to the Normal College in Livingston, but many towns wanted the school and Montevallo was selected. Tutwiler was offered the presidency of the new institution, but she decided to remain at Livingston.[44]

The University of Alabama at Tuscaloosa and the newer Alabama A & M College at Auburn did not admit women until the 1890s.[45] Alabama A & M began admitting some women in the academic year 1892–93, but the University of Alabama did not do so until Julia Tutwiler went to the board of trustees in 1893 and persuaded them to open the doors of the institution to women. Tutwiler pointed out that the federal lands had been given to provide education "for the youth of the state." She insisted that half of the youth had been deprived of their just share. Nowhere in Alabama, she pointed out to the trustees, could an intelligent woman get the equivalent of a university education. Respecting Tutwiler's opinion, the trustees voted to admit women of sophomore standing. For several years no housing was available for women on the campus so only a few women from Tuscaloosa were able to attend. Tutwiler met this situation by persuading the president to set aside a house on the campus for ten of her graduate students whom she would bring over from Livingston. The women under the supervision of Sallie Avery, a colleague of Tutwiler, kept house, did their own cooking, and won academic honors. Of the six awards the university granted in one year, the women won four of them. This confirmed Tutwiler's opinion that women were smarter than men. It was not until 1898 that women were admitted to all classes and all privileges on terms of equality with the men.[46]

A major project of the Alabama Federation of Women's Clubs was the establishment of university scholarships for women. The chairman of the scholarship committee, Conradine Skaggs McConaughy, expressed the feeling of the federation in 1899. "If we, a band of women one thousand strong, are more determined to educate the girls of our state, not many generations will pass before every hearthstone will be a school, every child an educated one, and then this great state will stand first for culture, first for morality and first in the hearts of her children."[47] As an ardent advocate of the importance of education, McConaughy constantly encouraged club women to use their influence in the cause of education. She pointed out that men spent their time developing the state's natural resources, but that women spent theirs "opening the minds of God's children." The women were very conscious of the importance of an education in rearing children. In 1908 the scholarship committee adopted as its slogan "Educate a man, you educate an individual; educate a woman, you educate a family."[48]

As early as 1898 the AFWC undertook to provide scholarships for the Alabama Girls' Industrial School at Montevallo, which had been established only six years earlier. The first scholarships were designed to provide deserving poor women with an education to enable them to be self-supporting. The federation collected the money from its members to fund the scholarships, which the recipients were expected to repay as soon as they had a job. At first the federation requested 5 percent of the first year's salary. Since most of these women obtained teaching certificates, the federation required the women to teach in the state for at least two years. This approach enabled the club women to provide women with an education and also to obtain qualified teachers for the state.

These scholarships proved to be difficult to fund. Originally the AFWC hoped that the scholarships would be self-sustaining, but this did not turn out to be the case. As with most scholarships, the rate of repayment was low. It also was difficult to collect enough seed money from the members. In 1902, for example, the AFWC, which had 1,500 members, donated an average of eleven cents per member to the scholarship fund. The chair hoped to increase that to thirty-five cents per member, which would provide an annual fund of $525 for scholarships, but even this proved to be impossible. The AFWC then turned to the General Education Board, which offered $1,000 if the club women could match the amount. The committee put forth its best efforts, but by 1903 had collected only $600. The additional $400 was raised by agencies in the Alabama Girls' Industrial School. By 1904 twenty-six women had received scholarships from the federation. Scholarships were also granted for women to attend the University of Alabama and later Southern Industrial Union at Camp Hill.

The money from the General Education Board was only a stopgap measure; still other sources needed to be found. The scholarships were becoming better known and were in greater demand as more women became interested in higher education. Older and more mature women began to apply. The scholarships now had a reputation and the recipients were known as the Federation Girls. The cost of attending colleges had also increased. In 1911 it cost $110 a year to attend Montevallo, $200 to attend the University of Alabama, and $70 to attend Camp Hill. By 1910 the committee realized that the only permanent solution was to establish an endowment fund; shortly after, the AFWC created a $10,000 scholarship endowment, the Margaret P. Coleman Endowment Fund, named in honor of its most zealous advocate. By 1913 the nature and purpose of the scholarships had changed. They were outright grants that did not have to be repaid and they were available for use at out-of-state institutions.

In 1914 the chair of the scholarship committee, Mrs. C. Clifford Adams, summed up the work of the committee by saying:

> The eagerness of Alabama girls to avail themselves of these opportunities for education is the best possible commentary on the Federation's scholarship work in the past and the strongest argument for pushing it in the future. As it now stands the A. F. W. C. has helped *eighty* young women . . . through its Scholarship Department. When we think of these young people whose lives we have enriched, do we not feel that our energies have been well expended, our money well invested?[49]

Another major interest of the AFWC was a dormitory for women at the University of Alabama. The Julia Tutwiler Annex was a popular place. The rates were so reasonable that many women whose resources were limited were eager to be accommodated, but there was room for only fourteen. The result was that fifty-seven had to be turned away in 1903. The women of Alabama were unable to take advantage of higher education because of inadequate dormitory accommodations. In 1907 the federation circulated a petition for a dormitory and lobbied the legislature for liberal appropriation. The legislature appropriated $100,000 for new buildings, but contrary to expectations, the trustees did not spend the money on a women's dormitory. The federation was convinced that coeducation was in danger at the university because the trustees were opposed to it.[50]

In 1910 the federation decided to petition the legislature for $40,000 for a dormitory and a course of study suitable for women. The next year the board of trustees appeared to agree with the AFWC and made a similar request of the legislature. By now the board was convinced that the policy of receiving young women as students was permanently established and that it was "clearly the duty of the State to make better provision for them." The board proposed that the university build a dormitory to accommodate 100–150 women and to offer courses in domestic science. The AFWC strongly supported these proposals in a petition to the legislature in January 1911. The federation felt that it was a reflection on the educational system of the state that the high schools had to seek teachers outside the state or else appoint women insufficiently trained to teaching positions. This situation could be remedied by providing adequate accommodations for the capable and ambitious women who desired to enter the university. The federation further argued that because of the "growing responsibilities laid upon women both by home and state . . . the most efficient education should be granted to the young women of the State." Both the federation's petition and the trustees' resolution received wide circulation.[51] The university received its appropriation but again did not use the money to build a dormitory. The federation felt it had been betrayed by the trustees.

Despite this defeat the federation embarked on an even more active campaign for a university dormitory for women. This time the members worked out an agreement with the president of the university and enlisted the assistance of other women's organizations. By 1914 the federation had an understanding with Pres. George H. Denny that the University would build the central unit of the dorm and the federation would raise the money for the second and third units. Making plans to raise $50,000 for this large undertaking, the AFWC launched a campaign for subscriptions and enlisted the help of other women's organizations—the Daughters of the American Revolution, the Daughters of

1812, the United Daughters of the Confederacy, the Alabama Congress of Mothers, and the Alabama School Improvement Association. "For the first time in the history of the State," said the chairman of the special committee, "have various organizations of women, with separate aims, come together as one power, rallying 15,000 strong to one single undertaking. For the first time have the women of the State banded together to seek from their men a gift for the women of the state." This united drive by the women was successful and a women's dormitory named for Julia Tutwiler was built in 1915. Once again the power and influence of organized women on behalf of other women was effective, but only after the greatest effort on their part.

Despite the obstacles, the club women had pursued their interest in the education of their children. As one member put it:

> The Federation is opposed to ignorance. We believe that intellectual and moral growth is not less indispensable than material progress. We believe that we can hasten the day when universal instruction, will no longer be a moot question in Alabama but an established fact. On our banner is inscribed "Let there be Light!" We work "to diminish the number of the dark, to increase the number of the luminous. This is why we cry, Education! Knowledge! To learn to read is to kindle a fire; every syllable spelled, sparkles!"[52]

By 1915 the women did not regard their work as accomplished, but realized that they needed to continue their efforts. When asked what did the schools of the state need, they answered "money," "money," and again "money." When asked what can the AFWC do? The answer was "agitate, educate, legislate." When asked what was the greatest need of the rural schools, the answer was "better schools," "better salaries," "better buildings," "better supervision," and "longer school terms."[53]

The AFWC was active at a crucial period in the history of the growth of education in the state. By their support of the expanded role for education and their belief in the importance of education, women were able to contribute their share to this important development. They founded the Alabama Boys' Industrial School. They created public support for education and its needs, and they actively worked with the department of education and the school improvement committees to achieve the goals. This interest in education was an entirely natural one for women, who saw themselves as wives and mothers concerned with children.

The women who led the Alabama Federation of Women's Clubs came from similar socioeconomic backgrounds, all being members of the growing business and professional middle class, with a few representatives from the old families. Of twenty women who played dominant roles, only nine were natives of the state, whereas eleven came from surrounding states, North Carolina, Tennessee, and Mississippi. Two actually were born in the North, in Ohio and Massachusetts. These women came to Alabama with husbands who moved into the state after the Civil War, being attracted by the economic opportunities of the New South. The federation was truly a statewide organization with members representing all areas. Of the twenty women leaders (seventeen of whom were presidents of the AFWC), seven lived in Birmingham, while three lived in Montgomery, two in Selma, two in Mobile, and others were from Auburn, Decatur, Montevallo, Tuscaloosa, and Troy. These women were very well educated for their day; more then half (twelve) of them attended a college or an academy (which often was only a finishing school). Of these, two graduated from Judson College in Marion, Alabama, and two others were graduates of Peabody Normal College in Nashville, Tennessee. Higher education was just opening up for southern women; the daughters of these leading women were more likely to graduate from a college or university than their mothers were. Indeed, one of the reasons women joined the clubs was to further their own education.

Virtually all of these female leaders were married and had children. The only one who was single was Mary LaFayette Robbins of Selma, the first president of the AFWC. Robbins pursued one of the few careers open to women; she taught English at the Noble Institute in Anniston, Alabama, and later was lady principal of St. Katherine's in Waynesville, North Carolina. Four of the other women also taught school before they were married, but none continued to do so afterwards. Middle-class women in the South virtually never worked after they were married.

Indeed, few of them worked before marriage; it was simply not socially acceptable. The husbands of these women were lawyers, clergymen, newspaper editors, judges, university professors, educators, business-men, and even governors who expected their wives to devote themselves to their homes and children. The women worked not only in the AFWC, but also in a wide variety of other organizations—the WCTU, the United Daughters of the Confederacy, the Daughters of the American Revolution, the Colonial Dames, the YWCA, the Southern Association of College Women, public library associations, and the Alabama Child Labor Committee—and some of them joined the suffrage associations. These female leaders were obviously women of education, talent, and intelligence who were devoted to their families, but who at the same time desired a wider role outside the home.[54]

Women created a separate space for themselves through their women's clubs, which provided them with an avenue to public life and affairs. The club movement allowed these women to engage in public life without abandoning domestic values. Their actions were viewed as an extension of the home. They did not see themselves as favoring women's rights or challenging the traditional role of women. Indeed, they felt obligated to use their influence nobly and faithfully to perform their wider mission as mothers and homemakers. They realized that they needed to keep the balance between the nearer and wider duties. They were convinced that they could meet the new demands of community life without sacrificing those of family life. These women did not see themselves as New Women and yet their roles were changing more than they realized.

4 BLACK WOMEN'S CLUBS, 1890–1920

*A*frican-American women began to organize women's clubs at about the same time that white women did. By the end of Reconstruction, black women were ready to create organizations and institutions that reflected their concerns as women. As a result, black women's clubs were established in a number of cities, usually centered around some local welfare or educational project. Following a pattern not unlike that of white women, these local clubs began to exchange information and delegates and to form large federations. Margaret Murray Washington was the preeminent leader of the black women's clubs in Alabama, not only in Tuskegee where she created the Woman's Club and the mothers' clubs, but also on the national level where she was an active organizer and leader of the National Association of Colored Women (NACW). From their women's clubs throughout the state, African-American women supported educational projects, social services, temperance, reform schools, and suffrage. In short, these women's clubs "did everything"; they saw themselves as the vehicle for the uplifting of the entire race.

The spur for a permanent national organization came from the outside. In 1895 lynchings in the United States had begun to arouse censure and protest from abroad. This was largely the result of the untiring campaign of an African-American woman, Ida Wells Barnett, whose speaking tour in Great Britain aroused an international debate over lynching and resulted in the formation of a British antilynching society. Rising to the defense of the white South, James W. Jacks, president of the Missouri Press Association, wrote to the British society in a widely publicized statement that "the Negroes in the country were wholly devoid of morality, the women were prostitutes and all were natural thieves and liars." This statement was the last straw for African-American club women, who had endured similar slanders in silence. It prompted the convening of the first national conference of colored women.

Citing the charge, Josephine St. Pierre Ruffin, a prominent black club woman from Boston, issued a call for a national convention in Boston. In July 1895 100 women from ten states met and created the National Federation of African American Women, which united thirty-six clubs in twelve states. Elected as president of the organization was Margaret Murray Washington, who had recently become the third wife of Booker T. Washington and the lady principal of Tuskegee Institute. Similar efforts to unite the clubs were being made by the National League of Colored Women in Washington, D.C., headed by the educator Mary Church Terrell. By the next year plans were completed to unite the federation and the league into the National Association of Colored Women, and after some debate as to who would head the organization, Terrell became its president.[1]

The National Association of Colored Women became an authoritative voice in defense of African-American womanhood, and it greatly spurred the growth of local and regional organizations. At the ninth biennial meeting in 1914, NACW represented over 50,000 black women in twenty-eight state federations and over a thousand clubs. The national federation movement provided encouragement, direction, expert leadership, and example. Like the club movement of white women, this movement was led by middle-class women, but unlike white club women, the members of black women's clubs were often working women, tenant farm women, or poor women.[2]

Black women's clubs were not welcomed into the General Federation of Women's Clubs. In 1900 Terrell, representing the National Association of Colored Women, was denied a seat at a GFWC convention. African-American women's clubs, therefore, occupied a truly separate sphere, rejected by white clubs but united by a sense of racial pride. The black women's club movement filled much the same function as the GFWC. Local clubs ran day nurseries, reading rooms, and welfare projects. The national federation set up departments to deal with major women's issues, such as suffrage, education, and women's employment. The black women's club movement also adopted a distinctive mission, the moral education of the race. By the turn of the century, these middle-class black club leaders staked out their role as moral beacons. Through the club movement, they intended to improve "home training" of children, provide racial leadership, and demonstrate that black women could form "an army of organized women for purity and mental worth." [3]

African-American women activists believed that their efforts were essential for reform and progress and that their moral uprightness was a steady rock upon which the race could lean. They believed that the black community was at a crossroads. Abandoned by the federal government, subjected to increasing violence, and shorn of political power, it would either be pushed into oblivion or would mobilize its resources and survive. Convinced that they could save the race, black women saw their role in almost apocalyptic terms. They were "the fundamental agency under God in the regeneration . . . of the race, as well as the groundwork and starting point of its progress upward," wrote Anna Julia Cooper in her *Voice from the South* (1892). At a time when their white counterparts were riding the wave of moral superiority that sanctioned their activism, African-American women were seen by whites as immoral scourges, as having all the inferior qualities of white women without any of their virtues. At this time the idea of a pure upright black woman was inconceivable. It was against this background that black women organized women's clubs.[4]

Beginning in 1890, the black women of Montgomery created the first club, Ten Times One is Ten Club, at the Congregational Church.

It was soon followed by other clubs until by 1904 there was a total of twenty-six clubs in Birmingham, Selma, Mobile, Tuskegee, Tuscaloosa, Eufaula, Greensboro, and Mt. Meigs. These clubs had a variety of purposes; some were young women's clubs, others were for married women, still others were musical clubs or literary clubs. Clubs in Montgomery and Birmingham supported hospitals; the two in Tuscaloosa had as their project the building of a high school. They had purchased land for $200 for the project. The five clubs of Montgomery created a city Federation of Women's Clubs that met quarterly. On one occasion Josephine St. Pierre Ruffin, the famous Boston club woman, spoke on "The Morality of the Race: Its Causes and Its Remedies." The Montgomery Sojourner Truth Club established an essay writing contest at the normal school. Prizes were awarded to the student who wrote the best essay on the history, conditions, or development of the African-American race. Many of the clubs celebrated the birthday of Frederick Douglass, the abolition leader. In 1899 these state clubs joined together as the Alabama Federation of Colored Women's Clubs, which thereafter held annual conventions.[5]

The most famous of these clubs in Alabama was the Tuskegee Woman's Club, which was organized in 1895 by Margaret Murray Washington. Washington was born in Macon, Mississippi, in 1865; after her father's death when she was seven years old, she went to live with two Quaker schoolteachers. She learned quickly and easily, sitting up late at night and getting up early in the morning to study. She began teaching school at the age of fourteen. After graduating from Fisk University in 1889, she accepted a position at Tuskegee Institute. She married the recently widowed Booker T. Washington in 1893 and collaborated with him in building Tuskegee, first as the director of girls' industries, later as dean of women. She played a leading role in the state and national women's club movement. She was the organizer and first president of the Alabama Federation of Colored Women's Clubs; she served as president of the National Association of Colored Women from 1914 to 1918 and as editor of *National Association Notes,* the official publication of the association. Washington understood the need to plot her course carefully to offend neither black nor white. Her position as Booker T. Washington's

MARGARET MURRAY WASHINGTON, FOUNDER OF THE TUSKEGEE
WOMAN'S CLUB, THE TUSKEGEE MOTHERS' CLUBS, AND THE ALABAMA
FEDERATION OF COLORED WOMEN'S CLUBS. *TUSKEGEE UNIVERSITY
ARCHIVES*.

wife made her views and position more acceptable by both races. It was largely through her efforts that African-American women from all social and economic classes began to create their own social service programs. She died in 1925.[6]

The Tuskegee Woman's Club was an exclusive organization composed entirely of women connected directly as teachers or indirectly as wives of teachers with Tuskegee Institute. Thirteen women attended the first meeting of the club in March 1895, which was designed to improve its members intellectually, morally, and spiritually. Margaret Washington recalled in 1899 that "I said nothing of my plan to Mr. Washington or to anybody else beforehand, because I was uncertain as to how the experiment would turn out, and I thought if I failed I should not want anybody to know it."[7] Meetings were held twice monthly on the Tuskegee campus and new teachers were encouraged to join. When the club celebrated its twenty-fifth anniversary in 1920, it had 130 members. The work was done through departments, some of the most important of which were temperance, night schools, community work, prison work, suffrage, Sunday schools, and mothers' clubs.[8]

The Tuskegee Woman's Club actually helped to create new communities and establish social services that were common in towns. One of its first actions was creating a community out of a plantation settlement by providing social and educational services for the rural poor people. The Russell plantation, located eight miles from Tuskegee, was populated by hundreds of tenants—men, women, boys, and girls. Many of the people working in the plantation had been recently released from jail, others were working out their time on the plantation. No real home life existed on the plantation. As Washington described the situation, the people had no idea how to bring up children; they had no idea about what food to eat; they gave no thought to moral or spiritual life. These people had simply been left to drift for themselves without any training or guidance, without any help from the people who owned the plantation.[9]

Women from the Tuskegee club went to this plantation on weekends for more than twelve years, going from cabin to cabin teaching Sunday school, conducting newspaper reading clubs for men, and organizing boys' clubs, sewing classes for girls, and mothers' clubs. In short, they did all things necessary to improve the physical, moral, spiritual, and educational life of the people. Ann Davis, a graduate of Tuskegee, moved into a cabin on the plantation and opened a school in 1898. Parents paid what they could toward the upkeep of the school and the county contributed fifteen dollars a month to Davis's salary. Davis taught household industries at the school and the students raised agricultural products on the nearby ten-acre farm. The state assumed responsibility for the school in 1906. As a result of the efforts of the club women, life on the plantation completely changed. The people had their schools and churches and had larger and better homes; they changed their ideals altogether. When the plantation was able to function on its own, the Tuskegee women ceased to be directly involved and devoted their time to other projects.[10]

Beginning in 1910 Tuskegee Institute conducted a night school as part of its extension program. It was designed for the men and women who worked during the day and who could attend classes only at night. The school offered the traditional academic courses in reading, writing, and arithmetic along with instruction in cooking, sewing, carpentry, bricklaying, and painting. Initially, the institute employed two academic and six industrial teachers. However, by 1912 the night school became too great an expense, causing the institute to announce that it could no longer support the school. At this time the Tuskegee Woman's Club assumed responsibility for keeping the school open eight months a year. By their support of the school, club women demonstrated that they realized the importance of industrial education and adult education for blacks.

The club scaled down the program, employing only two to five teachers, usually senior students from the institute who worked without pay. The women did employ a head for the school at twenty-five dollars a month. In 1912 there were 103 night classes and thirty-seven day cooking classes. The cooking classes were designed for women who were the heads of families or who were employed by white people as cooks. For persons who could not afford much time or money, the night school provided an opportunity to secure an education. Many people were able to earn a better living because of the skills they acquired attending the school. Special emphasis was placed on the history of the race, because as Margaret Washington said, "We believe that any school which does not teach children to know and revere their own men and women of note, fails in its duty." The history course proved so beneficial that the women encouraged the teaching of African-American history in all schools throughout the county. Children of the town also became an integral part of the program and received educational experiences that reinforced what they learned in public schools or in some cases substituted for public education.[11]

The club had a special interest in the men who had to live part of their lives in the Macon County jail. Regularly each Sunday morning club members visited the jail, distributed literature, talked with the prisoners, and learned the needs of their families. The men were provided with newspapers, books, and holiday dinners. Club members located their wives and children and offered assistance to them to keep the family together until the husband was released. The members even followed the men who were sent from the county jail to the state penitentiary at Wetumpka and offered support to them. Washington said that the club members "felt that because a man makes a mistake and gets into jail is no reason why he should give up, or be given up; so he is followed from year to year."[12]

Since alcoholic beverages were seen as destroying homes and engendering loose morals, the temperance movement appealed strongly to black women in their drive to strengthen home life. Instead of creating temperance unions, black women worked largely through the temperance departments of the women's clubs. Temperance meetings, lectures, and medal contests were held throughout the entire county and thousands of pledges were made. Margaret Washington felt that no "work of the club had been more productive of good than the department of temperance." The temperance department also campaigned against cigarette smoking and urged merchants not to sell cigarettes to boys.[13]

The club women also made a special effort to assist the authorities in maintaining railroad stations and improving travel conditions for African-American people. In Tuskegee the club cleaned both the black and white waiting rooms and supplied them with chairs and reading material. In the black waiting rooms they hung pictures of Booker T. Washington, Abraham Lincoln, and Theodore Roosevelt. Pictures of George Washington, Grover Cleveland, and Woodrow Wilson were hung in the white waiting rooms. The women's clubs in Montgomery provided a similar service.[14]

One of the most successful projects the Tuskegee Woman's Club undertook was the sponsoring of mothers' meetings or mothers' clubs. The idea for the mothers' meetings grew out of an experience of Margaret Murray Washington at the first Tuskegee Negro Conference in 1892. Booker T. Washington called this conference to provide opportunities for blacks to discuss their problems and to seek solutions. Nearly five hundred people attended. While Booker Washington was trying to give the farmers new ideas, new hopes, and new aspirations, Margaret Washington realized that once again women were being ignored. It was assumed that women had no place worth mentioning in important concerns of life outside the household. Indeed, women themselves did not realize that they had any interest in the practical affairs that were being discussed by their husbands and sons. The thought came to Margaret Washington that the place to begin her work was with the women of Tuskegee and the surrounding area. She realized that women came into the town on Saturdays seeking to vary the monotony of their hard and cheerless lives. She became determined to locate these women and utilize the time they spent in town to some good purpose.[15]

Washington organized the first mothers' meeting in the upper story of an old store that stood on the main street of the town. The stairs were rickety, but it served the purpose for a time and there was no rent to pay. For fear of opposition, Washington took no one into her confidence except the man who lent her the room. She wondered how to get the women to the meeting, then decided to send a small boy through the streets with the instruction to say to every black woman loitering about the streets: "There is a woman upstairs who has something for you." This appeal brought about a dozen women. Washington said: "That first meeting I can never forget. The women came, and each one, as she entered, looked at me and seemed to say, 'Where is it?' We talked it all over, the needs of our women of the county, the best way of helping each other, and there and then began the mothers' meetings." [16]

These clubs were aimed primarily at women who came to town once a week and learned their lessons in manners, dress, and morals from what they saw on the street. The purpose of these meetings was to create an interest among rural women for self-improvement, the betterment of their homes, and the development of their children. In this project the educated women of Tuskegee reached out to rural women who were less motivated to effect changes in their lives. Washington believed that teachers from Tuskegee Institute should spearhead the organizational process because they possessed the necessary skills. The idea spread quickly and by 1920 there were hundreds of women all through Macon County who had attended the meetings. Most meetings had an average of from fifty to seventy-five women present.

The topics of discussion included ordinary subjects pertaining to the care of the home, the rearing of children, the relation of husband and wife, show of affection for the children, and amusements in the home. Some examples were, "The part a woman should take in buying land and building a house," "The care of children," "The boy's place in the home," "The importance of close confidence between mother and daughter; father and son," "How to teach children respect for parents and sacred relations," and "The kind of teacher to have in a community." Washington recommended that the topics be given to the women at least two weeks in advance in order that they could have ample time to think about them. The mothers were also taught basic information concerning nutrition in order to provide better meals for their families. They were urged to plant vegetables and to conserve their food. They were taught how to buy food and clothing for their families in the most economical manner. Washington aided African-American mothers even further by writing pamphlets about uplifting black womanhood and the home. [17]

At one of the meetings, the question arose "Should women stand around on the streets?" The discussion brought out the fact that women had no place to sit down except on the curbs or in a store. The mothers' clubs decided to provide a restroom for women where they could sit and visit with each other. A model sitting room and bedroom were set up to show the mothers how a home should be kept. Women traveled long distances on foot to attend the meetings. They often brought their children with them because they could not leave them at home. Soon the children were so numerous that Washington decided to provide an educational experience for them as well. They were taught simple lessons and received practical talks on behavior at home and in the streets. The club also provided a small library with picture books and games.[18]

The Tuskegee Mothers' Club meetings brought about a marked improvement among the women in the matter of dress and care of the hair. The women stopped the old plantation habit of "wrapping" their hair; they ceased to go barefooted and sit on the street "in listless fashion indulging in a kind of reckless familiarity with the men." Very few of the women knew how old they were. Washington helped them determine their age by asking them to recall some incident in their lives near the time they were born. The women were quite delighted to learn their approximate ages. The program was especially helpful for one woman who was an original member of the club and never missed a meeting. When she first came she appeared to be old, had little idea how to dress, and could not read or write. Later she learned how to dress, how to keep a neat house, how to read and write, and looked twenty years younger. This transformation stemmed largely from the lessons she learned while a member of the Tuskegee Mothers' Club. Washington summed up the importance of mothers' clubs by saying: "Teach our women the sacredness of the hearthstone, teach our men to guard it with their lives, and you will in the next twenty-five years give to the country an entirely new civilization, so far as the Negro home is concerned."[19]

The mothers' clubs in the various towns acted as school improvement associations for the black schools. These developments paralleled the steps taken by the white women's clubs in 1905 when they organized similar associations. The purpose of these organizations was to break down the barriers between the home and the school and to bring about cooperation between the two. In 1904 even before white women organized school improvement associations, the Tuskegee Mothers' Club assumed responsibility for providing for the physical needs of the Children's House, the laboratory school for Tuskegee Institute. At first the main purpose of the club was to beautify the schoolrooms and the grounds. The women made the schoolrooms more attractive by installing new shades, clean white curtains, and maps. They provided playground equipment, swings, vaulting bars, jogging boards, seesaws, balls, bats, and games for rainy days. They hung pictures of famous African-American leaders—Toussaint L'Ouverture, Frederick Douglass, Paul Lawrence Dunbar, and B. K. Bruce—in the entryway.[20] In 1917 they undertook to provide 200 new desks for the school at a cost of $800, which they raised by selling chicken salad, ice cream, and cake. With contributions of twenty-five to fifty cents the Tuskegee Mothers' Club raised the necessary money. Fundraising in black communities was obviously more difficult than in the white community because of the limited resources, yet blacks were not deterred from trying to meet their own needs.[21]

African-American women were as equally concerned with the public schools as were the white women, but they had fewer resources with which to work. Alabama maintained a dual school system, one for whites and another for blacks, when the state did not have enough money to fund one system adequately. If educational resources for white children were inadequate, resources for blacks were often nonexistent. The largest discrepancy between whites and blacks was the money the state appropriated for each child. In 1918 only $2.45 per year was allotted for black children as against $19.90 for white children. The black school buildings were only 10 percent of the value of white schools. Black schools urgently needed trained teachers. Almost half (43 percent) of the school-age children were black, but they were taught by not quite one-fourth (23 percent) of the teachers. But even these teachers were poorly trained; 70 percent had only third grade certificates. African-American teachers received less than half of white teachers' salaries; white women made $363.00 per year as compared with $152.00 for black teachers. Only half of all black school-age children attended classes, the average term being less than five months.[22]

Black club women stressed the importance of education for women. The majority of the leaders had some education and most taught in the black public schools or colleges of the state. However, not all black parents believed in the importance of education, especially for their daughters. Many young women worked in the fields for years with the promise from parents of going off to school someday. Some finally realized that such a day would never come and they would run away to Tuskegee Institute or some other school. Other parents wondered what a girl could do with an education. Margaret Washington answered that women could build up the communities where they live, that they could maintain homes that are orderly and clean, that they could teach others what they had learned. As far as Washington was concerned the home and the family were the starting points for the improvement of the black people. "No people can rise above the source—the mothers of the land—and there at the fountainhead the work must begin. . . . [T]he mother should have a wide knowledge of all matters pertaining to the moral, spiritual and intellectual training of her children." Washington believed that black women never had proper training in the home. They were occupied in keeping the homes of white people and caring for the white children and families. "It now becomes our duty to teach our girls to sweep and keep house, and bake bread, and care for children and motherhood, and instill in them the desire to beautify their environments and contribute to the improvement of their communities." Washington felt that the purity and safety of African-American families rested with the women; what their families were, the race would be.[23]

Another prominent club woman who worked to foster education was Cornelia Bowen, who was principal of Mt. Meigs Colored Institute and the only female president of the Alabama State Teachers Association. Bowen actively worked to encourage African-American girls and women to obtain an education. She influenced the lives of all students who attended her school and was largely responsible for the success of the institute. The school had been established in 1888 by Edward N. Pierce of Plainville, Connecticut, who visited Alabama during Reconstruction and saw the need for black education. He bought the Carter plantation at Waugh and lent the former slaves $2,000 to build a two-story, eight-room school. With modest equipment and at small expense, the school elevated the whole community and became a "Great Light." Bowen addressed the needs of the community and gave selflessly to the students. When students lived too far away to return home at night, Bowen allowed them to live with her until her house became too crowded. At this point a new dormitory was built, which left the institute with a debt of $2,500. By the twenty-fifth anniversary in 1913, the institute employed five teachers and enrolled 300 boys and girls. They were taught not only to "read, write, and cipher" but to understand the importance of character by Bowen, who was described as the Mary Lyon of her race.[24]

Like the white women's clubs, the black women's clubs established a reformatory for boys. Since the Alabama Boys' Industrial School created by the Alabama Federation of Women's Clubs was for white boys only, the Alabama Federation of Colored Women's Clubs established a reformatory for black boys at Mt. Meigs in 1907. The motivation of the African-American women was similar to that of the white women— they wanted to keep youthful offenders out of the prisons and coal mines of the state. Josephine T. Washington of Montgomery, the organizer of the drive for the project, said that the reformatory was for "small boys and boys not quite so small, but all boys who linger still in the lap of childhood." The federation bought twenty acres of land and erected a five-room cottage that cost $2,000. The club women raised the money over a period of time from relatively small donations. A superintendent was employed and four boys taken in even before the building was completed. By 1912 the reformatory employed two full-time teachers and several others part-time and housed forty-four boys. During the first five years over three hundred boys had lived in the home and the estimated worth of the property had increased to $5,000.[25]

As early as 1911 the Alabama Federation of Colored Women's Clubs realized that they would not be able to continue providing the $2,000 a year needed to support the reformatory. The number of boys had increased to forty and the courts were adding to the number. The club women decided to ask the state to assume responsibility for the institution. Cornelia Bowen, Lillian B. Dungee, and Margaret Washington began a campaign to interest the legislature in the project. In 1912 the land, equipment, improvements, and the inmates were formally transferred to the state. The state assumed responsibility for the institution and its operation and appropriated $2,000 for that purpose. Gov. Emmett O'Neal appointed Bowen and Dungee from the Alabama Federation of Colored Women's Clubs to the board of trustees. The women regarded this as a victory. They felt that the efforts of the black womanhood of Alabama "had been recognized, endorsed, and adopted by the state" and the cause "for which they have long labored and sacrificed, is assured of protection and perpetuity." Alabama now had the Reform School for Juvenile Negro Lawbreakers and its inception came from the "loving and loyal Negro women of the state." The state provided less money for this school than it did for the white boys' industrial school. Hastings H. Hart of the Russell Sage Foundation said that the black boys "have not only made bricks without straw but they had made bricks without clay." The state appropriated only seven dollars per boy, yet with surpluses from this small sum they built a reinforced concrete dairy barn and other buildings. Hart recommended that the monthly allowance should be raised to $12.50 per boy, the amount at that time provided to the white boys' industrial school.[26]

The boys' reformatory at Mt. Meigs consumed a major portion of the time, effort, and money of the club women, but it was not their only project. Other projects included the establishment of the Girls' Rescue Home. Location and financing for this project were more difficult; it was not until 1921 that this home was established, also at Mt. Meigs. Continuing their interest in education, the club women created kindergartens whenever they could; they worked to secure playground equipment for black children; they desired to extend the school year to six months; they attacked illiteracy; and they encouraged students to learn a trade. In their concern with prison reform, they favored the separation of youthful offenders from hardened criminals, the creation of juvenile courts, and the abolition of the convict lease system. They created a Big Sister movement, which rescued children from undesirable surroundings and placed them in a new environment of love, sympathy, and protection.[27]

African-American women also supported the demand for the vote. There is no evidence that they created suffrage associations in Alabama, but they did work for suffrage through their various women's clubs. Indeed, black women had a more consistent attitude toward the vote than did white women. By the 1890s blacks tended to support a political philosophy of universal suffrage, whereas white women advocated a limited, educated suffrage. Black men also had fewer objections to women voting than did white men; suffrage challenged the black male's traditional role less than it did that of white males. White antisuffragists harped on the theme of true womanhood in its many variations, but by contrast few African-American women opposed the concept of women voting. The major exception were rural black women who regarded political education as secondary to activities and programs designed to improve the quality of life on an immediate, tangible level.[28]

Like white suffrage leaders, black women saw the franchise as a cure for many of their ills; sexual exploitation headed the list. They felt women needed the ballot to uphold their virtue and to foster sentiment in favor of their own protection. They also felt that woman suffrage would be a boon to education by providing them a voter's influence with legislators and school boards. Being able to vote would allow women to work for improved schools and compulsory education. African-American women were also interested in the vote because the vast majority of them had to work for a living. The most immediate concern, however, was the loss of the vote by black men and the charge that the men had "sold" their votes to white supremacist politicians. Disfranchised, racially conscious black women were highly critical of men who had the ballot but who did not know its value. Underlying these attitudes was the conviction that unlike the masses of black men, women would never betray the race if they had the power of the vote. Their exalted sense of themselves as a group extended to their feelings about the suffrage issue. Nannie Helen Burroughs, an African-American educator, said, "The Negro woman, therefore, needs to get back by the wise *use* of it, what the Negro man has lost by the *misuse* of it. She needs it to ransom her race." W. E. B. Du Bois applauded the greater tenacity of black women as a group. "You can bribe some pauperized Negro laborers with a few dollars at election time," he said, "but you cannot bribe a Negro woman." Evidently this thought also occurred to white supremacists in the South, especially in the states with a large black population, which gave them further reason for opposing woman suffrage.[29]

Margaret Washington, the best known black woman in the state, took a cautious approach to the suffrage issue. In 1913 she described herself as a "conservative" who had not paraded in the streets or gone on hunger strikes, as the more militant suffragists were doing by this time. She said woman suffrage had never "kept her awake at night," but she believed that before the United States could consider itself a democracy, it needed to be willing to trust its citizens black and white, men and women to be loyal to their government. She added that she was certain about one thing: "we are reading and studying the great questions which make for the good of the country and when the vote is given to women . . . we shall be ready to cast our votes intelligently and there shall not be the general accusation that our votes are for sale for all the way from a drink of liquor to two dollars."[30]

The leading African-American suffragist was Adella Hunt Logan of the Tuskegee Woman's Club, who supported woman suffrage as early as the turn of the century. Logan was born in Sparta, Georgia, in 1863. She graduated from Atlanta University in 1881 and began teaching school in south Georgia. She joined the Tuskegee faculty in 1883 and within a few years she became the lady principal. But she retired as a teacher in 1888 when she married Warren Logan, Tuskegee's treasurer. Tuskegee did not allow more than one member of a family to draw a salary from the institute's limited financial resources. She had six children, most of whom died before reaching adulthood. Logan soon became interested in the suffrage drive and worked for women's right to vote for nearly two decades. She was a life member of the National American Woman Suffrage Association as early as 1901. As a charter member and officer of the Tuskegee Woman's Club, she participated in many of its activities, but her major work was on behalf of suffrage. She led spirited monthly discussions at club meetings and established a large personal library on the subject, which she opened to all who were interested. She worked regionally and nationally within the National Association of Colored Women to educate her associates about suffrage. She helped establish a department of suffrage within the organization and headed it for sev-

ADELLA HUNT LOGAN, SUFFRAGE LEADER AND ACTIVE MEMBER OF THE
ALABAMA FEDERATION OF COLORED WOMEN'S CLUBS. *COLLECTIONS OF
THE HERNDON FOUNDATION.*

eral years. She died tragically in 1915 when she committed suicide by jumping from the second story of a building on the campus of Tuskegee Institute.[31]

Logan's thinking regarding the ideology of suffrage evolved over the period during which she was active as a suffrage leader. In a 1905 article she argued for suffrage on the basis of abstract justice, as other suffrage leaders of the day were doing. She quoted Jefferson's famous statement in the Declaration of Independence about governments deriving their just powers from the consent of the governed. She pointed out that women must obey the laws made by men; they must pay taxes levied by men; but they had no voice in writing these laws. She cited some of the benefits that accrued when women voted: better schools, less crime, better laws for women and children. She refuted some of the common objections to women voting: that women do not want the vote, that they are not interested in politics, that the home would be neglected, and that women are represented by their husbands. She concluded by saying that "If white American women, with all their natural advantages, need the ballot . . . How much more do black Americans, male and female, need the strong defense of a vote to help secure their right to life, liberty and the pursuit of happiness?"[32]

By 1912 Logan believed that more black women were becoming interested in studying public issues and in voting. Under the influence of progressivism, African-American women along with white women were beginning to realize that in order to be good housekeepers, they must be able to vote on such issues as pure food, sanitary and safe buildings, adequate school facilities, reform schools, and juvenile courts. "Colored women feel keenly that they may help in civic betterment, and that their broadened interests in matters of good government may arouse the colored brother, who for various reasons had become too indifferent to his duties of citizenship."[33] Logan felt that black women had the motivation and skills to contribute to the improvement of conditions in the black community.

The Alabama Federation of Colored Women's Clubs officially endorsed suffrage in 1910, but it was the 1913 convention that took decisive action under the leadership of Logan, who headed the committee on resolutions. The convention approved of a strongly worded resolution that favored unrestricted suffrage and looked forward to the day when "our broad country woman shall share with man the responsibility of deciding questions—social, economic, and civic—which have to do not only with her welfare, but with the deepest interests of those dearer to her even than herself." The leaders believed that when women were enfranchised, the African-American women would be equal to the situation—that they would be educated well enough to cast their ballots wisely. After the ratification of the Nineteenth Amendment in 1920, subsequent conventions continued to support woman suffrage, and black women were continually encouraged to organize in precincts and to teach women the value of their vote. They were encouraged to pay their poll taxes, because the ballot would be their only salvation. Their popular slogan was "A voteless people is a voiceless people." [34]

The black women's club movement had some things in common with the white club movement that preceded it. To a certain extent, black women were inspired by the success of the white movement. The two groups were organized in much the same way. The General Federation of Women's Clubs was the white equivalent to the National Association of Colored Women. The membership of both organizations consisted mostly of middle-class, educated women who were steeped in the Protestant ethic. Neither group questioned the superiority of middle-class values or ways of life. Both believed in the importance of the home and woman's moral influence within it. Black and white women saw the family as a microcosm and cornerstone of society. [35]

Nevertheless there were distinct differences between the two organizations and the perspective of women within them. For African-American women the club movement was a vehicle for their recognition as a distinct social and political force in the black community. They felt a special calling in the club movement that gave them a sense of exhilaration. They were able to achieve a sense of self-identity that they had not possessed before. White women had this same feeling, but did not have to depend solely upon the club movement for such recognition. They were already viewed as the moral leaders of the family and home, and as such were awarded a place of honor by society in the private sphere.

White women were trying to enlarge this sphere; they were frustrated by their exclusion from occupations and other activities for which their education and background had prepared them.

High on both organizational agendas were reform and aid to the poor. But with these goals also, the difference between the women's organizations were immediately apparent. White women had limited concern for working-class women or women who had to work to make a living. They did help the poor, but such activities were not new because helping the poor was one of the few socially sanctioned activities that could be performed outside the home. African-American women saw their mission as quite different. They did not hold themselves aloof from the masses, but understood that their fate was bound with them. They realized what Mary Church Terrell declared: "Self-preservation demands that [black women] go among the lowly, illiterate and even the vicious, to whom they are bound by ties of race and sex . . . to reclaim them."[36] Class did not separate black Alabama women; the club women reached out to working women, tenant farm wives, and poor women.

The differing missions of the black and white movements were evident in the people each group chose to serve. The African-American clubs represented the effort of the few competent on behalf of the masses. Their motto, Lifting as We Climb, reflected this position. The club movement among the black women had to reach all black women and lift them together as they moved upward. The black club movement was organized by women concerned with how to help and protect some defenseless woman, how to aid some poor boy to complete a much-needed education, how to lengthen the school year, how to instruct a mother in the difficulties of child training. White women might talk about going onward, but they were already uplifted.

African-American club women were deeply concerned about morality. As they saw it, moral women were the cornerstone of the good home and it was only through the home that a people could become great. More homes, better homes, purer homes were their goal. Black women saw themselves not just as messengers but as living examples. The mother in the home, as the teacher in the schoolroom, and the woman in the church set the standard for the multitudes. "The Negro home," said

Josephine Bruce, "is rapidly assuming the position designed for it. It is distinctly becoming the center of social and intellectual life; it is building up strength and righteousness in its sons and daughters, and equipping them for the inevitable battles of life which grow out of the struggle for existence."[37]

The black women's clubs placed great emphasis on education. Because the majority of women had to work, it was important for women to get an education. Their occupational choices were limited to teaching in the colored schools or performing domestic service. Education had a dramatic impact on women's status and quality of life because it enabled them to find employment in an area other than domestic work. It also shielded women from the sexual harassment that many of them confronted in white homes. Historians are only beginning to probe the effect that rape or the threat of rape had on black women. A major goal of black women's clubs was to provide women with dignified work and protection from sexual exploitation.[38]

The purpose of the National Association of Colored Women was summed up well by Margaret Washington. She said the goal was

> to build better homes, to establish good schools, to insist upon a cleaner and more intelligent ministry, to teach respect for the aged, to bring the child and parent closer together to each other, to bring man and woman, husband and wife to a realization of their individual responsibility and so to reduce divorce and separation, to make a fireside for a race, and last but not least the Colored Woman's duty is to teach herself self-control, to give the same lesson to all who come under her influence, revolutionizing communities and bringing about their civic salvation and so saving the race to itself.[39]

By 1920 African-American women of Alabama had created organizations that dealt with the problems of education, self-improvement, and community improvement. They established programs that provided for industrial education and adult education, they worked for better schools in their communities, they created mothers' clubs, they established a reform school for black boys, and they worked for temperance and suffrage. But most important, black women were united by a sense of racial pride. They had a distinct mission—the moral education of the race. These black middle-class leaders defined their role as moral beacons. Through the club movement they intended to improve the training of children and provide leadership for the race. African-American women showed that they were capable of identifying the needs of the black community and creating programs that were meaningful and enduring. In their efforts to provide social services they unified their communities.

5 CLUB WOMEN AND CHILD LABOR, 1903–1919

Alabama women joined with Progressive women nationwide in trying to alleviate the ills of society that were the result of rapid industrialization, especially the evil of child labor. The club women approached this problem with confidence, believing that they were pursuing their proper interest as mothers and homemakers. These earnest, wide-awake women were concerned with everything that related to the family. They felt that their best efforts should be aimed at the welfare of "the Woman, the Child, and the Home."[1] The drive to abolish child labor was ideally suited to the interests of club women. The two major leaders of this drive were Nellie Kimball Murdock of Birmingham and Lura Harris Craighead of Mobile, quintessential Progressive women who were involved in virtually every reform movement in the state.

The white women of the state played a large role in the long drive to abolish child labor. The Alabama Federation of Women's Clubs and the Alabama Woman's Christian Temperance Union put child labor high on their agendas, but it was the AFWC that played the dominant role. Black club women were not active in the child labor movement because black children were not employed. The club women were never entirely successful in eliminating the practice, but they were able to provide some protection for the children of the state. The state legislature passed child labor acts first in 1903, then successive acts in 1907, 1911, 1915, and 1919. The legislature was faced with the issue of child labor every time it met, which was only once every four years. The constitution of 1901 established the practice of holding regular sessions at these relatively infrequent intervals. Since the hottest political issue of the day was prohibition, child labor often was forced to compete with that issue for the attention of the legislators, especially from 1907 to 1915. Women were frequently in Montgomery filling the galleries and lobbying the legislators for one issue or the other. By 1915 women were also campaigning for the right to vote. The presence of women in politics was a wholly new experience for the state legislators. Often they were not quite sure how to respond to the changed situation.

The issue of child labor arose as early as 1887, when the state was just beginning to industrialize. A law was enacted prohibiting the employment of children under the age of fourteen and limiting those under sixteen to an eight-hour day. However, with the rapid industrial growth in the next few years, the pressure to use child labor, especially in the cotton mills, became intense and the law was repealed in 1894. Without a law, in the period from 1890 to 1900 there was a 386 percent increase in children under sixteen in the Alabama mills. By 1900 they constituted one-fourth of the textile workers. Their exploitation posed a major threat to the health and well-being of the state, although a comparatively small portion of the people knew about the existing conditions.[2]

Child labor was a national evil in 1900, and in terms of absolute numbers there were more children under sixteen working in the North than in the South. However, in the North the problem had been recognized and was being attacked, but in the South the opposite was true. Due to the work of Samuel Gompers of the American Federation of Labor (AFL) and the reformer Florence Kelley, laws were enacted in the northern states, most of which prevented child labor under sixteen. As a result, the number of employed children under sixteen was reduced from 15.6 to 7.7 percent of the work force between 1880 and 1900.[3]

Conditions in the South made the enactment of labor legislation highly unlikely. Manufacturing was a relatively new development and one that was strongly encouraged by the leaders of the New South as a solution to the economic problems of the area. The mill workers themselves were strong individualists who were unlikely to support labor unions. The southern public was not responsive to the need for legislation to correct this abuse. The legislature of Alabama made sporadic attempts to reenact child labor legislation during the 1890s. But the child labor acts that were presented in 1897 and 1899 did not receive serious consideration.

By 1900 the situation began to change. The WCTU and the club women began to show awareness of the issue; the growing employment of young children was new to the women and their sense of justice was outraged. Martha L. Spencer, the president of the WCTU, became the first to speak out publicly in opposition to child labor. The WCTU had gone so far as to sponsor the weak bill that had been introduced into the 1898–99 session of the legislature. These actions by the WCTU were soon followed by those of the Alabama Federation of Women's Clubs. At a meeting of the executive committee in Birmingham, the leadership of the AFWC learned of the absence of any law regulating child labor. The sympathies of the women were thoroughly aroused and all board members were requested to report the matter to their clubs and try to influence public opinion. The opportunity to support children touched the interest of club women as mothers. Moreover, the AFL and Gompers began to promote child labor legislation in Alabama. Child labor restrictions had a strong humanitarian appeal that would win support from people who would not under other circumstances support labor legislation. The leaders of labor were aware that they could secure allies from among the nonlaboring groups, such as women, for the enactment of such laws.[4]

In 1900 Gompers sent a special agent of the AFL to Alabama, Irene Ashby, a young Englishwoman. Ashby had been educated at Westfield College, where she was interested in industrial and social problems. She was sent to Alabama not as a labor organizer, but for the sole purpose of promoting child labor legislation. The Alabama legislature was in session and support existed for the restriction of child labor. The coming

of a special agent to work up anti–child labor feeling aroused the interests not only of the organized workers, but also of the more progressive
and liberal-minded people of the cities, who were found primarily in the
various women's groups. From December 1900 to January 1901 Ashby
conducted an investigation into the cotton mills of the state. She went
to sixteen cities and into twenty-three mills, asking a uniform set of
seventy questions of the superintendents, managers, operators, and persons living in close contact with mill life. She made the first thorough
investigation of child labor in any southern state and prepared a report
that showed that 430 children under the age of twelve were working
more than twelve hours a day in the Alabama mills.[5]

Since Ashby realized that labor unions had little political strength
in Alabama, she began to search out interested people who could use
her study to promote restrictions on child labor. She took her information to the Rev. Edgar Gardner Murphy, rector of St. John's Episcopal
Church, Montgomery, and sought his aid. Coming to Montgomery in
1899, Murphy was much impressed with the need to address the South's
social and racial problems. He had taken part in race conferences held
in 1900 and had written and spoken on the subject of race. He turned
to the child labor movement at a time when a person of ability and influence was needed as a leader to bring together the several groups that
were interested and to produce unity of action.[6]

In her role, Ashby was also an ideal person to serve as the advocate
for a child labor measure. Her presence in Alabama served to reassure
the socially elite women of Montgomery, Birmingham, and Mobile as
to their wisdom in advocating a labor measure. She was a person of education and found that she could meet the conservative classes on their
own ground. At the same time the local labor organizations were glad
to accept her as the representative of the AFL. When she succeeded in
securing the cooperation of the clergy, it looked as though her efforts
might be successful.[7]

A new child labor act was introduced into the legislature of 1901. This
issue had to compete with the major political concern of the day, which
was the disfranchisement of blacks. The Constitutional Convention of
1901 met concurrently with the legislative session. The child labor bill,

sponsored by Rep. A. J. Reily of Ensley and Sen. Hugh Morrow of Birmingham, provided for a twelve-year age limit except for children of widowed mothers or disabled fathers, in which case the age limit was ten. It also prohibited night work for those under sixteen, required all employed children to be able to read and write, and authorized the state employment of a factory inspector at an annual salary of $1,500. These standards were higher than those proposed in measures previously introduced in Alabama or in other southern states. At the same time this bill was introduced, a companion bill for compulsory school attendance was presented in both houses.[8]

The Reily-Morrow bill was the first one of its kind to receive any degree of public interest. Ashby reported that petitions favoring the bill came from Birmingham and some of the mill towns. Delegations of interested citizens went to Montgomery to lobby for it. Murphy, along with the Montgomery Ministerial Association, testified for the measure. Ashby observed, "The foremost women, both privately and in their clubs, gave it their support; the press . . . gave columns to the discussion of it and to interviews with me. The humanitarian and community aspect of the matter swept away prejudices, and the society and religious lion lay down with the labor lamb."[9] The Alabama Federation of Women's Clubs and the WCTU sent delegations to Montgomery, one of which was headed by Julia Tutwiler, the well-known reformer, who was the secretary for the National Society of Charities and Corrections. These actions were the beginning of active interest in legislation for the protection of women and children.[10]

With this public interest in the bill, the mill owners became aroused and began their own lobbying. Southern mill men did not reply to the reformers with straightforward laissez-faire arguments, but instead launched personal attacks on the advocates of reform. The lobbyists made capital of the fact that Ashby was a foreigner and charged that she was being paid by the eastern and English mills to make trouble in the South. They replied to Murphy's arguments with a degree of vituperation that amazed him and implied that he too was being paid by eastern mills. They later developed other arguments, used again and again. For example, they maintained that Georgia, with twice as many spindles, should restrict child labor before Alabama. They claimed that parents put pressure on the mills to employ their children. The mill owners claimed they feared that if the children were not given jobs, the parents would not work. They made use of the "idle hands" theory. This widely held view was that a compulsory education law should precede any restrictions on child labor, because without such a law unemployed children would not go to school and would get into trouble. The mills were seen as an education and good training for life. They taught children the discipline of hard work. The arguments of the mill owners were persuasive because the house committee rejected the bill by a nine-to-four vote and the senate by a five-to-two vote.[11]

The most important outcome of the legislative contest was the formation of the Alabama Child Labor Committee (ACLC) in 1901, with Murphy as chairman. The lack of newspaper coverage and public interest in the bill convinced Murphy and Ashby that a campaign to inform and arouse the people was essential if child labor was to be regulated. Murphy's first actions were to write a series of pamphlets that were to have national significance; they became the first body of printed material that presented arguments favorable to child labor legislation in the South. These included *The Case Against Child Labor, The South and Her Children,* and a series of ten personally taken photographs, *Pictures from Life: Mill Children in Alabama.* These presented, as words could not, the true plight of Alabama's working children. The publications became a major force in every state where the battle against child labor was waged. Written by a native southerner, a man who by birth and profession belonged to the conservative class, and moderate in tone, they succeeded in conveying what would have been impossible coming from another source. Murphy was recognized as a prominent child labor reformer in every section.[12]

Irene Ashby had an opportunity to carry on her own campaign of education. She was invited to address the state convention of the Alabama Federation of Women's Clubs, which met in Montevallo in May 1901. Her speech, "Child Labor in Factories," was easily the most significant aspect of the convention. Described as a magnetic and delightful speaker, she discussed the evils of child labor, especially in the South where so many children were employed in the cotton mills. She described the recent attempt to secure legislation that had failed, leaving ten-year-old children at work in the cotton mills and nearly one-third of the mill hands under the age of sixteen. "When she finished a burst of applause gave evidence of the fact that every man—there were many—and every woman present endorsed all she had said." [13]

As a result of Ashby's speech, the AFWC threw its wholehearted support behind the regulation of child labor. The federation adopted the issue as its major project for the coming year. The members further pledged themselves to persuade their respective clubs to make it their major business also. In this way child labor would become the special work of every club in the state as well as of the federation collectively. The federation further decided to collect data on child labor for the information of the clubs and the general public. Most important, they voted to endorse a bill to be presented to the 1903 legislature by the Alabama Child Labor Committee and pledged to work for its passage. In order to carry out these decisions, the federation appointed a special committee on legislation in 1902 with a large Montgomery membership so that a quorum could be assembled at a moment's notice. This committee prepared articles for the newspapers, interviewed legislators, and held joint meetings with the ACLC. They talked child labor early and late. Indeed, the legislative committee showed "admirable judgment and unflagging zeal" in their work. [14]

Irene Ashby left Alabama for a brief period and went back to England to marry a British soldier who was returning from the Boer War. When she returned to the South in the fall of 1901 as Irene Ashby MacFadyen, she came as a representative of the AFL but one invited by the Alabama Child Labor Committee. Murphy realized that popular opposition to organized labor would lead many to oppose a child labor bill if it appeared as a labor measure or as one coming from forces outside the state. MacFadyen's task was to travel around the state speaking to women on behalf of child labor and compulsory education. From October 1901 until the spring of 1902, she met with women's clubs and other organizations throughout the state. She was especially well received in Montgomery. The society editor of the *Montgomery Advertiser* covered her activities thoroughly in the social columns. She was popular with the society women and was a guest in the homes of prominent people. Thus through her relationship with the state labor committee and prominent women of Montgomery, MacFadyen made contacts with the leaders of organizations that enabled her to carry her message throughout the state.[15]

MacFadyen continued her association with the two major women's organizations that supported child labor legislation. She was invited to speak to the Alabama WCTU, which met at Fort Payne. At this meeting resolutions supporting child labor legislation were adopted and a committee appointed to cooperate with the Alabama Child Labor Committee. The Alabama Federation of Women's Clubs continued their work of educating the public in preparation for the next session of the legislature in 1903. She addressed public meetings at Tuscaloosa and Mobile, where she met members of the clergy and prominent politicians. At Auburn she spoke to the students at the polytechnic institute and to the local chapter of the DAR.[16]

It was only in Huntsville that she met any hostility. There were eleven mills in this area and the mill owners resented her advocating restrictions on child labor. She was refused admission to the Dallas and Merrimac mills. She found that the people were ignorant of conditions existing among the workers. However, she had an opportunity to educate them because the editor of the paper opened his columns to her and she wrote the leading articles for the week. She spoke at a large meeting at the Huntsville city hall in February 1902, where she met some opposition. Indeed, she even feared that she might be arrested.[17] She then returned to Montgomery, where she met one more time with her friends before she departed for South Africa in April 1902 to join her husband, who was stationed there in the army. The effect of MacFadyen's work was to arouse the interest of people who might otherwise have been ignorant or indifferent to child labor. She appealed especially to the women and through them to the voters. The publicity that she gave to the extreme cases of child labor was part of the drive to gain public support for the law.[18]

The club women and the WCTU cooperated with the Alabama Child

Labor Committee in their drive to educate the voters and the legislators of the state about the evils of child labor. All of their efforts were aimed at the meeting of the legislature in 1903. They hoped to get a child labor act through this session, because the legislature would not meet again until 1907. When the 1903 session of the legislature convened, a child labor bill similar to the 1901 version was introduced. The Alabama Federation of Women's Clubs even held a special session in Montgomery at the same time that the legislature met to be on hand to lobby for the bill. The meetings, held in the Court Street Methodist Church, were well attended not only by the delegates but by many women of the city.[19]

The theme of the convention was "A Little Child Shall Lead Them." The women of the federation said that it was the factory child who led them to Montgomery. They desired to "save the little children of Alabama from mill labor through the force of authority of law framed by the Legislature now in session. . . . Never before in the history of the South has our duty as women and mothers been so clearly outlined." One of their first acts was to give to each member of the legislature a copy of a pamphlet written by Lura Harris Craighead listing the arguments for and against child labor.[20]

The bill before the legislature had been introduced in January 1903 by T. J. Hall of Montgomery, a labor Democrat who had consulted with Samuel Gompers on the specific provisions. Since children of eight or ten years old worked in the mills, the bill proposed that children had to be twelve years old before they could be employed. However, an exception was provided. A child who was ten could be employed if he or she was an orphan or had a widowed mother. Other provisions limited the number of hours a child could work in a day or week. Violations would be punished by a fine of $25–$200. The Hall bill had been given publicity through the press and it was supported by the *Montgomery Advertiser,* which had become an advocate of child labor reform, giving support in the editorial columns.[21]

As the legislature convened, Edgar Gardner Murphy realized that chances for the passage of this bill were slim. The average lawmaker had little pressure to comply with popular wishes, since he would not be up for reelection for four years. Murphy was also concerned about the commitment of Lillian Milner Orr, president of the Alabama Federation of Women's Clubs. He was disturbed that Orr, in the summer of 1902, had been willing to support a voluntary agreement among the mill owners instead of a law prohibiting child labor. Murphy knew this approach would be ineffective. Agreements of this kind had shown that only the best mills complied, whereas those with the poorest conditions flouted the agreements. Voluntary agreements of the type proposed placed the honest mills at a disadvantage. Further, Murphy knew that Orr's father had been a major opponent of child labor legislation and she and her family were stockholders of Birmingham's Avondale Mills, which employed fifty-six children.[22]

Orr, as president of the federation, was obligated to support restrictions on child labor because that had been federation policy since 1900. But she and other women in the organization came from the socioeconomic class that was closely tied to the mill interests. Orr said that she realized there were two sides to every question. When she became president, she began to study the child labor issue and realized some very well respected people did not want restrictions placed on the labor of children. She listened to the mill managers and was convinced an agreement with the ACLC was possible. She said, "In the pursuance of this hope I held out a flag of truce to the mill men and opened the way for agreement with them." In short, she was willing to compromise and did not hold out for the measure as proposed by the Alabama Child Labor Committee.[23]

The ACLC and the AFWC decided to take half a loaf rather than none. A meeting was arranged between Murphy, Orr, and leaders of the mills. The compromise they agreed to included many of the features of the original bill. Murphy and the ACLC were able to maintain the age limit of twelve years with the exception of children of ten who had widowed mothers or dependent fathers. The difference came in the number of hours a child could work during the day or week. The compromise bill allowed younger children to work longer hours or at night. A statement of agreement to the terms was signed by Murphy representing the Alabama Child Labor Committee, the mill owners, and Orr as president of the Alabama Federation of Women's Clubs. However, Orr was not allowed to sign for herself because she was a woman and women had no legal standing. A man signed as her proxy. The AFWC and Orr received almost exclusive credit for the compromise.[24] Once the compromise was reached, little trouble was expected in getting it through the legislature. The house passed it with one dissenting vote, but it ran into difficulty in the senate. Opponents argued that the wishes of the parents should be respected, that the industry would be crippled, that dangerous precedents would be set, that the measure was class legislation, and that it would discourage outside investment because the South's chief asset was cheap labor. The bill aroused such a storm of protest that "it might have been supposed that the only thing that stood between the mills and absolute ruin was the labor of little children."[25] A motion to table was defeated by only two votes, but eventually it passed by a bare majority of six votes.

Even though the bill may have fallen short of ideal provisions, its enactment was a solid achievement. It marked the acceptance of the principle of public regulation and opened the way for more adequate laws. Its passage indicated a measure of awareness on the part of the legislators and the general public. Child labor was destined to remain an issue for the next two decades. The role that the federation played in the drive to get this bill adopted was without precedent. The women won a substantial victory and showed the political leaders how effective groups of organized women could be. Seldom before had the opinions of women been taken seriously by those in political and economic power. The women were powerful lobbyists; they filled the galleries and made their presence known. Holding the federation's convention at the time the legislature met to consider the bill was a smart political move. It was a totally new experience for the state legislators to be told how to vote by a group of women. Some of them did not like it. One senator remarked that the "ladies" had no ballots, but they had come near to voting this time and had apparently hypnotized some of the members of the senate.[26] Alabama women were learning the importance of political power and the techniques of using it.

Alabama's campaign for a child labor law was watched closely by other southern states. The 1903 law set a precedent that other states soon followed. As a direct result of his role in the Alabama campaign, Edgar Gardner Murphy achieved national prominence. His writings were widely read and he was in demand as a speaker. The Alabama campaign spread to other states and in 1904 the National Child Labor Committee (NCLC) was created, which set standards for child labor legislation in all of the states. Murphy was the first temporary secretary of this organization. He played a critical role in the founding and directing of its early policy. He had left Alabama in late 1901 to become secretary of the General Education Board, but he continued his interest in Alabama and in child labor.[27]

The campaign had energized the forces of the women in both the AFWC and the WCTU and encouraged them to continue to work for child labor restrictions. The law that Alabama adopted proved to be inadequate to prevent children from working. The problem of inspection and enforcement had not been solved and the age limit was seriously weakened by the exemption clause. As the AFWC kept track of the enforcement of the act, they shortly discovered that the law was being evaded and children under the age of twelve were once again working. Members of the federation went to Gov. William D. Jelks in 1904 and pointed out this problem. Jelks refused to take the women seriously. He responded that he would gladly take steps to prevent it if they could prove the law was really being abused. The women realized that they were in no position to do so and decided to use their influence to secure a law that provided for a state inspector. They pointed out that in Oregon the child labor law provided for a board of five inspectors, three of whom were women.[28]

In 1906 Braxton Bragg Comer, widely viewed as progressive, was elected governor and Alabama began to consider a multitude of social problems and solutions that were considered "advanced." The governor and the legislature began debating railroad regulation, public health measures, juvenile courts, education, prohibition, and child labor. Comer was the owner of the Avondale Mills and had represented the mill owners in the compromise legislation of 1903. He was viewed as being only lukewarm in his support of child labor legislation.[29]

Although Alabama had led in the fight among the southern states in

1903 for the regulation of child labor, by 1907 other states had enacted legislation that left Alabama at the bottom of the list in age limit for employment. The women of the state federation continued their interest in correcting this "deplorable condition." The Alabama Child Labor Committee once again sought the aid of the club women in lobbying the legislature for the passage of a new and stronger act. It wanted to raise the age limit to fourteen years, limit any exceptions to the age of twelve, and provide for a factory inspector to improve enforcement of the act.[30]

In 1907 two child labor bills were introduced into the Alabama legislature. One was written by the Alabama Child Labor Committee in consultation with the Alabama Federation of Women's Clubs and introduced by William L. Pitts of Perry. The other favored the interest of the mill owners and was introduced by A. K. Kirby of Madison. Both bills provided that no boy under the age of fourteen or girl under the age of sixteen should be employed, except in order to support indigent parents, under which circumstances the age limit should be twelve. The chief difference was in the power of enforcement. The Pitts bill provided for the employment of a factory inspector at a salary of $2,300 a year who would visit the factories four times a year. This provision was a major goal of the reformers. The Kirby bill did not provide for enforcement.[31]

The lobbyists for the Pitts bill were representatives of the Alabama Federation of Women's Clubs and the Alabama Child Labor Committee. These groups were assisted by Alexander J. McKelway, who was the southern secretary for the National Child Labor Committee. McKelway had come to the state as early as 1906 to aid in reorganizing the state committee, which had become inactive. The legislative committee of the AFWC testified before the joint House and Senate Committee on Mines and Manufacturing. Lura Harris Craighead spoke for the women and made a strong appeal for children who were forced to earn a living at an unreasonably early age under adverse circumstances.[32] The mill owners lobbied for the Kirby bill. After the hearings the bills were not acted on during the winter session of the legislature. But the legislature did pass a bill providing for the inspection of jails, almshouses, and cotton mills. This action alarmed the child labor reformers because they feared that this action might be seen as a substitute for a child labor act that provided for its own enforcement.

During the summer the reform groups, the state labor committee, the AFWC, and the National Child Labor Committee carried on a vigorous campaign. Murphy wrote an open letter to the legislature and pointed out that it was inconsistent to appoint a state game inspector at a salary of $2,500 and yet refuse to provide for a child labor inspector. In June Governor Comer received a report from Dr. Shirley Bragg, first inspector of cotton mills, which showed that the child labor law was being flagrantly violated. At this point Governor Comer got behind the child labor law.[33]

Eventually a substitute proposal was adopted that was a compromise, but one that was much more favorable to the manufacturers than the reformers wanted. In the final version, the age limit went back to twelve years but allowed for no exceptions. Abolishing the exceptions was a big step forward in real regulation, because the conditions of the exceptions were so hard to prove. Every mill appeared to have a large number of widowed mothers or helpless fathers who were dependent upon their children's labor. But the bill required all children between twelve and sixteen to attend school eight weeks a year, instead of the twelve originally called for, and it advanced the number of hours a week for minors from fifty-six to sixty. A major advancement, however, was that the bill provided for a method of enforcement. The government had the power to appoint an inspector who would visit the mills and prosecute the management for violations. Yet the new law was below the standard set by the ACLC and National Child Labor Committee. The legislative chair of the AFWC described the bill as a disappointment but not altogether a poor law. The opposition of the mill owners was simply too great to overcome.[34]

Popular interest in child labor reform reached a low ebb after the passage of the 1907 law in the Comer administration. The state child labor committee again became inactive. The women of the AFWC agreed "that Alabama, so far as its women could do it, was to have a rest from further reform bills, until the present dose had taken effect."[35] The 1911 legislature did consider child labor measures, but the public took little interest. The overriding issue in the state at that time was prohibition. The new child labor law that the legislature passed declared it a misdemeanor to "knowingly" employ children or to refuse to give information to the inspector. The inspector was required to inspect the factories four times a year.[36]

At this point, the child labor movement found a new leader in Nellie Kimball Murdock, who became president of the moribund Alabama Child Labor Committee. She revitalized the committee, which had earlier even refused to admit women to membership, and led the fight for two new child labor laws. Born in Boston, Murdock moved to Atlanta when she was an infant. She returned to Massachusetts for an education, graduating from Bradford Academy in Haverhill. In 1891 she married Lincoln Murdock and moved to Birmingham. As a young matron, she became interested in the Mercy Home and was elected to the board. With the WCTU and Mercy Home as a beginning, she reached out to all fields of social and civic work. She founded a literary club, the Amaranth Club, in 1897 and served as its president for fifty years. Through this club she became active in the Alabama Federation of Women's Clubs. Early in the century she developed an understanding of modern social work. She was the first probation officer of the Boys' Club in 1905; she assisted Judge Samuel D. Murphy in creating the first juvenile court in 1907 and worked actively in the field for more than a decade. She served on the board of the state Child Welfare Department when it was created in 1919. In addition to her activities on behalf of children, she was also one of the founders and active members of the Equal Suffrage League of Birmingham. She labored on behalf of working women by supporting equal pay, shorter hours, and better working conditions for clerks in the Birmingham stores. She served on the board of the WCTU and the YMCA and was president of the Travelers' Aid Society.[37]

The attention of child labor reformers was directed toward the National Child Labor Committee when it held its seventh annual conference in Birmingham in 1911. The state committee under Murdock's leadership hosted the meeting. The major topic at the meeting was

NELLIE KIMBALL MURDOCK, MEMBER OF THE AFWC WHO LED THE DRIVE
TO ABOLISH CHILD LABOR AND TO ESTABLISH JUVENILE COURTS. *FROM
THE COLLECTIONS OF THE BIRMINGHAM PUBLIC LIBRARY.*

uniform child labor laws. The chief attraction was former president Theodore Roosevelt, who was on a speaking tour of the South. Also in attendance was Jane Addams of Hull House and Julia Lathrop, a well-known reformer. Two suffrage leaders, Jean Gordon of Louisiana and Belle Bennett of Kentucky, attended the meeting and gave lectures of their own after the Child Labor Convention. Gordon said, "If the men of the South had taken the same interest in children that women have we would not have such disgraceful conditions here and now." She went on to assert that women could not be certain of abolishing child labor until they could vote and she urged the formation of a suffrage organization. Murdock heard Gordon's address and was convinced that she was right. Later in the year Murdock was instrumental in creating the Equal Suffrage League of Birmingham.[38]

The National Child Labor Committee felt greatly encouraged by its reception in Birmingham as compared with its reception two years before in Atlanta. In Birmingham 300 businessmen came to a luncheon to discuss child labor and at each of two mass meetings at least 1,500 people were present. Alexander McKelway, southern secretary of the NCLC, went to Montgomery with an exhibit on child labor. It was displayed in the hope of influencing the legislators. It presented the child labor problem as national rather than sectional, and with photographs illustrated the evils found in the cotton mill and canning industries.[39]

However poor the Alabama law may have been, its provisions for factory inspection did promote the regulation of conditions and, if nothing else, presented annual evidence that children were still employed in the mills in considerable numbers. The factory inspector, Dr. W. H. Oates, characterized the laws as "conspicuous by their ambiguity, inefficiency, inexplicitness and inadequacy."[40] In his experience he found parents indifferent to education and anxious to put their children to work.

The four-year period between meetings of the Alabama legislature gave the reformers an opportunity to promulgate new demands for improvement and to arouse the social conscience of the state. The early reforms had been directed against child labor in the one great offending industry, but with its expanding program and gradual changing standards the NCLC began to agitate for reforms in other occupations.

Murdock wrote in the *Child Labor Bulletin*, "Our law applies only to mills, factories and manufacturers, and is absolutely silent about all other forms of occupation for children, so that we have actually in the state children as young as nine years legally at work 12 to 14 hours a day."[41] The direction and the interest of the NCLC was beginning to change and include investigations into child employment in other areas.

By 1914 Murdock was able to arouse the local reformers from the apathy that had settled down after the meeting of the legislature in 1911. She was the most active member of the committee, which was really not functioning to any great extent. She was also trying to keep alive the interest of the Alabama Federation of Women's Clubs. The AFWC gave Murdock theoretical support, although for a time its actual activity was limited. There was some friction between the AFWC and the child labor reformers. Some of the prominent club leaders who were connected with leading manufacturers resented the constant criticisms of the cotton industry. Murdock herself was able to see and sympathize with this view and yet able to work with the conservative women in the federation.[42]

In the fall of 1914 Lewis W. Hine of the NCLC and eleven other investigators (ten of whom were women) undertook a statewide study of the child labor problem, not only in the cotton mills but in other industries as well. An effort was made to establish harmonious relations and a spirit of cooperation between the committee and the women's clubs. Murdock had an important role in this project. The investigation was concluded just in time for the material to be used in agitating for a new law in 1915. The NCLC sent Herschel H. Jones to Alabama to take charge of organizing the campaign and to work with other interested groups. He was elected secretary of the ACLC and organized the legislative program of the reformers. The results of the investigation were given publicity through the press. The evil conditions under which messengers worked at night were especially emphasized. Cotton mills, which had for fifteen years borne the brunt of the attack, were relieved somewhat, although certainly not exonerated.[43]

Another child labor bill was introduced into the legislature in January 1915. It was based on the uniform child labor law endorsed by the NCLC and the American Bar Association. It was commonly referred to

CHILDREN WHO WERE EMPLOYED BY THE MERRIMACK MILLS OF HUNTSVILLE, 1914. PINKIE DURHAM WAS AN EIGHT-YEAR-OLD SWEEPER; HIS SISTER ELIZA BEGAN WORK WHEN SHE WAS ELEVEN. *PHOTOGRAPHY COLLECTIONS, UNIVERSITY OF MARYLAND, BALTIMORE COUNTY.*

YOUNG GIRL AT WORK IN A TEXTILE MILL. THIS PICTURE AND THE PREVIOUS ONE WERE TAKEN BY LEWIS W. HINE IN 1914 WHEN HE INVESTIGATED THE STATUS OF CHILD LABOR IN THE STATE. *PHOTOGRAPHY COLLECTIONS, UNIVERSITY OF MARYLAND, BALTIMORE COUNTY.*

as the "women's bill." The proposed bill, which protected children in all industries except agriculture and domestic service, raised the age limit from twelve to fourteen years. It limited the number of hours and times of day that children could work. It provided for school attendance. Children under sixteen were required to attend school eight weeks out of the year, six of which had to be consecutive. The enforcement of the law was in the hands of the state prison inspector and his deputies.[44]

The women were busy interviewing legislators, distributing campaign propaganda, and studying the terms of the bill and the arguments to be used in its favor. They used the network of the AFWC to advantage. When club women found a legislator who opposed the measure, they would inform other club women in the legislator's hometown, who in turn would talk to him when he went home for the weekend. They made personal appeals to the men through letters, telegrams, and even telephone messages. The ACLC and the AFWC put up a child labor exhibit in the rotunda of the capitol, which consisted of pictures of children at work. The child labor exhibit emphasized the various employments of children, the ignorance of families allowing children to work, and the poor schools that were provided. These pictures were especially effective because they pulled the heartstrings of all who saw them. The women also offered answers to the question of what to do with families dependent on children for support; they refuted the notion that child labor furnished good training and kept children out of mischief. Some of the clergy took the matter up and preached sermons on child labor from the pulpits of both Montgomery and Birmingham. The demand for legislative reform had become widespread with the two major proponents being Lura Craighead and Nellie Murdock, both of whom testified at public hearings on the bill. Craighead stressed that women were not in politics, but that they "were seeking to do what they could to help humanity."[45]

Murdock believed that Alabama needed to pause in the advertising of its industrial greatness and consider what it should do to conserve its human resources. She thought that people would be willing to attack the child labor problem when they realized that they were wasting the citizens of the future. She saw several needs for the state. One was an enforceable compulsory education law. Another was a uniform child labor law in all the southern states so that child employers could not evade the law by simply moving across the line into the next state. And last, the state needed an adequate force of inspectors with a severe penalty attached to all violations. "Furthermore we need to recognize, as a state, the principle that no child under fourteen is to be reckoned as an economic asset, and that it is the community's burden to provide for the widow with children of tender years until those children have become old enough and well enough educated to become wage-earners intelligently."[46]

The mill owners argued that the bill was too drastic because it limited the hours children could work to forty-eight a week. If this happened, they argued that the whole mill would have to run on that schedule and it would drive the workers out of the state. Indeed, the manufacturers had enough strength to force a compromise and they absolutely refused to agree to a forty-eight or even a fifty-hour week for minors. Determined opposition developed and increased to such an extent that a conference was arranged with the representatives of the mill owners. In a desire for amicable adjustment, the federation had to yield to their demand for sixty hours or else risk losing the entire reform package. The legislature reluctantly agreed to this compromise and the bill was passed on the last day of the first session.

The new law was more comprehensive and detailed than any other proposal, and in spite of the amendments, it raised the standards of regulation. Murdock said, "This new law while not all we wanted is a great improvement upon the old, probably as good as that of any Southern mill state."[47] The most serious defect of this law was the school attendance requirement. Although the same legislature had passed a compulsory school law requiring children between the ages of eight and fifteen to attend school eighty days a year, the child labor law conflicted with this because it required only forty days' attendance. The continuation of enforcement in the hands of the prison inspector was another weakness. It placed a burden on a department whose primary function was not the regulation of employment of children.[48] These problems were eventually rectified in the 1919 act.

The Alabama Federation of Women's Clubs widened its interest in children by the creation of the Child Welfare Committee in 1914. This shift reflected the growing concerns of the nation as a whole toward children. Not only were Americans concerned with child labor, but now the interests had broadened to include the general welfare of children. One member pointed out that the federation, like the federal government, had provided for almost everything except its children. "Cow, cotton, corn, and cabbage have had millions spent for their protection, the child's welfare is now going to be considered."[49] The U.S. Congress had just created the Federal Children's Bureau at the insistence of women such as Jane Addams and Julia Lathrop, who became the first director.

Under the leadership of Nellie Murdock in 1916, the Child Welfare Committee broadened its agenda to include items other than child labor. Murdock was interested in improving the health of children by requiring a health certificate before marriage, providing information about proper nutrition, establishing a system of mothers' pensions, and providing care for handicapped and emotionally disturbed children. She had an even more ambitious project of establishing a state agency whose purpose was the welfare of children. In conjunction with the Alabama Child Labor Committee, Judge Samuel D. Murphy of the juvenile court, and the governor, she secured the services of Evelyn Beldin of the Federal Children's Bureau to tour the state and lay plans for a state children's bureau. Beldin came in March 1916 and visited seventeen counties, spoke in twenty-three towns, and held forty-seven meetings.[50] These plans bore fruit when the legislature voted to establish the Alabama Children's Bureau in 1919. The Child Welfare Committee roused the federation with these words: "Mothers, wives of Alabama, there is work ahead of us if we would win the children's fight. . . . Do you not hear the shuffling feet of the thousands with no mind to guide them? Do you not hear the other thousands yet unborn, who plead with silent tongues for the chance to be born well? If you do, work for the child welfare of this state."[51]

The interest of the Alabama people in child labor and the problems of regulation were now thoroughly aroused. Once again the women of the federation and the National Child Labor Committee united to remove the weakness in the 1915 law. Their goals for the 1919 legislative session were to shorten the working hours and to provide a sufficient number of inspectors. The cooperation of these two agencies had produced the 1915 law and it was through them that further reforms were to be made. Once again they were aided by an investigation; one into the status of children in the state was conducted with money from the NCLC and the Virginia McCormick fund.

The McCormicks lived in Huntsville and had taken an interest in social work among the mill people there, establishing YWCAs that were really settlement houses. The investigation dealt not only with child labor, but also with the larger problems of care and education for dependent, delinquent, and defective children. The child welfare investigation was a thorough piece of work conducted under the direction of the national committee's agent, Edward N. Clopper, with the aid of the University of Alabama and Lorraine B. Bush, the widow of a former factory inspector, who had been appointed to succeed her husband. Since she was familiar with the child welfare problems of the state, she was made a representative of the NCLC.[52]

Bush and the agent for the southern states of the NCLC, Wiley H. Swift, planned the legislative campaign for 1919. Gov. Thomas E. Kilby agreed to the proposed changes in the 1915 Child Labor Act. The prospect of another reform bill was no more pleasing to the cotton manufacturers than the previous one had been. They had hoped that the 1915 law would be final and they had been given to understand by Nellie Murdock that no new demands would be made in 1919. The NCLC had given no assurances and its representative went ahead with the preparations for a new bill.

Opposition to child labor reform and child welfare work had weakened to a remarkable degree in the four years after 1915. The two measures introduced into the legislature encountered very little opposition. The first was to decrease the number of hours worked to forty-eight and the second was to create a child welfare department with the enforcement of child labor laws under its direction. The measure passed without a dissenting vote in the house and only slight opposition in the senate. Alabamians now felt the need of such laws for the good of the state because they had also become conscious of their responsibilities toward the children of the state. The change in attitude was the result of years of effort on the part of a few people. Even the cotton mill men themselves had changed. They too agreed that a fourteen-year age limit was reasonable and they were trying to see that age records were correct and that the children got the required schooling. They felt that it was not good business to employ very young children.[53]

The law passed by the legislature in 1919 retained the same age limit of fourteen for work, but it cut down on the hours to meet the forty-eight-hour week provided for in the federal statutes. Most important, the enforcement of the child labor law was transferred from the hands of the prison inspector to the newly created Child Welfare Department. Bush, who was largely responsible for securing the laws of 1919, became the first head of the Child Welfare Department.[54] The women of the federation and the NCLC had gained virtually all their goals.

Because Alabama is conservative, reforms come slowly. The state did not respond quickly to the problems of child labor. Yet from 1900 to 1919 considerable progress was made. The changed attitude of the public was in itself a substantial reform. The conviction that child labor was an evil and that it was largely responsible for Alabama's stand in the scale of illiteracy grew during these years. No more could ten-year-old children be employed: rather, the age limit was set at fourteen. Instead of a sixty-hour week, they could work only forty-eight hours. Education was compulsory and employers were enforcing the educational requirements. Most important, the state had created the Child Welfare Department, whose sole responsibility was to care for the children.

Throughout the entire drive for the regulation of child labor women had played a dominant role in the process. The issue appealed to women as mothers and they felt entirely justified in taking up the cause in the name of the home and motherhood. Some strong leaders emerged. Irene Ashby MacFadyen of the AFL provided a useful role model for southern women. Here was a cultivated Englishwoman who could relate to the conservative, socially oriented southern ladies. She convinced them that she could be a lady and still be interested in child labor. The state leadership consistently came from the Alabama Federation of Women's Clubs, notably Lillian Milner Orr, Lura Harris Craighead, and Nellie Kimball Murdock. These women were civic-minded individuals who devoted much effort to the cause and, in the case of Murdock, gained national recognition. Murdock and Craighead were able to negotiate with the state and national labor committees and the mill owners on a basis of equality, unlike Orr who could not even sign her own name to the agreement that had been worked out.

The Alabama Federation of Women's Clubs was justly proud of its accomplishments in eliminating very young children from the labor force and requiring compulsory school attendance. It worked consistently from the 1890s to 1920 to achieve its goals. Writing in 1921, the president of AFWC observed: "It took more courage twenty years ago for a body of women to wait upon the legislature than it does these days, but with each succeeding legislature the courageous pioneers of the Federation waited at the doors of the statehouse in the interest of the children." [55] The hearts and minds of the women were committed to this cause over a longer period of time than were the hearts and minds of any other group. Their efforts culminated in the creation of the Child Welfare Department in 1919. By then the women recognized that the pioneer work of the volunteer had given way to the trained expert social worker. Lorraine B. Bush had training and experience that enabled her to became the first director of the Child Welfare Department, a state agency supported by state taxes. The club women had laid the groundwork and by 1919 the jobs they had been doing had become institutionalized and directed by professionals. Bush herself wrote in 1924 that "to the organized women [of the AFWC] should go credit for much of the advancement made during the decade, particularly in the field of child care." [56] In the process women themselves had changed; they were assuming larger roles in the society and economy. They became the new women of the New South.

6 THE SUFFRAGE ASSOCIATIONS OF THE 1890s

he same factors that made possible the creation of the WCTU in the 1880s and the women's clubs in the 1890s also aided in the establishment of the first suffrage associations in the state. In 1892 supporters of woman suffrage organized two associations, one at New Decatur near Huntsville and the other at Verbena near Montgomery. Since large numbers of women had been drawn into club work and temperance work, these suffrage associations profited from a coattails effect. However, the suffrage drive presented problems that other reforms did not. Suffrage was seen as far more radical than temperance, child labor, or education. For these reasons the first suffrage associations were weak organizations that lasted about a decade. Alabama women flocked to the women's clubs and the temperance unions, but the suffrage cause had fewer supporters in the 1890s.

The WCTU and the women's clubs were interested in reforms that correlated with their roles as wives and mothers. They saw their activities as an extension of the home and the private sphere. They in no way challenged the defined gender roles that separated the male sphere of the public world and the female sphere of the private world. They posed no threat to the patriarchal family. But suffrage was seen in a different light because it called into question all of the traditional activities of women. The suffrage movement demanded for women admission to citizenship and the public sphere of men. It demanded a kind of power and a connection with the social order not based on the institution of the family and women's subordination within it. By demanding a permanent, public role for all women, suffragists began to demolish the absolute, sexually defined barrier separating the public and private worlds. In the traditional or patriarchal family, a woman was expected to subordinate her individual interests to those of her family; thus a husband quite properly represented his wife at the polls, because a woman's interests were no different from those of her husband. But as voters, women would be able to participate directly in society as individuals, not indirectly through their subordinate position as wives and mothers.[1]

The WCTU had taken as its starting point women's position within the home. It listed the abuses women suffered there and it proposed reforms necessary to ameliorate their domestic situation. The WCTU spoke to women in the language of their domestic realities and they joined in enormous numbers. Because of its base in the private realm, the WCTU became the mass movement that the suffrage movement never did. However, in both the WCTU and the women's clubs, women had been introduced to extradomestic concerns. As a result their lives were changed. Instead of being wholly domestic, women had now been introduced to a world wider than the home and family. At this point suffragism no longer opened up such revolutionary vistas for women; they were already operating in the public world of work and politics. It was this enlarged vision that nurtured the creation of the suffrage movement.[2]

The demand of women to vote was made two decades before temperance unions and women's clubs were organized. Women had first issued the demand to vote at the famous Seneca Falls Convention in 1848. The Declaration of Sentiments of this convention listed a broad spectrum of grievances and demands that involved a major shift of attitudes toward women. To these antebellum women lack of the vote was only one part of a complex network of social and institutional oppression, involving marriage, family, employment, education, and religion. In 1848 enfranchisement was widely viewed as the most extreme of women's demands even by its supporters.[3]

Because the majority of the women's rights advocates had been active in the abolition movement, women had high hopes that they might gain the vote at the same time blacks were enfranchised with the passage of the Fourteenth and Fifteenth Amendments to the Constitution. Women's hopes were raised because their male colleagues in the abolition movement were, for the first time, influential in Republican politics. But these old associates, once sympathetic to women's rights, proved to be fickle allies. In their view, the fight for black suffrage was enough of a battle and woman suffrage was extra baggage. The Fourteenth Amendment, which injected the word *male* into the Constitution for the first time, was ratified in 1868. The granting of black male suffrage hammered home the powerlessness of women. Educated and enlightened women resented the vote being given to newly freed slaves who could not read or write.

As a result of their abandonment by their former abolitionist allies, women's rights advocates then created their own organizations. From 1869 to 1890 two suffrage organizations existed: the American Woman Suffrage Association centered in New England led by Lucy Stone and Henry B. Blackwell, and the New York-based National Woman Suffrage Association led by Elizabeth Cady Stanton and Susan B. Anthony. Both organizations sought to achieve the right to vote but they used different methods and organizational techniques. The American Woman Suffrage Association, regarded as the more moderate, pressed for action on the state level. The radical faction centering in the National Woman Suffrage Association did not confine itself to the demand to vote, but was concerned with a wide range of issues inherited from the Declaration of Sentiments. The national group eventually decided that the best route to suffrage would be an amendment to the federal Constitution. During the late nineteenth century neither group was able to attract a large female constituency and suffered perpetual failure at both the state and national levels.[4]

The first successes for woman suffrage came not in the East, where the associations were active, but in two western territories. Wyoming enfranchised women in 1869 and Utah in 1870. Neither of these territories was interested in women's rights. Wyoming gave women the vote in order to attract more female settlers, and Utah was interested in Mormon voters being able to outvote non-Mormon voters. In both cases conservatives made use of woman suffrage to consolidate their political position. These two cases remained anomalies; suffragists saw no success elsewhere.[5]

By the 1890s changes were taking place outside the suffrage movement that enabled it to expand and legitimize its role. As we have seen, a new world of organized women marked the beginning of the Progressive movement. These new women reflected a shared desire to participate in public life beyond the family. As a result, the suffrage movement was no longer an isolated phenomenon, but was one of several national women's groups that held conventions, elected delegates, ran campaigns, and lobbied for causes. The larger women's movement testified to their rising social consciousness and made the suffragists' efforts more legitimate. The split within the suffrage organizations was healed when the two groups united, creating the National American Woman Suffrage Association (NAWSA) in 1890. This merger was part of a larger trend toward federation in other middle-class associations. The new organization streamlined its operations by running more formal conventions made up of delegates from state organizations.[6]

It was during the decade of the 1890s that the suffrage campaign moved into the South. But the driving force behind the first stage of the suffrage campaign in the South was not a desire for women's rights; it stemmed instead from a desire to guarantee white supremacy. As in all issues in the South, race played a critical role in determining the strategy, even the timing of the southern suffrage movement.[7]

Woman suffrage could not even be considered by the whites of the South until the demand for women to vote was separated from the abolition movement. The pre–Civil War leaders of woman suffrage believed in universal suffrage on the theory that women and blacks had the same inalienable right to consent to the laws they obeyed as did white males. However, after the Civil War the historical connection between racial and sexual equality gradually faded until suffragists could argue that the two issues were really not related. By the 1890s racism had become so nearly universal in the nation that southern attitudes toward blacks were not unlike those of northerners. The National American Woman Suffrage Association began to separate the two issues during this decade, but the seeds had been sown earlier.[8]

The pre–Civil War woman suffrage leaders had been concerned with both their rights and those of the blacks. But after the war women discovered that they had to choose between the two causes. This dilemma was especially evident in the discussions leading to the adoption of the Fourteenth Amendment. The Stanton-Anthony wing of the suffrage movement insisted that the cause of human freedom would be set back by an amendment that inserted the word *male* into the Constitution for the first time. They believed that singling out black men made it harder for women to get the ballot. The Lucy Stone wing, on the other hand, argued that women ought to acquiesce in the enfranchisement of blacks, happy that one group had at least won its rights.[9]

Some former abolitionists actively collaborated with southern suffragists in developing a new rationale for suffrage, the most prominent of whom was Henry B. Blackwell, a Massachusetts abolitionist and the husband of Lucy Stone. In 1867 he published an essay, *What the South Can Do,* containing statistics that showed that there were more white women in the South than there were black men and women combined. Hence the enfranchisement of women would greatly increase the white majority in the electorate and thus ensure white supremacy. The aim of this stratrgy was to prove that the enfranchisement of white women would further, rather than impede, the power of a white ruling class that was fearful of black domination. In a society laden with class strife, imperialist venture, and colonization, the equality of all people was no longer taken for granted. White suffrage leaders accordingly dispensed with the theory of natural rights. Desire for an educated electorate and the preservation of Anglo-Saxon power overwhelmingly influenced NAWSA's call for enfranchisement. This in time became the single most important argument used in the South.[10]

By the 1890s then, NAWSA began to separate itself from the cause of the blacks. Old-timers like Susan B. Anthony could not go so far as to advocate withdrawal of political power from the blacks, but the time had passed when she believed that black suffrage and woman suffrage were interdependent. By the turn of the century Anthony and other suffrage veterans were making way for a new generation of activists in NAWSA. Included were southern white women and others who had not been weaned in the abolitionist or natural-rights tradition. Black women who favored suffrage soon discovered that it was not just racist politicians who put up obstacles to their enfranchisement. White women, including suffragists who should have been their natural allies, often became their most formidable adversaries; white suffrage leaders either acquiesced to or took advantage of the antiblack sentiment in the period.[11]

Events in the South brought about a changed policy on the part of NAWSA and paved the way for the creation of southern suffrage associations. The decade of the 1890s and the years immediately following were the years during which southern states disfranchised blacks. Mississippi led the way in 1890 with the Second Mississippi Plan, which provided for a poll tax, a literacy test with a property qualification, and an "understanding clause" as a loophole for poor whites. South Carolina (1895), Louisiana (1898), Alabama (1901), and Virginia (1902) also turned new constitutions to the purpose of barring blacks from politics. North Carolina (1900) and Georgia (1908) accomplished the same thing with constitutional amendments, whereas Tennessee (1890), Texas (1902), Florida (1889), and Arkansas (1891) legislated the poll tax as a prerequisite for voting.[12]

Disfranchisement became the order of the day because both the conservative and the independent wings of the Democratic party had begun to compete for the freedman's vote. Many blacks had been kept from the polls by force, intimidation, and chicanery long before legal bars were erected. But these informal sanctions could be easily breeched and white supremacy would be in danger. Since neither white faction was certain it could control the black vote, both became willing to make disfranchisement formal. Sen. Henry Cabot Lodge's force bill of 1890, which provided for federal supervision of congressional elections, served to confirm the white belief that legal disfranchisement of the blacks must be undertaken.[13]

Actions at the Mississippi Constitutional Convention drew the attention of southern and national woman suffrage leaders. The convention met at Jackson in August 1890. Of the many plans proposed for disfranchising the blacks, one included woman suffrage. The proposal was to grant suffrage for "every woman who owned, or whose husband owned, real estate in the value of $300." An amendment was added to this proposal that made education as well as property a requirement for female suffrage. It was widely believed that the idea of woman suffrage was gaining favor at the convention and might even be adopted unless other plans for disfranchising the blacks could be found. The proposal at the Mississippi convention was not adopted, but it did receive the support of two-fifths of the convention.[14]

Suddenly white suffrage leaders saw an opportunity that they did not even know existed. Proposals to enfranchise women had been brought to the floor of the Mississippi convention and had been given serious consideration with little or no organized female support. The suffrage leader who became aware of these possibilities in the disfranchisement movement was Laura Clay of Kentucky. Clay had been active in the Kentucky suffrage movement since 1888 and had achieved important gains in the state by 1890. At Clay's urging, NAWSA authorized the formation of the Southern Committee at its annual convention in January 1892. Events in the South convinced Clay that the region was the "most promising field" in the entire country for suffrage work. As a result of actions of the Southern Committee, suffrage organizations were established in virtually all the southern states by 1895. Because of these successes, NAWSA decided to hold its 1895 convention in Atlanta instead of the usual location in the nation's capital. NAWSA even sent its most able speakers and organizers—Susan B. Anthony, Carrie Chapman Catt, and Anna Howard Shaw—to tour the area before the convention. Out of deference to southern sentiment, Anthony asked Frederick Douglass, the famous black abolition leader, not to attend the convention because she feared that his presence would be an embarrassment for him and the southern suffragists.[15]

Some interest in woman suffrage existed in Alabama even before the Southern Committee was organized. The state had representation at the national association meetings during the 1880s and 1890s. Priscilla Holmes Drake of Huntsville was Alabama's representative, but most of her work was done through the WCTU because the women of the state were "awake on the temperance question, though still apparently unprepared for suffrage." Drake was a member of the board of the National Woman Suffrage Association and in the early days stood practically alone in the South as a worker for the suffrage cause. There is, however, no evidence of any real organizational effort until the decade of the 1890s.[16]

Alabamians became interested in woman suffrage as a result of the actions of the 1890 Mississippi Constitutional Convention. The legislature of Alabama, already considering ways to disfranchise the blacks, followed with interest the debate in the neighboring state of Mississippi. The editor of the *New Decatur Advertiser*, C. J. Hildreth, opened his columns in 1890 to the suffrage issue, thus arousing local interest. As a result of these efforts, Ellen Stephens Hildreth, wife of the editor, organized the first suffrage association in the state at New Decatur in 1892.[17] Hildreth, a member of the Alabama Women's Press Association, wrote articles not only for the New Decatur newspaper but also for the *Woman's Journal,* the official publication of NAWSA. Through her suffrage work, she was closely associated with Susan B. Anthony and Carrie Chapman Catt, both of whom visited in the Hildreth home. She was educated in St. Louis, where she studied new kindergarten methods. Later she served as the superintendent of the St. Louis public kindergartens. After moving to New Decatur, she established that city's first kindergarten. She wrote a book on clay modeling that was used in normal and kindergarten schools. She was also active in the women's clubs movement, establishing the Progressive Culture Club in New Decatur and later the Alabama Federation of Women's Clubs.[18]

Also in 1892 Frances A. Griffin created a second suffrage association at Verbena. This group appears to have been organized independently of the one in Decatur, because the two communities are geographically distant from each other. Griffin's background of long association with women's causes led her logically into the suffrage drive. Born in Wetumpka in 1843 and educated at Judson College, she taught school in Verbena and later in Montgomery. Leaving her career as a schoolteacher in 1885, she went to work as an organizer for the national Woman's Christian Temperance Union, among other tasks aiding Frances Willard in organizing Alabama. By the 1890s she added suffrage to her interests and soon was in demand as a speaker not only in Alabama, but in other southern states as well. In 1893 the suffrage organizations in New Decatur and Verbena joined together and created the Alabama Woman Suffrage Association, which affiliated with NAWSA. Hildreth was the first state president and Griffin the first secretary.[19]

By 1897 suffrage associations had been created in Huntsville, Gadsden, Calera, and Jasper; however, the associations that were the most active were the ones in New Decatur and Huntsville. The others appear to have existed largely on paper. The association in Huntsville was led by Alberta Chapman Taylor, who when she visited Colorado was impressed with the active role that women played in politics in a state where women could vote. In 1895 when Susan B. Anthony and Carrie Chapman Catt made their southern tour prior to the Atlanta convention, they visited New Decatur and Huntsville. The visits of these famous women aroused much interest in the state, but further work was hindered by the depression that engulfed the state following the Panic of 1893. The activity of these early organizations was also limited because of the strong antisuffrage sentiment that existed in the state. Women who supported suffrage at this time exhibited great courage. Under these conditions, suffrage activities were mainly educational. The suffrage leaders distributed copies of the *Woman's Column*, a national suffrage paper published in Boston, to some fifteen hundred teachers, ministers, and other prominent people in the state. The list was supplied by Hildreth, who had contacts through her husband as editor of the paper. Hildreth wrote a column in the *New Decatur Advertiser*, and Minnie Hardy Gist edited a similar column in the *Columbiana Chronicle*.[20]

Ellen Stephens Hildreth served as president of the Alabama Woman

Suffrage Association from its inception in 1892 until 1896. She and Minnie Henderson represented Alabama at the NAWSA convention in Atlanta in 1895. The second president was one of Alabama's most distinguished women, Virginia Clay Clopton of Gurley. In 1843 Clopton married Clement C. Clay, the United States senator from Alabama (1853–61). After his death she then married David Clopton, chief justice of the Alabama Supreme Court. She was the author of *A Belle of the Fifties* (1904), reminiscences of Washington society in the decade before the Civil War. Women such as Hildreth and Clopton added greatly to the prestige of the suffrage associations. Because of her age, Clopton was unable to be very active, but she did represent the Alabama association at the Tennessee Centennial Celebration in 1897 and spoke on suffrage. Opposition to woman suffrage was so great that the state leaders thought it best to do nothing more than distribute literature and present arguments in the press.[21]

The most effective and prominent state leader was Frances Griffin, who was in constant demand as a speaker and organizer throughout the region. In 1896 she gave a lecture on the National American Woman Suffrage Association to Arkansas women who were attempting to create their own associations. In May 1897 she made a six weeks' tour of Tennessee lecturing and organizing on behalf of NAWSA. She attended the first Tennessee suffrage convention in Nashville along with Clopton. This convention was held in conjunction with the Tennessee Centennial Exposition. Suffrage leaders were offered use of the Woman's Building for three days to present their cause. Griffin spoke at the first Georgia state convention, which was held in 1899 in Atlanta in the capitol building. This session was a breakthrough for women because in 1895 when the national convention of NAWSA requested to meet there, they were told that it was unconstitutional for women to use the building. Four years later the suffrage movement had enough of a following that the legislators decided that the women could at least be treated as residents of the state.[22]

In 1898 Griffin had an even more important speaking engagement. She was invited to New Orleans where the Louisiana Constitutional Convention was meeting. As in other states, the major purpose of this convention was to disfranchise the blacks and one method proposed was to enfranchise white women. No less prominent a speaker than Carrie Chapman Catt was invited to speak to the convention. While the convention was considering the issue, other suffrage leaders, including Griffin, Catt, and Laura Clay, spoke to the public and any delegates who might care to come. The lecture hall was crowded with men and women from all classes of society anxious to hear more about the topic of the day. The convention did not grant women the vote, but they did grant women property holders the franchise on questions of issuing municipal bonds or incurring debts. The suffrage leaders were disappointed, but this grant of partial suffrage was viewed, at least by some, as a step forward.[23]

Because of her state and regional reputation, Frances Griffin was the obvious person to succeed Virginia Clay Clopton as president of the Alabama Woman Suffrage Association in 1900. Julia Tutwiler, the famous educator and prison reformer, agreed to be state organizer. Because of Tutwiler's long and productive career, her name and influence carried weight that aided the suffrage cause. During the 1890s the suffrage association showed interest in issues other than the right of women to vote. They were greatly concerned with women's legal position; they desired to raise the age of consent for girls from ten to fourteen; they worked to increase women's inheritance rights, their property rights, and their right to be coguardians of children with fathers. These concerns continued to occupy the time and interest of suffrage leaders.[24]

By the 1890s, then, an organized southern movement with strong national support came into existence because leading suffragists, both in the North and South, believed the South's "Negro problem" might be the key to female enfranchisement. Southern suffrage leaders believed that as the men of their race and class cast about for a means of countering the effects of black suffrage, they might resort to enfranchising white women, just as conservatives in the West had made use of woman suffrage to gain their political ends. They even had hope that the South would actually lead the nation in the adoption of woman suffrage.[25]

The disfranchisement movement was the dominant political issue in Alabama all during the decade of the 1890s. On the surface, the Demo-

cratic party appeared to be in control, but its supremacy was more frag-
ile than it appeared. The party controlled the blacks primarily by fraud.
Democrats openly admitted—even boasted—that black votes cast for
the opposition were counted for the Democrats. In 1892 the Populist
candidate for governor, Reuben Kolb, made a bid for the black vote by
promising to protect blacks' political rights. He was denied election by
fraudulent voting in the black belt. As a result, Democratic leaders had
ample reason to fear Republican and Populist pledges of "a free vote and
a fair count." [26]

As usual in such situations, the Democrats turned to suffrage restrictions to escape their difficulties. The legislature passed the Sayre Secret
Ballot Act in 1893, which was designed to prevent blacks from voting by providing for a printed ballot that contained no party names,
making it difficult for illiterates to vote. At the same time Republicans
and Populists were prevented from assisting blacks in voting. This law
was responsible for the decline of the Populists and the decrease in black
turnout.

The question of calling a constitutional convention plagued Alabama
throughout the nineties. Most Democrats desired to replace the Sayre
law with a more permanent restriction of suffrage, but every faction
and interest group feared that a convention might damage its current
power. It was not until the conservative faction of Democrats took firm
control in 1900–1901 that a convention was finally called. As in other
states, only a small minority voted for disfranchisement. One black belt
politico is reported to have remarked, "All we want is a small vote and a
large count." [27]

The convention itself reflected the aims of its conservative, Democratic, black belt sponsors. It brushed aside all efforts at social reform. It
refused to strengthen the railroad commission or impose limitations on
corporate activity, refused to abolish child labor or the convict leasing
system, and it limited the government's ability to provide social services
by cutting the constitutionally set maximum state tax rate.

The suffrage restrictions adopted were designed to disfranchise most
blacks and uneducated and propertyless whites in order to create legally
a conservative electorate. The new restrictions included residency re-

quirements, a poll tax, a literacy or property test, and a "grandfather" clause. The only delegates to defend universal suffrage for both whites and blacks were the Populists and Republicans. Some contemporaries viewed these actions as a reform because thereafter elections could be honest. Actually, the results were that blacks were deprived of their suffrage to prevent the Democrats from stealing their votes.[28]

The Constitutional Convention of 1901 did consider enfranchising women. Frances Griffin, Virginia Clay Clopton, and others were ready to test the southern strategy of the NASWA. The convention reluctantly allowed Griffin to speak on the suffrage issue, and when Griffin began her speech, the gallery was packed with women. Those who could not get into the gallery were allowed to sit at the rear of the convention hall. According to the *Montgomery Advertiser*, the women "clapped their hands and waved their dainty handkerchiefs in approval of her remarks."[29]

Griffin addressed the convention for about half an hour on the subject "Shall Women vote?" She based her argument on the abstract principle of justice that governments derive their just powers from the consent of the governed. She maintained that women as well as men belonged to the governed and deserved to be recognized as citizens. The condition of woman had changed, she said, from being a ward of the state to being "an agent of intelligence where she touches the Government all the way along her life, and the Government touches her." Griffin believed that women should have a voice in the adoption of laws and the appropriation of taxes. In short, she argued that men and women should be equal in the eyes of the law.

Griffin also argued that men and women were different. She believed that women needed to vote because they should be able to speak for themselves, insisting that men by their very nature cannot speak for women. She said, "It would be as impossible for all men to understand the needs of women and to care for their interests as it would be for all women to understand the needs of men and care for the interests of them."

She refuted the common arguments against woman suffrage. To the objections that politics were too corrupt for women, her answer was that women would purify politics. Women were often viewed as not being able to vote intelligently, but she pointed out that a higher percent of women than men had a grade school education and that women were as capable of voting as recently naturalized citizens were. Others maintained that women should not vote because they do not bear arms, but her answer was that many men did not do so either, yet they could vote. Some men advanced the argument that voting would place an added burden on women. On the contrary, Griffin said, women's burdens would be decreased because they would be able to prevent some of society's problems that they currently spent much time repairing in their charitable work. Others suggested that only a handful of women wanted the vote. Her answer was, must all women be disfranchised because a few did not wish to vote?

She closed by pointing out that women needed to be able to protect themselves. They resented being classed with traitors, idiots, criminals, and children. She said that women wanted full justice before the law; they wanted equal pay for equal work. She stressed that there were some women who have no men to represent them. "My sisters are widows and I am an old maid; we have no representation at the polls. . . . I should like to remind you gentlemen that so long as laws affect both men and women, men and women together should make those laws."[30]

At the conclusion of the speech, Griffin was warmly applauded by the delegates as well as by the audience in the gallery. The press, however, neither sanctioned nor approved her efforts. One paper commented: "No matter how modest a constitutional convention is nowadays some female suffragist will find it out and insist on making a speech."[31]

After Griffin's speech, several ordinances were placed before the convention granting the franchise to women. The strongest support came from those who saw it as a check on black suffrage. "It would double the available white vote of the states and would not increase the Negro vote five per cent," declared R. M. Cunningham of Jefferson County. This was an argument that Griffin did *not* use, despite the motivating drive of NAWSA's Southern Committee; she did not seek to exploit the race issue as Laura Clay and others had done. However, there were even a few delegates who advocated woman suffrage on its own merits as Griffin did. Benjamin H. Craig of Dallas County argued that women who have no one to represent them and who own property should be allowed to vote on tax and bond issues. He described this as "equal justice, common and even-handed, to the women of the land." He pointed out that it had been done in Louisiana and other states of the union. Another delegate said that any woman who owned property had as much right to vote upon tax and bond issues as a man who owned property. He went on to say that granting women the vote was a "question of right, fairness and justice" not a question of poetry and sentiment.[32]

After some hours of debate, the delegates decided by a vote of sixty-five to forty-six to follow the Louisiana convention of 1898 by granting unmarried women property holders the franchise on questions of issuing municipal bonds or incurring debts. However, this victory was short lived. The next day the conservatives moved for immediate reconsideration and defeated the measure by a vote of eighty-seven to twenty-two, with most of the Populists and a few Democrats voting with the minority. Perhaps not to seem completely arbitrary, the delegates did agree that taxation without representation was unfair. Therefore, they adopted the provision that the husbands of women who paid taxes on $500 worth of municipal property could vote for their wives. A large majority of the convention opposed an outright grant of suffrage to women whether on its own merit or as a countermeasure to black suffrage.[33]

The delegates to the convention had traditional ideas about women and women's role. They did believe in the doctrine of no taxation without representation, but they held to the common view that women were represented by their husbands, sons, or fathers; and because men were the head of the household, their vote represented the entire family. The delegates believed strongly in the doctrine of the two spheres; indeed, the theory of southern civilization was that a woman was the "Queen of the Household" and the domestic circle. If women departed from this role, the delegates believed, they would lower the high standards that prevailed. The result might be the complete destruction of cherished convictions regarding women's sphere.[34]

The delegates further argued that voting would degrade women; it would involve them in the dirt of politics. It would be in opposition to the highest southern civilization where women were the loveliest on the face of the earth. They maintained that the finest southern woman was too pure, too refined to lower herself by going to the polls, where she would undoubtedly be put into contact with poor white women and black women. Rather than expose herself to such disagreeable contact, a southern woman should stay at home and leave those of low station and morality to vote alone. Emmett O'Neal, the delegate from Jefferson County, concluded by saying: "[I]n no age in history did any people ever create an ideal of feminine loveliness, sweetness, purity, and moral beauty which surpassed that of the South, an ideal upon the continuation of which depends the preservations of the high civilization that prevails in our section."[35] Male delegates were unwilling to modify the doctrine of the two spheres; they could not visualize women acting in such a public role as voters.

Thus in Alabama the southern strategy of NAWSA proved to be unproductive. Indeed, the plan failed to achieve success in any southern state. Frances Griffin and the other suffrage leaders were bitterly disappointed with the results. Griffin had devoted much time and work in Montgomery, hoping to bring sufficient influence upon members of the constitutional convention to secure some concessions for women citizens. The convention not only refused to grant suffrage to taxpaying women, but it gave to the husbands of women taxpayers the right to vote on the basis of their wives' property! It essentially gave men two votes while denying the vote to women. Women were still identified only as members of a family, defined only in relation to men. Griffin regarded this as an insult, although Hildreth looked on it as a partial victory.

By 1902 suffrage associations in only Decatur and Huntsville continued to function in the state, despite a well-publicized visit to Montgomery in 1901 by Carrie Chapman Catt, the president of NAWSA. Short reports were given in 1903 and 1904 at the conventions, but few tangible results could be reported. These reports mark the end of the first period of the state suffrage activity that had been maintained by a few devoted women.[36] However, other events were overtaking the suffrage drive. Women in Alabama were seeking a wider role outside the home; in fact, their definition of the home was changing. As we have seen, women of the WCTU had established the Mercy Home and were working for temperance education. Club women in the larger towns were taking an interest in social problems of the day. They created the Alabama Boys' Industrial School, they were working for improvements in the educational system, and they were leading the drive to abolish child labor. Griffin viewed all of this as a gradual advance for the suffrage sentiment and a general modifying of those opposed. She was right, but it would be almost another decade before the suffrage movement would be revived, this time motivated by a different force and under the leadership of a different group of women.

7 RE-CREATION OF THE SUFFRAGE ASSOCIATIONS, 1910–1914

The second stage of the suffrage movement in the South began nearly a decade later than the first and developed under entirely different circumstances. At this time few attempts were made to exploit the race issue strategically. The new organizations that were created were fueled by the reforms of the Progressive movement. Since Alabama women had begun to be active in a variety of reforms, they had learned how to organize, how to lobby the legislature, how to hold conventions, and how to achieve their goals. The leaders of the suffrage drive profited by the earlier experiences of these women. In fact, some of the same women were active in more than one organization. The suffrage argument now was that women needed the vote to ensure the adoption of these Progressive measures.

The first two suffrage organizations in the state can be traced directly to women's interest in two Progressive reforms, prohibition and child labor. The first state suffrage association was created in Selma in 1910 after the defeat of the constitutional amendment for prohibition in 1909. Mary Winslow Partridge and others had besieged the polls begging the men to vote for prohibition. When it was defeated, they decided that it was time to establish a suffrage organization to allow women to vote on issues that were vital to them. Another issue that Partridge was concerned with was a drainage problem in the city. She had approached the city fathers of Selma about it and had been ignored. Partridge wrote to the president of NAWSA, Dr. Anna Howard Shaw, to ask for advice. Shaw responded by saying: "I cannot express to you how happy I am that you are willing to begin the work in your State where little has been done for suffrage because of the great conservatism among the women of the South. I am very glad if they are now beginning to realize their absolutely helpless and unprotected position. We have the temperance agitation to thank for arousing a great many women all over the country." Partridge sent out a call in the Selma newspapers and in March 1910 six women came to a meeting at the Carnegie Library, where an association was created. By 1912 the membership had increased to eighty-one.[1]

The formation of the Birmingham Equal Suffrage Association came about as a result of the National Child Labor Conference held in Birmingham in March 1911. Among those attending were Jean Gordon, a Louisiana suffrage leader, and Belle Bennett of Kentucky. Following the convention, these two women gave lectures on equal political rights at the Hillman Hotel. Gordon asserted that women could not abolish child labor until they could vote. She made clear the close correlation between these two issues and she urged the formation of a suffrage organization. Nellie Kimball Murdock, who had long been interested in child labor and had recently become chair of the flagging Alabama Child Labor Committee, was impressed with Gordon's arguments and took action.[2]

Murdock held a series of study meetings at her home during which the women present considered creating a suffrage organization. One of these women was Pattie Ruffner Jacobs, whose interest in suffrage stemmed from an encounter with the mayor of Birmingham whom she approached with a plan to oversee the sewage disposal problems. The mayor received her but totally ignored her suggestions. She was convinced that if she had been a voter, the response would have been different. At a meeting in the directors' room of the chamber of commerce in October 1911 the Birmingham Equal Suffrage Association was formed with an initial membership of approximately seventy people.

Pattie Ruffner Jacobs was elected president, Ethel Armes second vice-president, and Murdock third vice-president. Greetings were sent from Jane Addams of Hull House, Jean Gordon of New Orleans, and Mary Winslow Partridge of Selma.[3]

With these two associations as a nucleus, Pattie Ruffner Jacobs sent out a call a year later to create a state organization. Women from the Birmingham and the Selma associations met at the parish house of the Episcopal Church of the Advent in Birmingham in October 1912 and formed the Alabama Equal Suffrage Association (AESA). Jacobs was elected president, Mary Winslow Partridge of Selma vice-president, Nellie Murdock corresponding secretary, and Carrie M. Parke of Selma recording secretary.[4]

The call to organize the Alabama Equal Suffrage Association was a call to all women and men of the state "who wish to further the cause of woman suffrage." The suffrage leaders stated that they intended to form an association in every county in the state in order that "women may give their untrammeled help as citizens in bettering conditions in our state and municipal governments." They hoped to promote "equal and exact justice," to improve the "civic, social, economic, educational and sanitary conditions in Alabama," and to mitigate "the cruelties of industrialism." Women were ready and able to help men with this heavy burden. Speaking like true municipal housekeepers, the suffrage leaders were concerned primarily with protecting the home by giving women a role in regulating the "food supply of every community, water, milk and meat inspection, all housekeeping conditions and school affairs, highways, lighting, drainage and sewerage systems." They were convinced that the enfranchisement of women was now at last stirring in the heart of the southern states. "It is coming like sunrise over Alabama—a great light, sound and sweet and wholesome, born of the desire of women for a chance to help in the world's work."[5]

Suffrage associations quickly followed in other cities. Huntsville was reorganized in November 1912 by Bossie O'Brien Hundley, who had been elected president of the Birmingham Equal Suffrage Association. Some of the same women in the earlier association were active in Huntsville. Virginia Clay Clopton, who by now was more than ninety years old, was the first president. However, she was shortly given the position of honorary president and Mrs. Milton Humes became the active president. Montgomery was organized in January 1913 by Mary Partridge, who was invited to speak and form a group. An association in Tuscaloosa was created when Jacobs and others from the executive committee of the AESA went there in July 1913. The suffragists drove the fifty-seven miles to Tuscaloosa in two automobiles, held the organizational meeting, and drove home all in one day. The president of the Tuscaloosa association was Marie Hale Losey, wife of an English professor at the University of Alabama. Thirty women signed "I believe in Woman suffrage" cards. By January 1914 associations existed in Greensboro, Pell City, Coal City, Cullman, Vinemont, and Mobile. At that date the Birmingham association was the largest, with 700 members.[6]

The most prominent leader of the Alabama suffrage movement was Pattie Ruffner Jacobs of Birmingham, a remarkably perceptive and unusual southern woman. Born in 1875 in West Virginia of parents who were staunch unionists during the Civil War, her parents moved to Nashville shortly after Pattie's birth. After graduating from the Ward Seminary in Nashville in 1893, she entered the Birmingham Training School for Teachers, where she studied for two years. Pattie proved to be the family's most original thinker as well as its most versatile and talented member. In a diary she kept between the ages of nineteen and twenty-two she showed a restless and independent spirit. She longed to "break away and do something really unconventional and new." She was able to fulfill this desire by studying art in New York from 1894 to 1896. After this period of independence, she returned to Birmingham and in 1898 married Solon Jacobs, a man who was ten years older than she. The institution of marriage troubled Pattie and she struggled with her fear of a marriage that was not carefully considered. Evidently she overcame these fears, because her marriage appears have been a most happy one.[7]

Jacobs became interested in the suffrage movement after her marriage. With her husband providing her with financial security and constant encouragement to pursue her many causes, she became active in many of the reform movements of the day—the abolition of child labor, the convict lease system, and elimination of prostitution—as well as

PATTIE RUFFNER JACOBS, CO-ORGANIZER AND FIRST PRESIDENT OF THE AESA, AUDITOR OF NAWSA, AND OPPONENT OF CHILD LABOR AND THE CONVICT LEASE SYSTEM. *FROM THE COLLECTIONS OF THE BIRMINGHAM PUBLIC LIBRARY.*

charitable and philanthropic organizations. She described these efforts as a "long, long voteless way of non-success in civic improvements" that led her into active suffrage work. As the major organizer and leader of the Alabama Equal Suffrage Association, she served as president from its inception until the ratification of the Nineteenth Amendment with the exception of a short period, at which time she was chairman of the critically important legislative committee. During the crucial campaigns of 1915 and 1919 she was the association's chief strategist. After 1915 she served as an officer in NAWSA and worked closely with Carrie Chapman Catt. When the vote was won, she found opportunity for increased political activity, becoming the first national secretary of the League of Women Voters, Alabama's first national Democratic committeewoman, and the first woman on the National Democratic Executive Committee.[8]

The major work of these new suffrage organizations was primarily one of education with their campaign directed first of all at the suffragists themselves. The women needed to be familiar with the arguments for suffrage and able to present a convincing case in support of the issue. They also needed to give one another the courage and strength of their convictions, especially in a hostile or indifferent environment. The second stage was to educate the general public by the publication and distribution of national and state literature and by publicity through the press. No state newspaper endorsed suffrage, but many were willing to carry a suffrage column written by suffrage leaders. Three newspapers, the *Birmingham News*, the *Montgomery Journal*, and the *Selma Times*, maintained special suffrage columns edited by suffrage leaders. Other papers such as the *Montgomery Advertiser*, the *Mobile Register*, the *Anniston Star*, and the *Tuscaloosa Times* devoted space to the issue on a fairly regular basis. Another approach was to establish a prize essay contest. Fifty dollars were offered as a prize for the best essay on woman suffrage written by any Alabama schoolboy or girl between the ages of fourteen and twenty.[9]

The suffrage leaders quickly realized the opportunity for publicity provided by the annual state fair in Birmingham. They selected October 5, 1912, as Suffrage Day at the fair and set up a booth where the leaders could display their Votes for Women sashes and buttons. The booth was furnished with wicker furniture donated by a local store and made inviting with chintz covers, pictures, posters, and bunting. A straw vote was taken on the question of woman suffrage, and from this unscientific survey 2,085 favored suffrage whereas only 515 were opposed to it. Most important, the suffragists distributed 15,000 pieces of literature. A surprise visitor to the booth was the labor leader John Mitchell, who happened to be in the city. Mitchell even made a talk in favor of suffrage. Jacobs felt that the association reached so many people that they should continue the project on an annual basis. The women were delighted with the amount of favorable sentiment they aroused. They had the exciting experience of bringing their message to the people of the state. Maintaining a booth at the state fair was so successful that the practice was copied at county fairs.[10]

Not all of the sentiment was favorable at the fair booth, however. The superintendent of schools, Dr. J. H. Phillips, visited the booth and saw Amelia Worthington distributing literature. Worthington, a young woman from a prominent family who was taking a teacher training course at the Powell School, shortly afterwards was suspended from the course for thirty days because of her suffrage activity. When asked about the action, Phillips replied that it was the policy of the board of education to require all teachers to refrain from any activity that would interfere with the efficiency of their work. Work at the Birmingham Training School for Teachers was strenuous and required all the time of its members, he maintained.

The Alabama Equal Suffrage Association came to the defense of Worthington. Since Pattie Jacobs was out of town, Ethel Armes responded by pointing out that the time required for suffrage work in no way interfered with other duties, but might be carried along with them. The suffrage association met only twice a month on Saturday and even the Suffrage Day at the fair was on a Saturday. Armes went on to say that Phillips's actions led many teachers to believe that any open declaration of belief in the principles of equal suffrage would cost them their jobs. She took the occasion to point out some unjust practices of the board of education regarding women: female teachers were paid less than the male teachers for the same work; and women could neither vote for the board members nor serve on it. The suffragists hoped to change these practices.

As a result of the ensuing publicity, Phillips backed down and reinstated Worthington. He said that she was "simply requested to conform." Receiving considerable publicity from the incident, the suffrage association was seen as winning a victory. Teachers in the school district probably were still fearful of letting their names be associated with suffrage because Phillips was clearly not in sympathy with the cause. He was the only educator in Alabama who refused to announce the essay contests that the AESA sponsored, a program popular in other schools. This refusal was just one more reason why the suffragists were displeased with Phillips and the public schools. The suffragists reasoned that they paid taxes and should have more voice in school policy.[11]

As a result of the Worthington episode, the drive of the suffrage association to push for women members of the school board gained new life. The AESA had earlier appointed a committee to prepare an amendment to the municipal ordinance that prevented women from serving on school boards. However, before the city could act on the amendment, a vacancy occurred on the school board. For the first time in the history of Birmingham, women sought an official position. The AESA prepared a petition listing the reasons why a woman should be appointed and suggested six names. No woman was appointed at this time, but in 1915 the legislature passed a law making it legal for women to serve on school boards.[12]

By 1913 equal suffrage had become a major issue in the state. Woman suffrage had more then a thousand advocates, whereas a few years earlier it had had almost none. Newspapers began to run editorials on the subject and readers began to respond. No paper came out in favor of the issue; most were mildly tolerant or else did not take the issue seriously. The attitude of the *Montgomery Times* was typical at the beginning of the suffrage drive. The editors candidly admitted that they had never been very enthusiastic about women voting. "We have always been of the opinion that as soon as the women . . . decided they would like to have the ballot, they will get it." However, the *Times* was willing to lend its columns to the suffrage cause in order for suffragists to educate their sisters. The editors did not feel that the votes of women could hurt the state, but on the other hand, they had no sympathy for "Rise Slave," "Shake off your bondage," "Fight for your rights," and other such wild and, as they saw it, foolish nonsense. As far as the editor knew, there were not any women slaves in Alabama. "Let it be well understood that this paper feels very kindly toward the women in their vote movement, but we shall not go crazy to please any of them." [13]

A similar attitude was expressed in another editorial. This editor believed that when the women of the state wanted the ballot, all they would have to do would be to ask. The men of the state, he insisted, had always done what was right for women. The editor maintained that men had not responded because women marched in parades or made speeches. He concluded that "Ours is one state where there will be no suffrage difficulties." [14] At this stage of the suffrage movement, men often expressed the attitude that they were gracious to women and if women wanted the vote, all women had to do was to request it. The southern man could always be depended upon to take care of the southern woman. But when the number of women increased and the demand became louder, men did not feel so gallant.

The suffrage organizations became even more effective when they were able to establish a headquarters in Birmingham. In June 1913 both the Birmingham and the Alabama Equal Suffrage Associations shared an office in the Cable-Shelby-Burton Building on Second Avenue. The room was on the fourth floor and had four large windows that opened toward the south with a view of Red Mountain. The walls were painted suffrage yellow and on them hung pictures of suffrage leaders, such as Susan B. Anthony, Anna Howard Shaw, Mary Johnston, and Pattie Ruffner Jacobs. Open from ten to five daily, the room was used as a reading room with all kinds of suffrage literature available as well as banners, postcards, and buttons. This large and comfortable room, staffed by members of the association, even had a telephone. The rent for the new headquarters was twenty-seven dollars a month, which was paid by contributions from members. Judge Oscar Hundley started the list with a twenty-five-dollar annual contribution, which was followed by other liberal contributions. [15]

It was Pattie Jacobs who conceived of the idea of a headquarters. She visualized that one of the purposes of the headquarters was to provide the working women of the city with a place to have lunch and rest during the noon hour. Tea was provided at a penny a cup. Jacobs not only intended to arrange a comfortable place to eat lunch, but hoped to involve the working and business women of the city in the suffrage movement. The working women came in substantial numbers. Beginning with fifteen "regulars," the numbers grew until sixty women ate their lunch at the headquarters on an average day. Since the downtown department stores did not maintain restrooms or lunchrooms for their female employees, the women were grateful to the association for providing such services. By 1917 the suffragists were forced to abandon the service because the owners of the building objected. Nellie Murdock then negotiated with the department stores (primarily Loveman, Joseph, and Loeb where ninety percent of the women worked) who agreed to provide lunchrooms for their employees. Murdock further persuaded the downtown merchants to agree to close their stores at noon on Thursdays during the summer, providing the saleswomen with a half-day holiday. The suffrage club, 850 strong, promised not to do any buying on Thursday afternoons. They also pledged themselves not to shop between noon and two o'clock on any day, so as to give the "girls" time for an unhurried lunch.[16]

By these actions the suffragists showed they were not only concerned with middle-class women but, unlike club women, were sensitive to the needs of working women. They expressed their interest in other women's issues by the resolutions they adopted at their annual conventions. They strongly pushed the concept of equal pay for equal work. This resolution was especially for the female public schoolteachers, who received 25–50 percent less pay than male teachers did. They supported raising the age of consent for girls from twelve to twenty-one years. They advocated the right of trade unions to organize and supported the eight-hour day and minimum wage for women. They favored a plan for mother's compensation and also desired to make mothers coguardians of children with fathers. The suffrage association joined with the Alabama Federation of Women's Clubs in the drive for making women eligible to serve on school boards, and as county and state school superintendents as well. They also supported the AFWC in their drive to restrict child labor and to enact a compulsory education law.[17]

By 1913 Pattie Jacobs, Bossie Hundley, and other suffrage leaders were beginning to see results from their efforts to make suffrage a political issue in the state. By this time the Selma association was three years old, the Birmingham association two years old, and the state association had just held its first annual convention in Selma. Because of the publicity the women had generated, political leaders began to state their opinions on the subject. One of these was Rep. Thomas Heflin, who came out in opposition in February 1913. Heflin expressed the commonly accepted view of women. He said that the "home is a sacred place. It is the most important place in the world. God has set it apart as the sweet and peculiar sphere of woman." Heflin felt that as a daughter, sweetheart, wife, or mother, a woman "can accomplish infinitely more in the sacred precincts of home for the moral uplift and for good government than she can equipped with all the power of a woman suffragist babbling about the ballot box." It would be a sad day, he argued, when the queen of the home tired of the duties of women and preferred to make political speeches and exercise the ballot. He said his position was that "it is not best in the long run that woman should vote; not best for woman, not best for man, not best for the home, not best for the government."[18]

Pattie Jacobs took on Heflin in a long letter to the editor of the *Birmingham Age-Herald*. She said that woman suffragists were as much concerned with safeguarding the home as Heflin was. Jacobs asked about those women who had no home. She pointed out that 20 percent of all women were employed and the number was increasing. "If our social conditions were ideal and every girl happily married to some man who could support her, the question of woman suffrage might be of much less concern." But she insisted that the lack of direct political influence constituted a powerful reason why women's wages were so low. She objected to Heflin describing women as "*babbling* about the ballot box." She maintained "that women were praying for it, working for it with such dignity, skill, patience and persistency of effort that no thoughtful man can belittle." Futhermore, she added that even though woman might be "the best creature" as Heflin said, "her opinion is worth nothing to her city, her state, her nation."[19] Later Jacobs responded to the belief that a woman as queen of the household was too pure to vote:

> However much these chivalrous gentlemen may wish it were so, that southern women might be called roses and lilies which toil not, they must know that their compliments do not provide equal pay for equal service . . . that their flowers of speech do not help us secure a co-guardianship law. . . . The pedestal platitude appeals less and less to the intelligence of the southern women, who are learning in increasing numbers that the assertion that they are too good, too noble, too pure to vote, in reality brands them as incompetents. . . . We are not queens but political and industrial serfs.[20]

The Alabama Equal Suffrage Association received wide attention as a result of the forty-fourth annual convention of NAWSA, which met in Washington in December 1913. At this meeting Jacobs made a major address and she and others had an opportunity to reply to Heflin at a congressional hearing. The delegates to the national convention from Alabama were four prominent suffrage leaders from Birmingham: Pattie Ruffner Jacobs, Bossie O'Brien Hundley, Amelia Worthington, and Nellie Kimball Murdock. In addition, there were four delegates from Huntsville, including the president (Mrs. Milton Humes) and Mrs. Felix Baldridge, and one delegate from Cullman. These delegates from Alabama received much attention because their enthusiasm and youth indicated a brighter outlook for suffrage in the South.

Jacobs was asked to make one of the major speeches at the convention. In her address she maintained that southern women did want the vote, contrary to the assertion that they were not interested. She maintained that she was a living refutation of this charge, which had even been made in the halls of Congress. She said, "It is an indictment of the Southern woman's intelligence, which I resent. Nor is my position unique, original or lonely—there are thousands of us." She went on to say that the women in all of the southern states "are stirring, are realizing that the vote is the only honorable, dignified and sure means of securing recognition of their aspirations and of their needs." She felt that it "is a wonderful thing to have convictions so strong that you must stand up and be counted; you must go out and do battle for them. It is a privilege to be born, to live in such soul-stirring times; to understand that communion of interests, that mutual responsibility which the solidarity of the woman suffrage movement indicates."[21] Jacobs was given a tremendous ovation when she made the statement about the indictment of women's intellect. Her remarks were seen as strong words for a southern woman. Her speech and picture appeared in newspapers in the East and South, and she was hailed as a new apostle of the New South. At last the daughters of the South were shoulder to shoulder with their sisters of the North.

This was not Jacobs's only time in the spotlight. When the suffrage leaders left their convention and moved to the halls of Congress, they had an opportunity to testify before the Rules Committee of the U.S. House of Representatives. They were urging the House to create a committee to consider woman suffrage. The Rules Committee also heard testimony from the National Association Opposed to Woman Suffrage, whose representatives came to Washington fresh from their own annual convention in New York City. The antis, who spoke first, regarded suffrage as "misleading, utterly useless and absolutely unnecessary." Tom Heflin of Alabama was asked by the antis to make the closing statement at the hearing.

Heflin was well prepared for his speech. He was lavish in his praise of women who opposed suffrage by eloquently comparing them to the sun, moon, stars, and other heavenly bodies. He declared that the demand for the ballot came not from the modest, home-loving women of the country, but from those women who were the restless dissatisfied products of unhappy homes. He further said that woman suffrage would create sex antagonism and destroy sex sentiment. Suffrage would cause disturbances in the family and was the enemy of the Christian religion and the American home. He concluded by saying: "When I heard you good women yesterday pleading with all the earnestness of your gentle nature that the ballot be not thrust upon you; when I heard you talking of your mission in the world and your duties in the home, I felt like I was attending an old fashioned love feast, and I said in my heart, thank God for these gentlewomen, for the home loving women of America."[22] Heflin was warmly applauded at the conclusion of his speech.

The Alabama women had an unusual opportunity to reply to Heflin face to face. They had often asked him to debate, but he declined to do so. Jacobs, Hundley, and Baldridge all made short statements. Jacobs said she was happy to have the opportunity to refute the charges that women of the South did not desire to vote. "We are very tired of being considered different from other women," Jacobs declared. "We are not angels, or lilies, or roses or even moons." This last statement brought about a round of applause and laughter from the audience. Hundley declared that many men and women in the South agreed with Lincoln when he said, "I go for all sharing the privileges of government who assist in bearing its burdens by no means excluding women." Baldridge took a shot at Heflin and began by saying, "I regret that I am not one of those 'mannish women' of whom Mr. Heflin spoke, if he meant those who had been trained in house speaking, but I came directly from the home to tell the gentleman from Alabama who represents all of our women, that the women of the south do wish the ballot in order that they may protect the home." This clash between the suffrage leaders and Heflin received wide publicity. It took considerable courage for these women to respond to Heflin as they did. All three of them showed that they were thoroughly familiar with the issues and were prepared for appropriate responses.[23]

Events were taking place at the national level that were to change the direction and course of the woman suffrage movement and were to force the Alabama suffragists to make some hard decisions. At the 1913 convention a split developed within NAWSA that had been in the making for some time. Suffragists disagreed over whether to continue to work for suffrage at the state level or to put their efforts behind a federal amendment.

From 1896 until 1910 no new states had adopted woman suffrage. During these years six state referenda were held and all of them lost. Only Wyoming, Colorado, Idaho, and Utah allowed women to vote.

Support for the federal amendment was at a low ebb. Anna Howard Shaw became president of NAWSA in 1904 and attempted to fill the leadership vacuum left by Susan B. Anthony. Shaw was a gifted speaker who was unmatched in eloquence and effectiveness, but she was not a capable administrator. She served as president until 1915, during which time she greeted any and all signs of initiative on the board as signs of potential insurgency. Initiative in the suffrage movement fell to the states, and victories were won in Washington (1910), California (1911), Oregon (1912), Kansas (1912), and Arizona (1912) with little or no help from NAWSA. Women could now vote in six western states with a total of forty-five electoral votes for the presidency. The suffrage movement was becoming a political force to be reckoned with. Just before the NAWSA convention of 1913, the state of Illinois granted women the right to vote in presidential elections, which added twenty-nine electors to the suffrage column for a national total of seventy-four. Illinois was also significant because it was the first state east of the Mississippi River to grant any suffrage to women.[24]

At first the board of NAWSA paid little attention to these new developments. But some members of the national board began to demand that they develop a political strategy to take advantage of what was clearly a new opportunity. Between 1910 and 1915 the board was in turmoil and experienced considerable turnover. For a time it appeared that the board might destroy itself through internal conflict regarding policy.

The controversy centered around the tactics and philosophies of two young women, Alice Paul and Lucy Burns, who had lived in England and had taken part in the militant movement there. These two women returned to the United States in 1910, worked briefly in Pennsylvania, then in 1912 offered their services to NAWSA for the purpose of organizing a new drive for a national amendment. The board welcomed them and sent them to Washington as the Congressional Committee. They organized the successful parade of 5,000 women in Washington on March 3, 1913, the day before Wilson was to be inaugurated. The march attracted thousands—so many, in fact, that when Wilson arrived he was told that the people were all watching the suffrage parade. The parade dramatized the suffrage cause as nothing else had done, but crowds in town for the inauguration became rowdy and hassled the women. The Washington police could not control the situation and called in troops from Fort Belvoir. Congressmen became indignant and called for an investigation. A delegation from Alabama walked in this parade and carried a banner; there is no evidence that they were molested.[25]

Shortly after the parade, differences between the philosophy of the members of the board and that of Paul and Burns became obvious. These two young women had raised money and created a separate lobbying group, the Congressional Union (CU), which demanded as its goal the immediate passage of a federal amendment. They also were ready to hold the party in power responsible if no action was taken on suffrage. They reasoned that since the Democratic party controlled the presidency and both houses of Congress, it should be held responsible for policy decisions. They proposed to organize women to oppose Democrats in the suffrage states.

At this time NAWSA still supported the state approach as opposed to the federal amendment. In addition, they had always had the view that they needed to follow a nonpartisan policy because the Congress was composed of men of both parties who would be needed for the necessary two-thirds vote in both houses. At the 1913 convention the board withdrew its support from Paul and Burns. The Congressional Union went its own way, eventually becoming the National Woman's party. For the second time the suffrage organization was divided. The split was similar to the earlier cleavage between the National and American Woman Suffrage Associations when the Lucy Stone wing emphasized moderation and tried to avoid extreme actions that might alienate friends, whereas Stanton and Anthony were prepared to press ahead and adopt more radical positions. Now NAWSA was following a more conservative approach and the Congressional Union the more radical. The CU took up an issue that was dead, brought it to life, and generated excitement in Washington while NAWSA was plodding along with no new ideas.[26]

Not only was the national suffrage movement split, but the southern suffragists were divided over policy and strategy. Kate M. Gordon of Louisiana was adamantly opposed to an amendment to the federal Constitution because she feared federal control of elections. She felt that the only way was for the southern states to amend their own constitutions. Gordon had served on the national board since 1901 and played an active role in that organization. But by 1908 she had developed a strategy to force southern lawmakers to adopt woman suffrage amendments to their constitutions. To build up a specifically southern suffrage movement, she desired to work toward a Louisiana law enfranchising only white women. In 1909 she resigned from the board to avoid acquiescing any longer in NAWSA's advocacy of a federal amendment. By 1913 she organized the Southern States Woman Suffrage Conference (SSWSC) in New Orleans and tried to get other southern states to join. At this point the leaders of NAWSA did not oppose Gordon's organization; indeed, it was even listed on the letterhead of NAWSA. The Alabama association had to decide whether it wanted to join the SSWSC and work toward the enfranchising of white women only. The decision does not appear to have been a difficult one. At a board meeting in 1914 the leaders decided not to join Gordon's conference. The Alabama suffragists never openly used racist arguments to advance their cause.[27]

It was at this point in the national and regional scene that the suffrage drive in Alabama began to gain momentum. The Alabama suffragists continued to follow the leadership of the national organization, although they cooperated with the Congressional Union on several occasions, first by marching in the 1913 parade and also by writing letters to members of Congress. The Alabama suffragists did attend some meetings of Gordon's Southern Conference, but did not subscribe to her radical views. Jacobs and others believed that the first step in Alabama was to petition the state legislature to adopt a constitutional amendment enfranchising women. Since southerners were consistent supporters of states' rights, they automatically objected to anything that resembled pressure from the federal government. The legislature of Alabama was scheduled to meet on its four-year cycle in 1915 and the suffrage leaders began to lay plans to request the legislature to amend the state constitution. Unless Alabama wished to have its women enfranchised by a federal amendment, it would need to act quickly.

8 CAMPAIGN FOR A STATE AMENDMENT, 1914–1915

The Alabama Equal Suffrage Association met for its second annual convention in Huntsville in February 1914, just shortly after the NAWSA convention of December 1913 when Pattie Jacobs and other delegates were greeted with such enthusiasm and had the opportunity to refute the antisuffragist arguments of Representative Heflin. The state had such strong leadership that it seemed to lead the South in support of suffrage. The region was awakening to the issue of woman suffrage; all southern states except South Carolina had active suffrage organizations. Laura Clay had achieved support in her drive in Kentucky, as had Sarah Barnwell Elliott in Tennessee and Kate and Jean Gordon in Louisiana. Florida, Arkansas, and Georgia had also created organizations. At the time of the Huntsville convention, Alabama had organizations in eleven cities or towns: Selma, Birmingham, Huntsville, Montgomery, Mobile, Tuscaloosa, Greensboro, Vinemont, Cullman, Pell City, and Coal City.[1]

Huntsville was especially pleased to host the convention because it was there that one of the first suffrage associations had been established in the 1890s. In fact some of the women involved earlier were still active suffragists. One of these pioneer suffragists was Anne Buell Drake Robertson, who was the daughter of Priscilla Drake, the first Alabama suffragist, who was active as early as 1868. Other long-time suffragists were Virginia Clay Clopton, who in her nineties was the oldest living suffragist in the state; Mrs. Milton Humes, who with Clopton had invited Susan B. Anthony and Carrie Chapman Catt to the state in 1895; and Alberta Chapman Taylor, who had established Huntsville's first association after having visited Colorado, where women could vote. Clopton, as life president of the Huntsville association, presided over the opening session and delivered the welcome from the local association. She was thankful that the suffragists were not "constrained to labor in secrecy with locked doors and stopped up key holes" as they had been compelled to do in the past. She based her argument for suffrage on the injustice of women paying taxes yet having no voice in how these taxes were collected or spent. Such a woman as Clopton, who was known as the Queen of the South, lent prestige to the suffrage cause.[2]

The most important action at this convention was the decision to petition the 1915 state legislature to adopt "an amendment to the State Constitution to enfranchise Alabama women on equal terms with Alabama men." This resolution marked the beginning of political action by the suffrage associations. In the past the suffragists had confined their actions largely to education by distributing literature and publicizing the issue through the newspapers. The association had had "ever recurrent requests for literature to be used for papers, speeches and debates from ministers, mayors of towns, school teachers, club women and from children" seeking information on every aspect of suffrage work. But now the association moved to pursue a more activist course, making plans for a political campaign to marshal support for a constitutional amendment. The legislative committee under the leadership of Bossie O'Brien Hundley created a statewide organization listing key people in all counties. A major project was to interview all candidates for office, asking their opinion of woman suffrage. The convention adopted the slogan Woman Suffrage for Alabama 1916. Bossie Hundley pledged twenty-five dollars to finance the campaign and suggested that every association within the state contribute its share.[3]

The enfranchisement of women was not the only issue that the women considered. Nellie Kimball Murdock, first vice-president of the Birmingham association and chairman of the Alabama Child Labor Committee, spoke on the need to regulate child labor, another issue that the 1915 legislature would be asked to consider. She described the conditions in the state and pointed out that once women had the vote, they could abolish child labor. The convention went on record as supporting the upcoming bills for restricting child labor and establishing compulsory education. The convention also adopted resolutions favoring other women's issues: paying women equally with men for equal work, establishing an eight-hour day and minimum wage for women, making mothers co-guardians with fathers, and raising the age of consent from twelve years to twenty-one years. The consistent support of these issues indicated the breadth of understanding that the suffrage leaders had regarding the position of all women in the state.[4]

Pattie Jacobs was very optimistic about the future of suffrage because she saw sentiment for the issue "bubbling up and crystalizing all over the state." In addition to the associations already formed, she was receiving daily requests from the rural areas of the state to form associations, a situation which made her believe "that public sympathy is with suffrage throughout the state." She pointed out that at the NAWSA convention just a few months earlier, "Alabama was considered the wonder of the convention" because of the enormous progress the state had made since the AESA was created less than a year before. By 1914 nine states had full suffrage, twenty-one states partial suffrage, but in eighteen states women had no voting rights at all. Even though Alabama was among the eighteen, Jacobs hoped that the state would be redeemed in 1915. She pointed out that women of the state could gain the vote by one of two ways: either by a federal amendment to the United States Constitution or by a "voluntary act on the part of the men" of the state in amending the state constitution. She saw no reason why the state should not recognize women as individual human beings instead of defining them as wives, mothers, and daughters of men.[5]

Like all good politicians, Jacobs presented an optimistic view about her cause to the press, but she was more candid when she wrote a letter to NAWSA about the status of the organization in January 1914 just before the Huntsville convention:

> When the facts concerning suffrage conditions in Alabama are set forth in cold type, they will I'm afraid expose our weakness instead of our boasted strength—& how thoroughly commonplace like women every where we are, instead of the clear, original strategists we ought to be. The fact is, we haven't done anything unique or picturesque (it would be disastrous here) but have been content to plod along making haste slowly—Naturally, we are not out of the "argument stage"—for little or no pioneer work was done in Alabama by the earlier suffragists. We are practically virgin soil; we are an illiterate state; the negro problem we have with us always. So our "campaign" has been one of education along suffrage lines—no politics yet, although it is changing.[6]

Despite the brave talk and the newspaper publicity that the suffrage cause received, the statewide membership stood at barely one thousand; moreover, fewer than thirty delegates attended the Huntsville meeting and the total amount spent in that year was $74.76. Clearly it was going to be an uphill battle for support.

The Alabama Equal Suffrage Association received much needed support and publicity from a meeting of the executive committee of NAWSA in Birmingham in March 1914 shortly after the Huntsville convention. The national executive committee held its meetings in different cities in order to get to know state and regional leaders and to gain wider exposure. Birmingham was the first southern city to be selected. Alabama women were disappointed that the president of NAWSA, Dr. Anna Howard Shaw, and the vice-president, Madeline Clay Breckenridge of Kentucky, were not able to attend the meeting, but other prominent women were present. Jane Addams, founder of Hull House in Chicago and a leader of the child labor reform movement, was there. She encouraged Alabama women to work for suffrage in order to abolish child labor. Addams visited the local mining and industrial operations to learn about their welfare work. Mary Ware Bennett, secretary of NAWSA who was responsible for the editing and publishing of suffrage literature, attended the meeting. Also present were Caroline Rurtz Rees and Mrs. James Lees Laidlaw, auditor of NAWSA.[7]

These visitors were given a warm greeting when they arrived at the railroad station. They were met by members of the Alabama association, many of whom knew the visiting women from national conventions. The local suffragists wore their yellow sashes that read Votes for Women. They evidently caused quite a stir when they pinned on the bright sashes over their stylish suits. Word spread through the train station like an electrical spark that the women suffragists were going to invade the depot. Southerners were not accustomed to having women behave in such a fashion in public.[8]

The schedule of events was designed to provide as much public exposure as possible for the suffrage issue and the leaders. A mass meeting was held on March 9 at the Jefferson Theater, which was transformed into a festive auditorium with Votes for Women pennants and yellow bunting decorating the stage. The theater was filled to overflowing. The petition addressed to the 1915 legislature was launched by Bossie Hundley, legislative chairman of AESA, and local suffrage leaders began the process of circulating copies of it. The ushers were young women wearing white dresses with yellow sashes signifying the suffrage cause. On the following morning the executive committee held its meeting at the headquarters of the AESA in the Cable building. At noon the women attended a luncheon at the country club sponsored by the board of trade of the chamber of commerce at which the president of the board, Robert W. Ewing, presided. The board of trade welcomed the visiting dignitaries, but they did not endorse woman suffrage at Cable hall. The day's events were concluded with a rally for the suffragists. Pattie Jacobs, Bossie Hundley, Nellie Murdock, and other women were the active hosts and participants at these various sessions.[9]

The suffrage leaders worked hard to make this occasion one in which all of Birmingham cooperated and participated. They invited leaders from other clubs to take part in the events even though they may or may not have been sympathetic to the suffrage cause. They hoped that this meeting would be viewed as a civic affair, not just as a suffrage gathering. This approach was effective because all of Birmingham wanted to be hospitable to the prominent women. Jacobs said, "We look upon the visit of these women as a matter of civic interest and welfare. I am glad to say that my efforts have met a response which proves again Birmingham's splendid civic pride and progressiveness." Jacobs was extremely astute to use this occasion to create broader support for the suffrage cause, to cast as wide a net as possible for suffrage. She said: "Our definite goal is the enfranchisement of Alabama women. In our ranks are no social lines drawn and no religious distinctions. We have no political faith, all parties being admitted. Nor do we confine ourselves to women, for this great movement of which we are a part is not a woman movement, but a human one." [10]

Just before the meeting of the executive committee, several newspapers ran a story suggesting that these women were coming to Alabama in order to defeat Oscar W. Underwood, running for the United States Senate against Richmond P. Hobson. Both men were long-time members of the United States House of Representatives. Hobson was one of the few representatives who was in favor of enfranchising women with a federal amendment; he also favored a nationwide prohibition amendment. Underwood was opposed to a federal amendment enfranchising women, but he said that he favored action by the state. However, he added that the women of the state needed to make it clear that they wanted suffrage enough to work for it. Underwood had just voted against creating a committee on woman suffrage in the House. On the prohibition issue, Underwood was a local option man. [11]

The local newspapers maintained that northern women, who resented the actions of the House in opposing the creation of a special committee, were invading the South to attack Underwood in his own state. The primary election (which in the South was the deciding election) was less than a month away. The executive committee of NAWSA was described as a "number of well advertised women, who at present have no family or domestic duties to interfere with their political excursions." The article went on to say: "They, in their advocacy of woman's suffrage by an act of congress, are coming to Alabama to help Captain Hobson and to try to defeat Mr. Underwood because he stands for the State's assuming control of the suffrage privileges of its voters." The article described the "spectacle of a car load of Northern women, ignorant of our condition and indifferent to our ultimate welfare" invading the state on behalf of Captain Hobson.[12]

The accusation prompted a letter of denial from Anna Howard Shaw to Pattie Ruffner Jacobs. Shaw described the rumor as being totally unfounded, because NAWSA had a long-established nonpartisan policy. The organization, Shaw said, had never taken part in any local political issue or used its influence in behalf of any candidate. The visit of the executive committee, Shaw maintained, had to do only with the issue of woman suffrage and had no bearing on state politics. NAWSA had a campaign of its own, which was more important to NAWSA than any partisan political campaign.[13] The public might or might not have believed Shaw's disclaimer, but the local suffrage leaders decided that the situation was sufficiently tense to alter their campaign plans until after the April 6 primary election. They temporarily ceased circulating the suffrage petitions and abandoned the plan to distribute yellow ribbons on the downtown street corners.[14]

From February 1914 to August 1915 Alabama suffragists were totally involved with their campaign to gain the vote by state action. The time seemed right. Suffrage was gaining momentum nationwide and was going to be an issue in the 1916 presidential election. The national Democratic party would be forced to take a stand. The chances were strong that it would follow the leadership of Pres. Woodrow Wilson and declare that suffrage was an issue that should be left up to the states. This was a position taken by many Democratic leaders, including William Jennings Bryan, Champ Clark, and most important, at least for Alabama, Oscar W. Underwood.[15]

At this point NAWSA still supported state action. However, the Congressional Union was pushing the federal amendment with a degree of success. For the first time in the twentieth century, Congress actually debated and voted on a federal amendment. But it was defeated in the Senate by a vote of thirty-four to thirty-five in March 1914 and later (January 1915) by a vote of 204 to 174 in the House. The rejection by the Senate prompted an editorial in the *Birmingham Ledger:* "Alabama will consider the subject more willingly now that the national administration has decided that there shall be no federal interference. The advocates of women suffrage now know where they stand and will direct their efforts. The vote of the senate was formal notice that there will be no amendment of the national constitution for years, if ever. Thousands of men will consent to woman suffrage under this decision who would never consent to the amendment." [16] Whatever other states might feel, clearly state action was more appealing to Alabamians than action by the federal government ever would be.

Pattie Jacobs and other suffrage leaders felt that the prospects looked bright for favorable action by the 1915 legislature. Jacobs believed that, when the question was put to the men of the state, they would grant women the franchise. No legislature in the history of the state had ever been put on record on the question of suffrage. The suffrage leaders planned to give the legislators an opportunity to voice their opinions and submit the question to the voters. They were in the process of conducting a campaign that would ensure that no member of the legislature was ignorant on the subject of suffrage. Jacobs said, "No member of the legislature can go to the capital saying that the women of Alabama do not want suffrage or that they have not had any opportunity to inform themselves on the subject." She pointed out that if the legislature failed to act in 1915, by the time the 1919 session came around, the United States Congress might have passed a federal amendment. She said that she believed that the men of Alabama had enough pride to bring the state into the suffrage fold willingly and not be forced to act by the federal government. [17]

Other women and men of the state felt the enthusiasm also. The number of state associations increased from seven in February 1914 to twenty-six associations by June and to thirty-four by November. The amount of money also increased. Instead of working with less than one hundred dollars, the association's income was nearly one thousand dollars. Two men's associations were formed, one in Cullman and the other in Birmingham. An important ally was gained when the powerful Alabama WCTU endorsed woman suffrage at their 1914 convention. Assistance was also forthcoming from NAWSA. The annual convention in Nashville in November 1914 made the decision to concentrate on Alabama because the prospects looked hopeful. It was also influenced by the fact that the legislature was meeting in 1915 and would not meet again for another four years. Two prominent southern suffrage leaders, Madeline Clay Breckenridge of Kentucky and Lillian Johnson of Tennessee, agreed to make a speaking tour of the state. In February 1915 NAWSA sent Lavinia Engle to the state as a field representative. Anna Howard Shaw, the president of NAWSA, made a trip to the state and spoke to the legislature and the association.[18]

This campaign was well organized and executed by the association. The newly elected president of the Birmingham association, Mrs. H. H. Snell, said that a campaign year was always fraught with difficulties and dangers and the suffragists would need to have "wise, cool intelligent leadership" to guide them through the "ridicule, injustice, doubt and despair" they would experience. In the early months of 1914, the women began to circulate petitions which requested that the state constitution be amended to confer upon women the same right of suffrage conferred upon men. Women carried these around the state in every public gathering, especially at city and county fairs. They even conducted door-to-door campaigns in the cities. The Birmingham association observed Petition Day one day each week. By the time the petitions were presented to the legislature in August 1915, they had collected 10,000 signatures.[19]

Bossie O'Brien Hundley, legislative chair of AESA, was in charge of the campaign. Hundley had been active in the suffrage drive from the beginning, serving as president of the Birmingham association after Jacobs became president of the state organization. She was the daughter of the first mayor of Birmingham and the wife of Oscar Hundley, a judge and prominent member of the Progressive party. Jacobs described Hundley as "young and very handsome, lives in a beautiful house in the fashionable 'South Highlands' of Birmingham." She went on to say that Hundley was a "dear little girl . . . full of initiative & has energy & enthusiasm necessary to carry to successful fruition much suffrage work."[20]

Hundley approached her job in a thoroughly professional manner. Shortly after the May runoff election, she secured a list of the men who had been elected to the legislature and sent suffrage literature to them as well as a year's subscription to the *Woman's Journal,* the official publication of NAWSA. In July 1914 she sent a questionnaire to each legislator requesting information about his occupation, religion, political party, veteran status, marital status, and views on woman suffrage. One of the newspapers printed a series of articles, "Early Glimpses of the Next Legislature," giving biographical and political information that Hundley said was "more interesting than accurate." The articles also included a picture that Hundley studied so she would be able to recognize each individual. From this information, she organized a card catalogue with information on each legislator. In this manner she learned who were friends and who were enemies of suffrage. Apparently at that point the women did not have many friends. But more important, the legislators knew that there was an active suffrage association and there were women who did want to vote.[21]

The suffragists continued making speeches on any and all occasions. Pattie Jacobs, as the best-known suffragist, was in demand as a speaker. In January 1914 she was invited to Mobile, where she spoke at the Cawthon Hotel to a large audience of women and men. The Mobile association was still in its infancy and Jacobs was able to attract forty-nine new members. In May 1914 she spoke in Anniston at the Alabama Presbyterian College. She was invited by the Euphians, a local club that was studying current issues. Bossie Hundley did not wait to be invited, but got in her car with other suffragists and made a trip from Birmingham down to Auburn and Opelika, stopping at numerous towns including Sylacauga and Childersburg. Their goal was to establish associations and distribute literature. She spoke in churches and courthouses and always opened her program with prayer. A trip such as this is remarkable because in 1914 few people owned automobiles and even fewer risked driving on the state's unimproved roads. It is more remarkable that a woman would attempt such a feat. Actually, Hundley did not drive herself on this trip, but evidently she did know how to drive and was enthusiastic about her Hudson Six. Even women who were fearful of speaking (and many were) could aid the cause with a "voiceless speech." Under this system women simply turned several cards or leaves printed with arguments in favor of vote for women and answered questions.[22]

BOSSIE O'BRIEN HUNDLEY, CHAIR OF LEGISLATIVE COMMITTEE OF AESA
WHO LED THE 1915 DRIVE TO OBTAIN THE RIGHT TO VOTE. *FROM THE
COLLECTIONS OF THE BIRMINGHAM PUBLIC LIBRARY.*

As the suffrage leaders presented their arguments to the public, they emphasized two principles: justice and expediency. Justice was the older argument. Women deserved the vote as much as men because they must obey laws and pay taxes and therefore should have a voice in how these laws are established and the taxes levied. Women had just as much intelligence and were as well informed as men. They were just as loyal to their country. In other words, women were human beings and deserved to be treated as such; they should not always be identified as someone's daughter, wife, or mother. In this argument suffragists were saying that men and women are essentially alike and should be viewed so in the eyes of the law.[23]

The argument from expediency was newer; it stemmed from women's involvement in progressive causes. According to this argument, women wanted the ballot because they were different from men. They wanted to be able to vote in order to be better wives and mothers, in order to protect the home. They needed to be able to make decisions about pure food, fresh milk, clean water, and adequate drainage. Women were still primarily wives and mothers, but the world had changed and they needed the ballot to protect the home and family. Women also had different views to bring to politics because women were different from men.[24]

This shift in argument has been seen by historians as a narrowing of the women's movement. Women began by talking about justice among human beings and ended by talking about what women could contribute to politics as women. Women began by challenging women's sphere and ended by accepting women's special role. Observers of the modern women's movement have tended to feel that women needed to make a choice. Either they were like men or else they were unlike men. They could not have it both ways. Historian Nancy F. Cott has made it clear that women of this earlier period did not see a dichotomy. They could talk about being treated as equals with men, then in the same breath speak of the differences between the sexes and women's special contribution. They simply recognized that the paradox existed. Women wanted a sexual equality that included sexual differences and saw no contradiction between the two.[25]

These southern suffragists had an image problem. When they entered a new community, they seldom found enthusiasm and oftentimes encountered downright hostility. Ladies simply did not speak out on political questions. The public was so unaccustomed to seeing women in public roles demanding the right to vote that they expected a "militant freak." Men were certain that they were going to see aggressive, "mannish" women. When Pattie Jacobs spoke in Mobile, the headline read, "Pretty, Brainy Suffragette Surprises Those Looking for Woman With Hatchet." The newspaper went on to comment, "Mrs. Jacobs carried neither hatchet or pistol. She neither wore a man's hat nor was she masculine. Instead, she presented a splendid picture of a true woman, a noble mother, and a deep thinker." [26]

An important part of the strategy was to try to show that voting was not in conflict with the behavior of a lady. The picture of Jacobs that was often in the newspaper was that of a gracious, attractive southern woman who was concerned with her home and children. She was described as being one of the most popular society women, the mother of two children, and noted for her charming personality, culture, and versatility. She and other women dressed in the style of the day, which included skirts down to the floor, wide-brimmed hats, and gloves. When Jacobs spoke in public, she always wore an evening gown and appeared every inch the lady she was. Hundley was pictured in her garden with her little daughter and assured readers that she found her greatest enjoyment in making salads or desserts in her kitchen. [27]

The long-awaited session of the legislature convened on January 12, 1915, in Montgomery. This productive session faced several major issues of the Progressive Era. In addition to woman suffrage, the legislators dealt with prohibition, child labor, and several major educational reforms. The legislators tackled the most controversial issue first, prohibition. They adopted a statewide prohibition law that replaced the earlier local option act. The governor, Charles Henderson, vetoed the bill, but the legislators quickly passed it over his veto. This major issue then settled, the lawmakers turned to other matters. Next the session adopted a child labor act that raised the age limit to fourteen years and put enforcement in the hands of the prison inspector. The educational reforms passed included a compulsory attendance law, authorization for the school districts to levy a tax, and enlargement of the duties and powers of the superintendents. Since these were all issues that women were advocating, the capitol was covered with women filling the galleries and lobbying for their favorite reforms. The WCTU flocked to the chambers pressing for prohibition. The Alabama Federation of Women's Clubs set up a child labor exhibit in the rotunda of the capitol. The lawmakers had never seen so many women in Montgomery.

On the day the session opened the suffragists joined the other women. They opened their campaign headquarters in the Grand Theater building, which provided comfortable offices and lay on the route from the downtown hotels to the capitol building. The windows were conspicuously plastered with suffrage posters. Elsewhere in the town the women displayed a suffrage map in the elevator of the hotel in which most legislators stayed and suffrage literature was left in the lobby. They were perpetually seen talking with one or another of the lawmakers. There was nothing amateurish about the suffragists' lobbying techniques.[28]

The woman suffrage bill that was introduced read, "The right of the citizens of this state to vote shall not be denied or abridged on account of sex." Since this proposal was to be an amendment to the constitution, it would require a three-fifths vote of both houses before it could be submitted to the people. The bill was introduced into the house on January 22 by Rep. J. H. Green of Dallas County, who had requested the honor almost a year before. Green was an engineer on the railroad that brought the women to the Selma convention in 1913. He had long been a supporter of women's rights and looked forward to pushing the measure. The bill was referred to the House Committee on Privileges and Elections. A similar bill, introduced into the senate by H. H. Holmes, was referred to the Senate Committee on Privileges and Elections. A careful poll had been taken by the women and they believed that fourteen of the eighteen members of the house committee favored the bill, as did all but one of the senate committeemen.[29]

On the afternoon of January 28, the suffragists were given a hearing at a joint session of the senate and house committees on privileges and elections. This hearing was attended by a large delegation of women

SUFFRAGIST LEADERS ON THE STEPS OF THE CAPITOL BUILDING IN
MONTGOMERY LOBBYING THE STATE LEGISLATORS DURING THE 1915
CAMPAIGN. *ALABAMA DEPARTMENT OF ARCHIVES AND HISTORY,
MONTGOMERY, ALABAMA.*

from various parts of the state. The gallery of the house was crowded and many members of the legislature attended. Bossie Hundley, the chair of the AESA legislative committee, presided over the two-hour hearing, although she was so hoarse from campaigning that her voice was scarcely audible. Pattie Jacobs spoke first on the history of the suffrage movement in the United States. She was followed by Lavinia Engle, field representative of NAWSA, who spoke about the progressive legislation that had been adopted in states where women could vote. The women even had the support of the highly respectable United Daughters of the Confederacy (UDC). Mrs. Chappel Cory, president of the UDC, spoke on "What the vote will mean to the morals of the state." Julia Tutwiler, the veteran reformer who was aging and in poor health, spoke about the need for women to be able to vote in a world that was once again at war. (World War I had begun in August 1914.) Rabbi B. C. Ehrenreich of Montgomery also spoke, as did Representative Green, who said that those who opposed woman suffrage were of two types: either they believed voting would lower the standards of women or they were whiskey politicians.[30]

After this presentation, Hundley asked for questions from the members of the legislature, but there was only ominous silence. The committees met in executive session and the house committee voted an indefinite postponement for the bill. The women were astounded because of the earlier promises of the legislators. The senate committee did make a favorable report and the bill was set to be considered on the twenty-fifth legislative day. The suffragists were determined that the legislature would actually consider the bill and be forced to register a vote.[31]

The women had an opportunity to support the amendment before the entire legislature in a joint session on February 5. At this time Dr. Anna Howard Shaw addressed the legislature. She spoke of the patriotism and devotion of southern women, especially those of the Civil War period. Women of the South, she believed, had paid for and earned their freedom. She stressed that the purpose of the proposal was not for the legislature to pass judgment on woman suffrage, but to decide to put the issue to the voters for their decision. The next week a new bill was introduced into the house by Rep. Sam Will John of Dallas County.

This bill was not referred to a committee, but was to lie on the table for three readings and then come up for a vote. However, before the bill was given a second reading, the legislature adjourned until July, five months later.[32]

The interim period was used by the suffragists not for rest, but for additional work. They hoped to secure promises from the requisite three-fifths of the legislators to support the bill at the regular session. Personal work by individual suffragists continued, and the legislative committee renewed its efforts. The Recess Joint Committee on Judiciary took an interest in the pending suffrage bill and asked that the suffragists submit a brief in behalf of the constitutional amendment. Bossie Hundley wrote a brief that presented the case in a concise and thoughtful manner. She reminded the men that they would not be committing themselves to woman suffrage, only to the principle that the people of the state be allowed to decide for themselves whether women should vote. She pointed out that this was the first time in the history of the state that women had asked to be enfranchised. The national Democratic leaders had said that suffrage was a matter properly left to the states. Now Alabama had an opportunity to act. Hundley maintained that there was much support for suffrage in the state. There were fifty-three suffrage associations, and the cause had been endorsed by the Alabama WCTU, the Alabama Congress of Mothers, and the American Federation of Labor. Because woman suffrage was increasing nationwide every year, it was in the interest of Alabama men to solve this problem in their own way and not wait for a federal amendment. She concluded by saying, "The Alabama women only want what belongs to them and they want the Alabama men to give it to them."[33]

The legislature reconvened on July 13 and on July 30 the suffrage issue was considered by the senate, giving some idea of the feeling of the senators toward the issue. Sam Will John of Dallas County endeavored to secure immediate action on the suffrage resolution. The senate refused to do so and a debate followed as to when the issue would be discussed. At one point a motion to postpone the measure indefinitely deadlocked at fifteen to fifteen. The lieutenant governor, John R. Kilby, broke the tie by voting against the postponement. After many motions, it was decided to debate the issue on the fortieth day of the session. This date was near the end of the session, which meant it might not be considered at all because of the shortage of time. But at least a date was set. The women had not anticipated this kind of fight, but they came out with flying colors. Hundley said, "I am well satisfied with the result." [34]

Meanwhile, the House Committee on Privileges and Elections, which had failed to take action in January, finally held a meeting, but many of the supporters of suffrage were not present. By a six to five vote the committee decided against submitting the issue to the house. Representative Green, who had introduced the bill, was not present at the meeting. Bossie Hundley put on a brave face by saying, "It would take more than an adverse committee report or the perfidy of any number of men whom the women . . . had cause to believe to be their friends, to cause any disappointment on their part." The women had received promises from fourteen of the eighteen members of the committee that they would vote in favor of the bill. They felt betrayed by men whom they had regarded as their friends. [35] The *Age-Herald* of Birmingham put words into Hundley's mouth in an article in which it was implied that she said, "All men are liars." Instead, she had replied with the phrase of John Paul Jones, "We have just begun to fight." The newspaper issued an apology the next day. Hundley may have felt the statement was true, but she was too much of a politician to make such a statement. [36]

This defeat turned out to be short lived, because on August 11 the caucus of the house voted to recommend that the bill be removed from the adverse calendar. The house then voted to follow the recommendation of the caucus. This action indicated a change of heart on the part of the legislators. [37]

While the legislature was considering the suffrage bill, Bossie Hundley had an opportunity to engage Tom Heflin in a debate of sorts. Hundley had been trying for some time to persuade the congressman to debate face to face, but Heflin refused to be drawn into such an encounter. But both were on the same platform at a barbecue in Wetumpka on August 12, 1915. Hundley spoke first in support of suffrage, and she was followed by Heflin, who was to make the major speech of the day. Just as an offhand comment, Heflin said that if he could be convinced that a majority of the women of the state wanted the vote, he might be willing to waive his "objection to the fad." At this point, Hundley interrupted him and asked to make a comment. Heflin smiled broadly and executed a chivalrous bow in making assent to the request. Hundley said, "The gentlemen surely knows that his proposition is neither frank nor practical. He knows it would be impossible to hold such an election as he suggests. The constitution makes no provision for any such referendum." Heflin did not respond directly but told a little story that made the point that women control men anyway. He concluded by saying, "Boys, if you give the women folks the ballot, you ain't got a chance."[38]

As the day for the vote approached, the women stepped up their pressure on the legislators. On August 10 they gave each member of the legislature a yellow miniature sunflower signifying hope. Huge vases of sunflowers adorned the speaker's desk. A huge banner swinging over the railing of the gallery read "Alabama Women Want the Ballot on the Same Terms with Alabama Men." Smaller banners read "Justice, not Favors" and "Votes for Women." Women filled the galleries of the capitol and overflowed into the hallways. They were especially evident on the steps of the capitol, where two women stood holding a huge Votes for Women banner. Other women, dressed in white dresses, large hats, and suffrage sashes of yellow across their chests, were distributing suffrage literature.[39]

The day before the vote was to be taken, an event occurred that was a blow to the suffrage cause. On each legislator's desk in the morning was an anonymous pamphlet entitled "A Protest Against Woman's Suffrage in Alabama." The pamphlet maintained that "Woman Suffrage is the most dangerous blow aimed at the peace and happiness of the people of Alabama and white supremacy since the Civil War." The author went on to say that the majority of women did not want to vote, because the vote was the least of their demands. These women wanted "full fledged citizenship, with all the duties and obligations of man, such as holding office, sitting on the juries, etc." Suffrage, they said, would strike a blow at the most sacred traditions of the South. It would be granted at the expense of home and home life. "The avowed purpose is to break the 'Solid South' by means of the votes of black women." The pamphlet raised the specter of blacks voting, which was always a threat in the South but had not emerged to any great extent in the campaign before now. It also levied a scurrilous attack upon Anna Howard Shaw and other suffrage leaders and completely misrepresented their purposes.[40]

At first Jacobs and Hundley thought it best not to reply to such a contemptuous anonymous attack, but then changed their minds. Almost overnight, in the days before photocopying, they produced a response. In their "Reply to the Anonymous 'Protest Against Woman's Suffrage in Alabama,'" they did their best to respond to the charges, but mainly made the point that all the legislators were being asked to do was to submit the amendment to the voters. They also reminded the legislators of the 10,000 people who had signed the petitions and the sixty-seven suffrage organizations in the state. But the reply could not undo the damage that had been done. The women learned later that the pamphlet had been written by Joseph E. Evans and others from Selma after the Selma Bar Association took a stand against suffrage.[41]

On the day of the vote, Representative Green who had introduced the woman suffrage legislation announced that he would not support the amendment. He decided that he would oppose the bill he had been supporting for more than two years. The newspaper described Green as seeing a great light and turning his back on woman suffrage. Green believed that the AESA was an integral part of a political organization having for its object the reenfranchisement of the blacks of the South. He was convinced that suffrage would destroy the social fabric of American family life and reduce man to the pitiable state of being merely the father of the children of women. The women were astounded because Green had been a supporter of woman suffrage for twenty years and had asked to have the honor of introducing the legislation. He even reiterated the request on two occasions. If the women had had any idea that he would change his mind, they would have asked others of their friends to introduce the measure. Jacobs described Green's defection as a "terrible blow."[42]

On the day that the vote was scheduled, the prospects looked dim. In addition to the distribution of the pamphlet and Green's change of heart, many suffrage friends were absent. Jacobs and Hundley realized that they could not gain the necessary three-fifths majority, so they asked to postpone the vote for a day. This postponement gave Jacobs and Hundley an opportunity to prepare their reply to the "Protest."

When the vote was held the following day, many of their friends were still not present. The vote was fifty-two yeas and forty-two nays, twelve votes short of the necessary three-fifths majority. With this action, the suffrage question was, for all practical purposes, dead in the 1915 legislature. When the senate finally acted on September 1, the vote there showed less support, twelve yeas and twenty nays. The suffragist leaders put up a brave front. Pattie Jacobs said, "We are not in the least discouraged. On the other hand, we feel distinctly encouraged and expect to go right ahead in the fight, going before every legislature that convenes in Alabama until the whole suffrage question is settled and settled right." She went on to say, "Fifty-two men stood by their guns there in the chivalrous manner for which Alabamians are famous, protecting the helpless women of the State, though it is true that if all the legislators had made good their promises we would have won a real victory instead of a moral victory that we achieved."[43]

The suffragist leaders really believed that the legislature would be willing to submit the amendment to the voters. They thought that they had the votes in the legislature and anticipated the real battle being a statewide vote on the amendment. They turned out to be wrong. However, the women showed political maturity in the organization and execution of their campaign. Establishing a firm base in their sixty-seven associations, they gained statewide support in circulating their petitions and gathered 10,000 signatures. They systematically organized information on the legislators, which allowed them to be effective lobbyists. They were able to gather their followers and have a presence when needed. In short, they conducted a thoroughly professional campaign.

The suffragists had succeeded in gaining a certain amount of legislative support, at least in the way of verbal promises. Both Jacobs and Hundley attested to this fact in their accounts of the campaign. But the male legislators were inexperienced in dealing with female lobbyists. They might not have known how to say no to a lady. They might have been such perfect gentlemen that they felt more comfortable giving the women the impression that they agreed with them. Clearly woman suffrage was an issue that most of them did not want to deal with. They would much rather have disposed of it by indefinite postponements or tabling the measure. But Hundley and others forced a vote on the measure and the legislators had to be counted. Despite their avowed support of states' rights, it turned out that the men did not want women to vote either by state or federal action.

The suffrage issue never had broad-based support in the state or among the legislators. The *Age-Herald* conducted a survey in October 1914, which found that suffrage would be overwhelmingly defeated in the next legislature.[44] Between October 1914 and August 1915 the women made some headway with the legislators. But their support was shallow; it evaporated quickly under pressure. Considering the situation, it was surprising that suffrage received a majority vote in the house. Since the issue was new, there was not enough time to build up strong statewide support. Indeed, it was so new that people did not take it seriously. Opposition did not form until a measure had some chance of success.

The argument of the 1915 campaign was twofold: women should be given the vote because it was just to do so and women needed the vote to carry out Progressive reforms protecting the family and the home. Suffrage leaders did not use the race issue in their arguments; they did not appeal for the right to vote to maintain white supremacy. It was the opponents of suffrage who raised the race question in their anonymous protest. From then on, what little chance suffrage had was doomed; almost no argument could be effective in the face of perceived danger to white supremacy. When the issue came up again for the 1919 legislature to consider, the debate turned entirely on the race question.

9 FINAL YEARS OF THE SUFFRAGE DRIVE, 1916–1919

fter the legislature defeated the suffrage amendment in 1915, the Alabama Equal Suffrage Association had to chart a new course. The majority of Alabamians preferred state action to federal action, but the legislature had had its opportunity to enfranchise women and chose to reject it. Now the state suffragists began to support the federal amendment as the only course of action. This change coincided with a similar change at the national level.

In 1915 Carrie Chapman Catt became president of the National American Woman Suffrage Association. She assumed that leadership role at a crucial time; the board had had no clear strategy and was unable to take advantage of the changing political situation. Anna Howard Shaw had been an excellent speaker, but she was an ineffectual organizer. Under Catt's leadership NAWSA became a coherently organized association built upon a mass base, which worked closely with local, state, and national members. Catt supported careful, low-keyed lobbying in a ladylike manner. She put forward her "winning plan" in 1916; this provided that each state would have specific responsibilities in the drive for a federal amendment.

Alice Paul and the Congressional Union were also well organized and constantly active as they continued their drive for a federal amendment. Both Paul and Catt were representative of a new type of professional organizer. The day of the amateur reformer was over. The CU tried to develop a base in the country, but met with limited success, especially in the South. CU members believed in dramatic action, the symbolic gesture that made headlines. As the Congressional Union moved further in this direction, NAWSA tried to separate itself from these flamboyant activities and to keep the distinction clear at least in the minds of congressmen.

Woman suffrage became an issue in the election of 1916. Both the Democrats and Republicans supported suffrage in their platforms, but proposed to gain it with a state-by-state approach. However, during the campaign the Republican candidate, Charles Evans Hughes, endorsed the federal amendment. Democratic Woodrow Wilson also supported woman suffrage, but was ambiguous about the method to achieve it. In this election women voted in states that had a total of nearly one hundred electoral votes. In fact the votes of women in California, Idaho, Utah, and Arizona were credited with giving Wilson his narrow victory in the election. Once women started to be an electoral force, politicians sat up and took notice.

By 1916 the drive for woman suffrage had taken on new life. The issue had become a legitimate one in the eyes of a larger number of Americans. Both political parties were forced to deal with the issue. The period of stagnation was over; a corner had been turned. The existence of the militant Congressional Union was decisive. They used their shock tactics of marches and pickets and other dramatic protests to gain publicity, while the more conservative NAWSA carefully developed its organization based on congressional districts to influence congressmen. Neither organization had much use for the other, but they complemented each other well. In the atmosphere of progressivism the question was no longer whether women would have the vote but when. Catt thought it would take six years, but World War I speeded up the process and it took only four.[1]

The revitalization of the national suffrage movement was reflected in the Alabama Equal Suffrage Association also. The 1915 legislative campaign gained much publicity for the suffrage issue. Even though the campaign was unsuccessful, suffrage was now a major issue and women and men flocked to the suffrage associations. The AESA saw substantial growth and activity for about a year and a half, until the United States entered the First World War. The leaders increased the number of associations more than threefold; they organized the state into congressional districts; and NAWSA sent a paid organizer into the state. The association published a newsletter twice a month, which kept the suffragists informed of state and national activities. The newspapers of the state devoted much space to the suffrage issue, with thirty-four of them publishing a biweekly press bulletin and eight publishing weekly suffrage columns. The women maintained four traveling suffrage libraries in circulation. They organized automobile parades and mass meetings in virtually every part of the state. However, the entrance of the United States into World War I in April 1917 brought almost all of the suffrage activity to a halt. The women shifted from their suffrage work to a variety of war work, which occupied them until the war was over in November 1918. This hiatus proved to be disastrous to the suffrage organization. When Congress passed the Nineteenth Amendment in 1919, the women had difficulty waging a campaign for ratification.[2]

After the legislative session of 1915, the Alabama Equal Suffrage Association had to make a decision about supporting the federal amendment, which by now NAWSA was pushing. Even though virtually all southerners preferred action at the state level, the decision was not difficult. Pattie Jacobs skillfully led the state suffragists to support the federal amendment and made its ratification their goal. The fear of a federal amendment was always that it would reopen the entire question of blacks voting. Once again southerners feared that the federal government would interfere with their state election laws, as had been done during Reconstruction. Since they were consistently opposed to anything that appeared to endanger white supremacy, they saw a federal amendment and white supremacy as mutually exclusive. Jacobs gave her answer to this fear at a congressional hearing in 1915.

If this amendment is adopted it in no wise regulates or interferes with any existing qualification (except sex) which the various State constitutions now exact. It leaves all others to be determined by the various States through their constitutional agencies. It is a fallacy to contend that to prohibit discrimination on account of sex would involve the race problem. The actual application of the principle in the South would be to enfranchise a very large number of white women and the same sort of negro women as of negro men now permitted to exercise the privilege.[3]

She went on to say later that in areas where a black majority existed, black women would be prohibited from voting by the poll tax and the literacy test just as black men were restricted. Jacobs saw white supremacy to be compatible with the federal amendment.

Not all southern suffragists agreed with Jacobs. Kate Gordon of Louisiana saw a necessary connection between the maintenance of white supremacy and the continued right of southern legislators to exercise complete power over local elections. With the goal of enfranchising only white women, Gordon had created the Southern States Woman Suffrage Conference (SSWSC) in 1913. Alabama suffragists never joined Gordon's conference and openly broke with her in 1915 over her opposition to the federal amendment. Gordon was critical of Alabama suffragists for their support of the federal amendment and saw this position as responsible for their 1915 defeat in the state legislature. She set herself up as the spokesperson for southern suffragists, a fact that Jacobs and others resented. At a meeting of the Alabama suffrage association in October 1915, the board adopted a strongly worded resolution reasserting its allegiance to NAWSA and protesting the attitude of Kate Gordon in assuming to speak for Alabama suffragists. Once again Jacobs showed her political skill in steering the association to uphold the federal amendment and the position of NAWSA.[4]

Changes occurred in the Alabama Equal Suffrage Association at the same time that NAWSA was being transformed. Pattie Ruffner Jacobs resigned as president because she was elected second auditor of NAWSA in 1915. This was a great honor for Jacobs and Alabama. At the time of her election, the director of the Birmingham Chamber of Commerce wrote to Carrie Chapman Catt expressing pride in the recognition given to Jacobs. She worked closely with Catt and other national leaders and was a valuable lobbyist for NAWSA. Thereafter, she was often absent from the state on national business. She continued, however, to serve the Alabama association in the crucial position of legislative chair and usually attended the board meetings, but she was no longer involved in the day-by-day affairs of the state. But when it came to the important ratification campaign in 1919, Jacobs once again assumed the presidency of the state organization.[5]

After four years under the capable leadership of Jacobs, the association had to find a new president. At the convention in Gadsden in 1916, Carrie M. Parke of Selma was elected to fill that position. Parke was a founding member of the state association and had served on the board from the beginning. She appears to have been a wise choice to lead the organization during this period in which suffrage was becoming a legitimate issue endorsed by both parties. She understood the rapidly changing events and gave every evidence of knowing how to implement NAWSA's new organizational plan in Alabama. However, she was at a distinct disadvantage because she lived in the small town of Selma instead of in Birmingham, which had been the headquarters of the association ever since its founding. Birmingham had approximately 1,500 members in 1917, which made it the largest and most important association in the state. Logic would dictate that the president should come from Birmingham if possible. Bossie O'Brien Hundley was also nominated at the 1916 convention. She was from Birmingham and had held the important position of legislative chair during the 1915 legislative campaign. She was a capable organizer who had shown her ability in lobbying the legislators. But in the election Parke received forty-five votes and Hundley thirty-two. The convention evidently felt that despite her remote location, Parke would make a better president. Hundley was appointed to serve as chair of the printing committee, but she was never again as active in suffrage work.[6]

After Parke's election, the state headquarters were moved to Selma, offices were opened at the Albert Hotel in March 1916, and the association engaged an executive secretary. The plan was that the state association would pay the rent of twenty-five dollars a month for the office and the salary of twenty dollars a month for the secretary, while the Selma association would be responsible for the maintenance of the office. Parke hoped to make the headquarters into a resting and meeting room for Selma women following the model of the Birmingham headquarters. This plan met with a degree of success. Every Saturday the women of St. Paul's Episcopal Church held a market there. The office was also used as a distribution center for clothing and food for those who were left destitute by the summer floods of the Alabama River. However commendable these projects were, the financial responsibility proved to be too great for the association. Parke made the decision to close the headquarters in November because too few of the local associations contributed money to pay the rent. The secretary was maintained, but her hours and pay were reduced. Parke felt her services were necessary to keep up with the correspondence with fifty to sixty local associations, eleven chairs of committees, and six officers. The secretary also typed the Alabama Suffrage Bulletins and the press releases. Maintaining an office in an out-of-the-way location like Selma was problematical at best, but the assistance of a secretary was a wise investment.[7]

The years 1916 and 1917 were busy times for the suffrage association. By 1916 NAWSA had a plan of action that it encouraged each state to follow. The Alabama suffragists made every effort to cooperate. They organized according to the political district plan of NAWSA, which prescribed a chair in each of the state's congressional districts in addition to the usual county chair. NAWSA hoped to standardize all state organizations in order to be able to mobilize any state in any direction on short notice. Parke pointed out that an organization based on local associations was satisfactory in the early stages of the movement, but was not adequate when the cause matured and entered the campaign stage. Once again the Alabama association was attempting to move beyond the educational stage to the campaign stage. In order to assist them in this endeavor, NAWSA sent an organizer to the state, Lola C. Trax of Baltimore, who worked from April through June 1916. She made a circuit of the state speaking every day except Sunday and holding meetings in towns where suffrage had never been discussed before. Trax felt that there was a noticeable change in the attitude of the public in the kinds of questions that were asked. She attributed this change to the recently adopted suffrage planks in the platforms of both political parties. The national conventions of the Democrats and Republicans were held in June, at which time they both came out in favor of woman suffrage. At the request of NAWSA women from Alabama even marched in the parades preceding both conventions.[8]

Following up the activities of Trax, women traveled over the state making speeches and holding meetings whenever possible. Parke was in demand as a speaker and traveled widely across the state. She and others often took automobile trips as a way of dramatizing the suffrage issue, since automobiles were still something of a novelty in the state. A new approach was to hold a suffrage school at which lectures were presented over a several-day period on the history of the suffrage movement, techniques of organization, press and publicity work, and public speaking. Mrs. J. O. Bonelli conducted suffrage schools in Tuscaloosa, Alexander City, Selma, and Livingston during 1916. The largest suffrage school was held in Birmingham immediately following the annual convention in February 1917. This school was led by three suffragists sent by NAWSA, Mrs. H. A. Wilson and Anne Doughty, both of New York, and Mrs. T. T. Cotnam of Arkansas. Over two hundred people attended this school, which also included a mass meeting held at the Tutwiler Hotel. During both the convention and the school the hotel was decorated with yellow pennants that bore the slogan Ballots for Both. Across the balcony in the ballroom hung a huge banner, "Alabama Women Want the Vote on the Same Terms as Alabama Men."[9]

Carrie Parke knew that because the spoken word could not be delivered every day or every week, the association needed to provide the printed word. The Alabama Suffrage Bulletin was begun in October 1915 as a part of the work of the press committee. Originally it was a monthly publication, but later was issued twice a month. The editor was Amelia Worthington, who earlier had nearly been suspended from a teacher training course in Birmingham because she was a suffragist. The bulletin contained news of the branches of the various local associations and was designed to bind the organization closer together during the letdown following the legislative campaign of 1915. After the first year Worthington doubted whether the bulletin was a success because it did not pay its way and because she felt too few people read it. But her doubts evidently were overcome because it continued to be published until 1919.[10]

The goal of NAWSA by 1916 was passage of the federal amendment to the Constitution. Both NAWSA and the Congressional Union were working to persuade United States representatives and senators to vote in favor of the amendment. Alabama suffragists openly favored NAWSA's policy of supporting the amendment. The state leaders were constantly encouraging all members to study the amendment and to be able to answer objections concerning it. And Alabamians had many objections. They mostly centered upon the fear of black votes and the danger to states' rights. Both of the United States senators, John H. Bankhead and Oscar W. Underwood, were opposed, as were almost all of the U.S. representatives.

Jacobs realized that the suffrage movement was in a difficult situation in Alabama. NAWSA supported the federal amendment, which was on the verge of being adopted, but which created almost insurmountable problems in terms of states' rights. Events were moving rapidly and the South was in danger of being left behind. As a way of gaining some momentum, she and others on the board considered other approaches. Jacobs proposed requesting municipal or presidential suffrage as a first step. Several states had enfranchised women to vote in presidential elections by an action of the legislature. Illinois was the first to do so in 1913; it was followed by North Dakota, Nebraska, Rhode Island, Ohio, Indiana, and Michigan in 1917. However, this step was essentially precluded in Alabama because the legislature was not scheduled to meet again until 1919. Jacobs did present a suffrage resolution to the state Democratic committee in the summer of 1916, but the committee refused to take any action on it. It was a difficult period in which to chart a course of action.[11]

Since none of these options appeared to be viable, as early as the convention in Birmingham in February 1917 Jacobs suggested that women should attempt to register to vote for publicity purposes. Later a rationale was presented for such action by E. Q. Norton when he addressed the Mobile Suffrage Association in September 1917. Norton said that women could not be deprived of the ballot because they were already citizens and citizens could not be deprived of their rights. Because both the federal constitution and the Alabama constitution were based on the principle of equality, women were entitled to vote. Following this line of reasoning, women should attempt to register and if they were denied that right, then they should bring suit and let the courts decide the issue. Two possible methods of procedure were proposed. One was to attempt to register in several parts of the state simultaneously or the other was to have only one attempt, which would be used as the basis for a "friendly" suit. Susan B. Anthony used this line of reasoning in 1872 when she attempted to vote, but it did not prove to be a viable approach. There was no reason to believe that this old argument would have any more success than it had earlier, but the Alabama suffragists were seeking some action that would gain them attention.[12]

The Congressional Union under the leadership of Alice Paul began to picket the White House in January 1917. As Wilson went for his afternoon drive, the pickets waved signs bearing his own words on democracy before him. On inauguration day in March 1917 thousands of women walked slowly around the executive mansion. The nation was shocked by such action, especially as it continued after the United States entered World War I in April 1917. Attacks on the president became more provocative in the summer of 1917. NAWSA was sure these militant tactics hurt the cause, but the National Woman's Party (as the Congressional Union was now called) insisted the reverse was true. The Alabama suffragists were critical of these actions, which they regarded as unladylike. Parke said, "In our organization work, we have endeavored to avoid spectacular and sensational publicity, believing that Suffrage is sufficiently established in Alabama to warrant more constructive methods."[13]

In the spring of 1917 the newly created National Woman's Party (NWP) attempted to organize in the South, including Alabama. Both Alice Paul and Beulah Amidon, national organizer for the NWP, came to the state to establish a branch of the NWP and to seek support for their more militant methods. The NWP was convinced that Alabama women had not tried to bring pressure to bear upon their representatives and senators to change their opposition. They saw Heflin as their chief opponent. Paul spoke at an organizational meeting held in Birmingham on May 19, 1917, at the Tutwiler Hotel, which was one of the largest assemblies of suffragists ever held in the city. Pattie Ruffner Jacobs and other members of the AESA were present to respond to Paul's statements. Paul demanded that the Democrats be held responsible for failing to adopt an amendment enfranchising women. She also defended the pickets at the White House, which she believed kept the issue before the president and the Congress. She pointed out that England and Russia were enfranchising women during wartime and asked how long must American women wait for liberty.[14]

Jacobs opposed the tactics and arguments of the NWP. She made every effort to separate NAWSA from the National Woman's Party in the mind of the public, pointing out that NAWSA had two million members, while the NWP had only a few hundred. She especially opposed the policy of holding the party in power responsible and pointed out that many Democrats had supported suffrage. Most of all, she believed that it was a "waste of energy and effort in maintaining two suffrage organizations, both working for the Federal Amendment." Alabama suffragists had been successful largely because they had maintained a united front in making their demands on Congress. In her opposition to the NWP, Jacobs had the support of the *Birmingham News,* which described the NWP as "anti-administration and anti-Democratic."[15]

The National Woman's Party did appoint a committee headed by Mrs. H. L. White, but it appears to have existed only on paper. Indeed, the Birmingham leaders claimed that they did not permit Paul to organize. There is no evidence that the National Woman's Party engaged in any activity in the state, but the national leaders did lobby the Alabama representatives and senators on behalf of the federal amendment and found that they were still opposed. In October 1917 the AESA adopted a resolution objecting to the National Woman's Party and expressing resentment at their coming into the state. The Alabama suffragists re-affirmed their loyalty to the president and condemned the picketing of the White House as an embarrassment to the administration at a crucial time. The AESA called upon its members to repudiate the pickets and their actions because such tactics were not compatible with the methods of southern women nor acceptable to the southern public. Perhaps because of this experience, the state board decided in January 1918 not to attempt to register to vote because it was undignified and a futile method of publicity.[16]

By mid-1917 the Alabama Equal Suffrage Association was stronger than it had ever been and, as it turned out, stronger than it ever would be again. Its members had been entirely faithful to NAWSA and its goals. They had rejected the militant route taken by Alice Paul and the National Woman's Party and the sectional racist approach of Kate Gordon's Southern States Woman Suffrage Conference. They attempted to reorganize their political structure along the lines proposed by NAWSA. They were committed to work for the federal amendment; they organized the state into the congressional districts and county units as outlined by NAWSA; they gained publicity by means of a regularly published newsletter and press releases; and they increased the number of local associations. These activities began to pay off in endorsements by various organizations. The Alabama Educational Association endorsed the principle of woman suffrage in 1917. The resolution was introduced by Dr. J. H. Phillips, superintendent of the Birmingham public schools, who had earlier opposed the movement. The Alabama Federation of Labor not only supported the principle of equal suffrage but also supported the federal amendment. Later the Alabama Farmers' Union at its convention adopted a resolution favoring votes for women.[17]

But when the United States entered World War I, the situation completely changed. This was the first all-out war the nation had faced and women were encouraged to contribute to the war effort. The suffragists faced a dilemma. The suffrage drive was gaining momentum, the federal amendment was gaining supporters in Congress. But the war changed the context in which the suffrage campaign would be conducted. If the suffragists took part in the war effort, they would have less time for their suffrage work. On the other hand, if they did not aid in the war programs, they could be accused of being slackers, a fact which would hurt their drive for the vote. Catt and NAWSA had seen the possibility of war being declared and in February 1917 had decided to pledge service to the government in the event of war; however, they also decided to continue the suffrage effort without relaxation. The National Woman's Party decided that individual members could do as they liked, but the organization itself would take no part in war work.[18]

Suffrage leaders in Alabama did not even debate the issue of what to do. They all knew that support of the war was the only choice. They did hope that if they could play a sufficient public role then the suffrage cause would be aided. Pattie Jacobs said that "Suffrage work was in no wise suspended but the more active forms of propaganda were held in abeyance." In actuality most of the activities of the suffragists were confined to war work. The women had an opportunity to show their support of the war effort and also suffrage on June 5, 1917. This day had been designated as Men's Registration Day in Birmingham when men signed up to volunteer for work. Pattie Jacobs and seventy-five other suffragists answered the call of the city commission to act as registrars. They served with the same authority and recognition as men. Their prompt response to this public role aided the suffrage cause.[19]

On the same day a parade was held in honor of Gen. Leonard Wood, who was visiting the city. This parade contained a women's section and for the first time in the history of Birmingham women marched in the streets. Wood and his escorts led the parade and the women followed immediately behind. The suffragists, who were first, were led by a woman dressed as Joan of Arc riding a white horse. She was escorted by six other women on horses, all of whom wore banners declaring Equal Suffrage. Following them was a suffragist dressed as Columbia carrying a large Alabama flag. Marching behind her was the main body of the suffragists, eight abreast in a group more than a block in length. They wore white dresses with yellow sashes over one shoulder. They were followed by the Red Cross workers, almost all of whom were suffragists. Following them were the members of the Daughters of the American Revolution and the United Daughters of the Confederacy. Birmingham had never witnessed women in such a visible role. It is difficult to imagine how such an event could have taken place without the leadership of the suffragists.[20]

A major center of women's activity during the war was the Woman's Committee of the Council of National Defense. Dr. Anna Howard Shaw was appointed chair and she in turn asked the presidents of the state federations of women's clubs to be the chairs in each state and instructed them to organize their states. Eleanor Gary Hooper, president of AFWC, called a meeting to be held in Montgomery at the Exchange Hotel on June 14, 1917. Fifteen women representing twelve organizations attended. Carrie M. Parke represented the Alabama Equal Suffrage Association and volunteered the services of the AESA to conduct the war service registration drive for women. Registration day for the state was set for August 15. At that time 16,000 women registered throughout the state. Women were asked to volunteer for any work they thought they could perform. Women of sixty-five stood in line with girls of sixteen before the crowded registration booths to pledge their services anywhere Uncle Sam needed them. Nearly every woman was ready to take advantage of the special training courses offered through the Woman's Committee of the Council of National Defense. The registration cards were filed with the council and proved helpful when the Red Cross or other organizations needed volunteers.[21]

In addition to these activities of the suffragists, Alabama women were involved in a number of other activities. Pattie Ruffner Jacobs served as chair of the Alabama Women's Liberty Loan Committee and also as a member of the National Woman's Liberty Loan Committee. This last appointment was considered an honor not only for Jacobs, but for Alabama as well. In September 1917 the Birmingham association organized a You-Knit unit of the Red Cross, which met at suffrage headquarters. While the women knitted, another woman read letters from a Canadian soldier who had served in France for two years. These letters were full of the atmosphere of trench warfare, which lent an added impetus to the flying needles. Suffragists cooperated with the civic associations in farewell demonstrations to the men who were drafted. As the men left Birmingham for training camps, the suffragists gave them small packages of tobacco and matches. In addition women took part in the meatless and wheatless days in order to conserve food.[22]

During 1917 women both in the nation and in Alabama were bending their efforts toward the war, but the momentum of the national suffrage campaign continued. Indeed, women's contribution to the war effort strengthened their claim to vote. Woman suffrage also gained support because of the new role of the United States as the leader of democracy. Since the nation was fighting a war to "make the world safe for democracy," denying women the right to vote was a contradiction. The suffragists achieved a great victory in November 1917 when New York adopted a constitutional amendment enfranchising women. As well as being the largest state, New York was the first state east of the Mississippi to give women the full right to vote. It was also the home of Susan B. Anthony and Elizabeth Cady Stanton. Women who came to Washington to lobby found they received a warmer reception after the New York vote.

The House adopted the Eighteenth Amendment in January 1918; with the establishment of nationwide prohibition, another obstacle to suffrage was removed. The liquor interests had long feared that women voters would enact prohibition, but if prohibition was coming anyway, then there was no need to waste time and effort fighting woman suffrage. As far as many of the "wets" were concerned, their chief objection had disappeared. All Alabama congressmen voted in favor of national prohibition even though it violated their states' rights principles. This, however, did not prevent them from arguing against woman suffrage on the basis of states' rights. Women did, of course, point out this contradiction. Southerners tended to use the states' rights argument when they preferred not to address the real issue.

On January 10, 1918, the U.S. House of Representatives voted in favor of the federal amendment to enfranchise women. The galleries were packed with tense, waiting women; sick congressmen were brought from their beds to vote. Only six members failed to vote, which indicates how important the measure had become since the 1915 vote. The measure was adopted with 274 in favor and 136 opposed. Eighteen percent of the southern congressmen voted in favor as opposed to two percent in 1915. All Alabama representatives except one opposed the measure, despite the appeal from Wilson to vote in favor. As the women left the galleries, someone began singing the doxology. The halls of Congress reverberated with the sounds of "Praise God from whom all blessings flow." The battle for the Senate proved to be more difficult. Suffrage supporters knew that they were two votes short and postponed the voting until September hoping to pick up the extra votes. But this turned out to be impossible. After five days of debate the vote was still two short of the necessary two-thirds. Both Alabama senators, John H. Bankhead and Oscar W. Underwood, voted against the measure in 1918 and again in 1919.

It was not until 1919 that both houses of Congress finally voted in favor. The war ended in November 1918 and by 1919 Wilson was in Paris negotiating the Treaty of Versailles. The House once again adopted the amendment during May with a vote this time of 304 to 89. The percent of southerners who voted in favor rose to thirty. One Alabama congressman, William B. Oliver of Tuscaloosa, supported the measure. With a favorable vote on June 4 the Senate bowed to the inevitable, but just barely. During this debate, Senator Underwood made a long speech on June 3 in opposition to the amendment. Now the women moved to work on the ratification process.[23]

While these national events were taking place, Alabama suffragists were trying to balance the demands of war work with those of suffrage. They did manage to carry on a minimum of suffrage work during 1917 but it was obviously difficult. The association distributed to voters thousands of copies of the speech of U.S. Senator John Shafroth, a gift of the Leslie Suffrage Commission.[24] They requested 2,000 copies, but were sent 10,000; to distribute these in a constructive manner turned out to be a challenge. The association found it difficult to keep its 1916 pledge to spend $10,000 for work in the state as well as give $1,000 to NAWSA.

The Alabama suffragists circulated petitions favoring the federal amendment and interviewed all of the representatives and senators. Each congressman was assigned a "suffrage Godmother" who corresponded with him, sent him *The Woman Citizen,* and kept him informed on the status of the federal amendment. When New York enfranchised women in November 1917, the Birmingham association held a victory luncheon and invited Senator Underwood and Representative Huddleston, who voted in favor of creating a woman suffrage committee in the House. The rest of the Alabama delegation remained steadfastly opposed to suffrage. The women lobbied the two senators when the votes of the Senate became crucial, but with no effect. Amelia Worthington said, "Bankhead is old and perhaps cannot learn new things; but Underwood should know better." [25]

Oscar Underwood's position was that suffrage was a state question. He maintained that he was not opposed to women voting, if such a change could come through a state statute rather than through the ratification of a federal amendment. He believed that federal action would violate the Jeffersonian principles he had learned at the University of Virginia. He wrote in a letter:

> I deeply regret that many of our people at home do not realize that the very basis of our civilization in the South is the control of the suffrage. . . . [A] great many of those who favor the Anthony Amendment . . . overlook entirely the fact that the border states . . . have unlimited manhood suffrage, and with unrestricted female suffrage, the vote of the Negro in those states will almost assuredly make them permanently Republican. With these states in the Republican column there is not much hope of the Democratic party electing its candidates for president in our lifetime. [26]

Basically Underwood held traditional views about women that he cloaked in racist and states' rights language. He was offended by the hordes of women in the capitol building lobbying for suffrage and was relieved when they finally left. [27]

Beginning in 1918 the Alabama suffrage association experienced real difficulties in conducting any suffrage business. The state organization that had carefully been built up seemed to disappear. One local organization after another disbanded, board members received no answer to their letters, and no chairs existed for many districts. All locals reported they were unable to pursue suffrage work during wartime. The best the women could do was war work in the name of the suffrage associations. This was a situation that was to last until the war was over in November 1918.[28]

Equally important was the difficulty in charting a course of action for the organization. Events on the national scene in 1918 were leaving Alabama behind. If the U.S. Senate adopted the suffrage amendment, as the House had just done, then the state suffragists would work for ratification of the federal amendment. Until the Senate took action, Jacobs, as legislative chair, felt that there was little she could do. But if the Senate did not pass the amendment, then Jacobs wanted to prepare to ask the upcoming 1919 state legislature for primary or presidential suffrage.

Jacobs received some encouragement for this course of action from a member of the National Democratic Committee from Alabama, Edward Smith, who believed that eventually the Senate would pass the amendment, although he doubted that it would be ratified by the Alabama state legislature. He suggested that he would be willing to support primary or presidential suffrage in the state. However, several state lawyers who favored woman suffrage pointed out that securing even partial suffrage would require a statewide referendum. Jacobs felt that it was as difficult to hold an election for partial suffrage as full suffrage and, hence, was not inclined to choose that route. What Jacobs probably also knew was that the day of partial suffrage had passed because full suffrage for all women was too near.

The situation in Alabama was even more discouraging because of the policy on campaign plans for ratification adopted by NAWSA at a conference in Indianapolis in April 1918. At that time the states were divided into three categories: hopeful states, fighting states, and hopeless states. NAWSA put Alabama in the "hopeless" category and was not prepared to offer any assistance in the ratification campaign. Jacobs was displeased with this description of the political situation in the state. She may have viewed it as a reflection on her leadership, since it was she who had played the major role. She was doubtless disappointed that after all the work she had done for NAWSA, they were not prepared to aid Alabama. Jacobs asked Carrie Catt whether she thought the Alabama association should press for ratification, if the Senate acted before the 1919 session of the legislature, and run the risk of a defeat. Catt's advice was to try for ratification. But timing was important. Would the Senate act before the legislature met? If the Senate delayed its action, the legislature might adjourn before it could consider ratification. In the end the Alabama suffragists decided to work for ratification of the federal amendment in the state even though the prospects appeared bleak.[29]

The Alabama delegates to the national convention in March 1919 learned that the federal amendment was likely to be passed by Congress in time for action to be taken on its ratification by the legislature of the state, which had been called to meet on July 8, 1919. They went before the national board and secured the promise of definite help, which was to consist of literature, press work, and organizers. The national association did even more than it promised and the state suffragists made heroic efforts to live up to their part of the contract.

On May 1 the campaign was under way, although the amendment had not yet been submitted. Pattie Jacobs, who once again was president, appointed a ratification committee with Adele Goodwyn McNeel of Birmingham as chair. The committee appointed county chairs in fifty-three counties and organized the Men's Committee of One Hundred. Headquarters in Birmingham were equipped with some paid workers and many faithful volunteers who began the distribution of literature and press work. NAWSA sent three organizers to Alabama to work as lobbyists. Press work was systematically carried on, with some of the material originating from national headquarters but most of it being produced in Birmingham.[30]

The situation in 1919 was much different from that of 1915 when the women had asked the legislature to adopt a suffrage amendment to the state constitution. At that time the suffrage organizations had only recently been established and the issue was so new that it had not been debated in the press and by the public. No newspapers endorsed the suffrage issue and few major political leaders were even sympathetic to the proposal. There was no organized opposition. The great majority of Alabamians were uninformed on the subject and tended not to take the subject seriously. The appeal to the state legislature to pass a con-

MEMBERS OF THE AESA AT WORK DURING THE 1919 CAMPAIGN. THOSE IDENTIFIED ARE (1) LILLIAN R. BOWRON, (2) MRS. H. E. PEARCE, (3) PATTIE RUFFNER JACOBS, (4) MRS. CHARLES BROWN, (7) MRS. W. D. NESBITT, AND (8) MRS. JOHN R. HORNDAY. *FROM THE COLLECTIONS OF THE BIRMINGHAM PUBLIC LIBRARY.*

stitutional amendment was entirely within the traditional states' rights beliefs of southerners.

By 1919 the subject of woman suffrage had become a legitimate issue in national politics. It had been endorsed by both the Democrats and Republicans, had become a major political issue, and a federal amendment was on the verge of being approved by both houses of Congress. The chances of it being ratified were good to a large extent because by 1919 women could vote in twenty-one states and politicians could no longer ignore them. The political leaders and the voters of Alabama had not kept pace with the rest of the nation. Most Alabamians still had great difficulty in seeing women in roles other than traditional domestic ones.

But suffrage had gained some support since 1915. During the ratification campaign of 1919, several major newspapers publicly endorsed woman suffrage: the *Birmingham Age-Herald*, the *Birmingham Ledger*, the *Mobile Register*, and the *Montgomery Journal*. The papers that opposed it were the influential *Montgomery Advertiser* and the *Birmingham News*. The suffragists were also able to gain the public support of several major political figures: John C. Anderson, chief justice of the Supreme Court; W. D. Nesbitt, state chairman of the Democratic Executive Committee; former U.S. senator Frank S. White; Judge S. D. Weakley, legal adviser to the governor; former governor Braxton Bragg Comer; and Dr. W. B. Crumpton, secretary emeritus of the Baptist Mission Board who led the fight for prohibition. The Alabama Federation of Women's Clubs finally endorsed the amendment in 1918 after Jacobs persuaded them to amend their constitution permitting them to take a stand on a political issue. Other endorsements came from the Alabama Educational Association and the Montgomery Business and Professional Women.[31]

The most important difference between the two campaigns was that by 1919 organized opposition had developed and the argument turned on different issues. Organizations opposed to woman suffrage had been created in New York and Massachusetts as early as 1895 and eventually extended to some twenty states. The most influential opposition organization by the time of the ratification drive was the National Association Opposed to Woman Suffrage, formed in New York in 1911 and headed by Mrs. Arthur M. Dodge.[32]

DO YOU KNOW

THAT

11 White States, Full Suffrage
1 Dotted State, Statutory Suffrage
  (Presidential and Municipal)
19 Shaded States, Partial Suffrage
17 Black States, NO SUFFRAGE

ALABAMA

Is one of seventeen states out of the forty-eight, where women can not vote on any question?

Do You Know
that women have equal suffrage with men in Wyoming, Colorado, Utah, Idaho, Washington, California, Oregon, Kansas, Arizona, Nevada, Montana and Alaska; in Norway, Finland, Australia, and New Zealand, and have partial suffrage in other countries?

Who Can't Vote!

Children, Insane, Idiots, Aliens, Criminals and Women.

WILL our boasted Southern chivalry still class the women of Alabama with these?

HELP US to make Alabama the first Southern State to give its women equal political rights with its men.

HELP US
1. By organizing an Equal Suffrage Association in the place where you live.
2. By joining the one already organized in your town:
3. By contributions of money.

Apply for Further Information and more Literature to

Alabama Equal Suffrage Association,
Headquarters

 1818 Second Ave., BIRMINGHAM, ALA.   (Over)

Price, $1.50 per 1,000

A southern antisuffrage movement developed more slowly. The first antisuffrage organization of importance to be created in the South was formed in Selma, Alabama, in 1916. The Alabama Association Opposed to Woman Suffrage had as a motto Home Rule, States' Rights, and White Supremacy. It was created in response to the suffragists' legislative campaign of 1915. The president was Nell V. Baker and it shortly claimed a membership of 1,000. They protested against having the issue of Votes for Women thrust upon them and affirmed their belief that the men of Alabama would always love, honor, and protect their women as long as they remained within the sphere to which nature and God have assigned them. This group appears to have engaged in little activity.[33]

A much more active organization was the group that was formed to fight the ratification of the Nineteenth Amendment in June 1919. This group called itself the Woman's Anti-Ratification League of Alabama and made its headquarters in Montgomery. Mrs. James S. Pinckard was selected president and Marie Bankhead Owen, the daughter of Senator Bankhead and a bitter foe of suffrage, was the legislative chair.[34] They chose as their motto Alabama for Alabamians and soon claimed a membership of more than 1,200 women. The league held meetings, listened to speeches, and wrote letters. They were aided by well-known men such as Cong. John H. Bankhead, Jr.; Judge John R. Tyson and Judge E. Perry Thomas, both of Montgomery; Martin C. Calhoun, an attorney from Selma and grandnephew of John C. Calhoun; and J. Lister Hill who was then a young attorney from Montgomery, later a U.S. senator.[35]

The argument of the antis centered on their support of states' rights and white supremacy, two issues which southerners had supported since the Civil War and Reconstruction and which continued to shape southern politics until well after World War II. The leaders of the league said in one of their first petitions that they were "unalterably opposed to all interference by the federal government with the internal domestic laws of Alabama, and deem it essential, for the preservation of social order and the maintenance of white supremacy, that the right of the state to regulate its own domestic laws shall be forever preserved to its own citizens, free from all outside interference."[36] State legislators received a strongly worded letter from the league signed by Pinckard, as executive chairman, and Mrs. Charles Thigpen, as legislative chair. The letter described the league members as "home-loving women of Alabama ambitious to preserve the blessings of free government in our state to ourselves." They believed that the suffrage amendment was conceived fifty years before by Susan B. Anthony for the very purpose of destroying white supremacy. They went on to say that the Anthony amendment was a "wolf gnawing at the vitals of both state and national government. It is the seed from which may spring untold misery in the future. The fifteenth amendment is not dead. It only sleepeth. Why arouse it from its slumber?"[37]

These two themes were presented again and again in various forms during the campaign, sometimes with reason and logic and at other times with hyperbole and emotion. The issue of women voting was seldom discussed on its merits; in fact those opposed to the amendment often said they favored votes for women but simply did not want it accomplished by federal action. J. Lister Hill held this position. He said that he was not opposed to woman suffrage, but was opposed to the Anthony amendment because of its danger to the right of local self-government. He said, "give congress the power to say who your state voter shall be and you give it the power to say what your state government shall be." Even some of the women who worked for the Anti-Ratification League said they favored women voting but did not want it forced on them by the federal government. An editorial in the major opposition newspaper, the *Montgomery Advertiser*, feared that the state would be forced to surrender control of its electorate if the amendment were adopted. Opponents could even find support from Sen. William Borah of Idaho, who favored suffrage but as a strong supporter of states' rights did not want it achieved by federal action.[38]

Judge E. Perry Thomas who opposed the amendment gave the argument a slightly different twist. He said that it was not a question of giving the ballot to the women of Alabama, but whether it was to be given by the federal government. He did not believe that it was necessary to amend the United States Constitution to give women the vote. The state already had the power to do so. Alabama was ready to do this, he claimed, when a majority of the state's women desired it. "When

these women want the ballot we will give it to them and to that end
we do not need the Susan B. Anthony amendment, no Carrie Chapman
Catt dogma, nor Dr. Jane Addams' experience."[39]

But in the same breath with the states' rights argument was expressed
the fear that Congress would have the power to enforce the amendment
and black women would be voting along with white women. Opponents
feared that the ballot would be opened to all women regardless of color.
In this light, the amendment was seen as a threat to "the established
civilization of the South." It was seen as opening the door once again
to the experience of the Reconstruction period when the Congress attempted to enforce the Fourteenth Amendment. As one editorial writer
said, it required more than thirty years to limit the suffrage of black
men: "It was a long, long fight with bloodshed and travail. . . . Honorable men stole votes, burned ballot boxes, they languished in jail. . . .
Alabama wants no repetition of that fight. . . . Why should we run the
grave and unnecessary danger of losing what our fathers gained for us?"
In short, the amendment was seen as a threat to white supremacy.[40]

On July 12, 1919, the most harsh words and rabid vituperations were
uttered at a meeting at the courthouse in Montgomery of the men's
league to oppose the Anthony amendment. Judge John R. Tyson, a respected constitutional lawyer, said that he wanted to strip all of the
charm that supporters and friends had tried to throw around the Nineteenth Amendment through deception and misleading phrasing and
hold it up for all to see its real meaning. He termed the amendment to
be the "Blood brother of the Fourteenth and Fifteenth Amendments,"
which were "conceived in inequity and born in sin based on hatred and
frenzied desire of carpetbag scalawaggery, dominated by the most de-
praved considerations for racial equality."

Tyson and two other speakers, Judge Thomas and L. H. Brassell,
united in denouncing the amendment as "unnecessary, unwise, and the
most monstrous act ever thrust upon a people for approval." It was a
challenge to all the principles of southern manhood. "Let this amendment be ratified by the United States," shouted Brassell, "and there will
no longer be need for Old Glory and its field of blue shedding its rays
from the forty-eight stars representing the sovereign States of America,"

but there would be one star typifying the Washington government as it cast its blight on the rights of the people. Another speaker, Martin C. Calhoun, said, "Any Southern State which ratifies this amendment will repudiate the principles for which the Confederate soldier struggled through four long years" and might just as well "dismantle every monument which has been erected to the heroic memory of the 'men who wore the gray.' "[41]

The proponents of suffrage attempted to respond to the more rational of these objections, specifically the fear of black women voting. Pattie Jacobs was joined by Chief Justice John C. Anderson of the Alabama Supreme Court in maintaining that the same voting restrictions that applied to black men would also apply to black women. Anderson said, "The amendment cannot and is not intended to qualify any women to vote. The qualifications are still left with the states." The legislatures were free to make whatever restrictions they desired regarding voting qualifications. Jacobs said, "There will be no wholesale enfranchisement of negro women if the Susan B. Anthony amendment is ratified. . . . [T]he same qualifications which men must possess to become voters must also be held by women before they can legally become qualified electors." In short, the poll tax and the literacy test would still be legal.[42]

Other suffrage supporters were more critical of the opponents and pointed out the hypocrisy of their arguments. One editorial writer said that there was no danger to the South except that which existed in the imagination of the opponents. He maintained there would be no lowering of the high standards of southern womanhood by the mixing of the races at the polls. This argument was made largely by those who wanted to defeat woman suffrage. They represented the reactionary element of the party that did not want women voting under any circumstances or conditions. Another writer maintained that the opponents were trying to evade the issue and were clutching at straws in their attempt to prevent the legislature from ratification. The opponents revived the black problem and flaunted it to the ignorant masses as a danger signal. Furthermore, by appealing to racial hatred and prejudice, opponents of the amendment were trying to create an issue that was in itself dangerous to the public welfare.[43]

The two Birmingham newspapers that supported suffrage provided comprehensive arguments which greatly benefited the suffrage cause. The *Ledger* believed that the women of America wished to vote and deserved to do so. They did half of the work of life and bore half of the responsibility. There was no reason why they should not have an equal share in the selection of public officials. The combined wisdom of both men and women was needed in order to conduct the affairs of state. The editorial writers pointed out that women would use the ballot as a means to impose safeguards about the homes and the health of the children of the nation. The *Ledger* saw no ulterior consequences to be dreaded—or, no change except that the white women of the country who helped the nation win the war would help guide the ship of state in times of peace. The editor wrote that the right to vote was a matter of justice. Another editorial writer said, "There can be no argument against women's suffrage based on a fair and impartial study of the question. Justice is its own excuse for being and no amount of quibbling will lessen the just claim of the nation's women to the ballot."[44]

The federal amendment was passed by Congress on June 4 and sent to the states to be ratified. The Alabama legislature met on July 8 and was one of the first southern states to consider the measure. Suffrage was the overriding issue in the legislative session that was just beginning in Montgomery. The proponents and the opponents filled the halls of the capitol building as they lobbied the legislators. The state Democrats found themselves in a difficult position. A majority of them were not in favor of the federal amendment, but they were strongly pressured to ratify by the national party. The national Democratic party was fearful that if southern Democratic legislatures failed to ratify, the Republicans would gain credit for woman suffrage. National Democrats were so concerned that on July 12 President Wilson telegraphed Alabama governor Thomas E. Kilby to encourage him to support ratification. Wilson said that he thought woman suffrage was based on justice and expedience and was a needed reform.[45]

In addition Josephus Daniels, who was the secretary of the Navy and a southerner, sent a long message to Adele Goodwyn McNeel, chair of the ratification committee of the Alabama Equal Suffrage Association, setting forth the merits of the amendment. Daniels said: "The South has nothing to fear from the amendment but it would be a loss to southern chivalry and southern prestige if our section of the country halted this great reform. I earnestly hope that the people of Alabama will take the lead of southern States east of the Mississippi and follow the wise leadership of Texas and Missouri and other progressive commonwealths. There is no doubt of its ratification. Let Alabama lead and not follow." Homer C. Cummings, chairman of the Democratic National Committee, also appealed for favorable action. Alabama congressman A. G. Patterson, after meeting with the National Democratic Committee, made it clear that state Democrats should carefully study the changed economic and political situation in the nation. In short, it was not good politics to oppose suffrage. Southern Democrats should not continue to stand defiantly in the roadway and challenge approaching reform.[46]

A hearing on the suffrage issue was set for July 16. From nearly every county women journeyed to Montgomery to speak for or against the amendment. The galleries were packed with enthusiastic women, the suffragists wearing their now familiar yellow sashes and the antisuffragists wearing crimson and white. The predictions were that the antisuffragists had enough votes to defeat the measure. Each side was allowed an hour and one-half to speak.

The suffragists, speaking first, brought out the best-known and most eloquent speakers, who repeated the now familiar arguments. Chief Justice John C. Anderson assured the legislators that the Constitution of 1901 that prevented black men from voting would be equally effective against black women. Carrie M. Parke pointed out that women had been treated as irresponsible children too long and now desired the vote as a right, not as a favor. W. D. Nesbitt, chairman of the Alabama Democratic Committee, reminded the legislators that they should stand by the policies adopted by the national Democratic party. Dixie Bibb Graves of Montgomery said that women of the state felt that the vote was a privilege they should share with men. Mollie Dowd, a businesswoman from Birmingham, spoke for the Alabama wage-earning woman. Pattie Jacobs, who was given an ovation when she was introduced, pointed out that in only a month eleven states had ratified the amendment and encouraged Alabama to "come into the fold." Judge S. D. Weakley said the antiratification league had injected passion into the issue by playing black women against white women.[47]

The antisuffragists surprised the joint session by refusing to address the legislators in person. Instead, they presented a memorial, which was read by Sen. James B. Evins. The announcement drew hisses and jeers from the suffragists, who had to be called to order by Lt. Gov. Nathan Miller. The antisuffragists said that they declined to appear before the session "to argue a political question in which the discussion may become acrimonious." To do so "would be to do the very thing which . . . we seek to avoid having thrust upon us." The women felt it would be "personally embarrassing to them to assume the unfamiliar and distasteful role of political gladiators." The memorial went on to say that they were home-keepers and mothers of children who sought to discharge their duties not by voting and holding office, but by instilling into their children love of country. They pleaded with the legislators that they be protected from this device of northern abolitionists, which would strike down the barriers "between the Anglo-Saxons and those who mongrelize and corrupt" them. They said that they opposed the amendment because the women of the state did not want to vote. They feared that it would nullify the work of those "wise and patriotic men who have purified the ballot box from the contamination of negro votes." They concluded by saying:

> Gentlemen, our welfare is in your hands. You may, if you will, thrust us from the quietude of our home into the contaminating atmosphere of political struggle, but we feel the strong assurance that in your protecting care we, our institutions and our sheltering laws are safe; and that you, on our behalf as well as your own, will decline to surrender our great state's control of her own electorate into hands that may be regardless of our welfare, our happiness, our safety and our great traditions.[48]

This appeal of the opposition was effective because it fit in with the traditional southern idea of women who were in need of protection. The *Montgomery Advertiser* described presenting the brief as an effective tactic and praised the women's confidence in the justice and fairness of the men of Alabama. The majority of the senators also agreed because the next day the amendment was defeated by a vote of thirteen to nineteen. For all practical purposes the amendment was dead even though the house had not yet acted. House action did not come until September 17. During the two-month period the suffragists continued working trying to gain a favorable vote. Once again President Wilson sent a telegram urging favorable action. The state Democratic committee met and by a vote of twenty to thirteen adopted a resolution favorable to suffrage. Even this action was not enough to change votes. Jacobs maintained that a majority of the house members were pledged to vote in favor, but after it had been defeated by the senate, the legislators did not feel bound by their promise and the measure was defeated by fifty-nine to thirty-one.[49]

The 1919 ratification contest turned on the race issue, unlike the 1915 campaign. Once the race issue was raised, the suffrage cause was doomed in Alabama. The suffrage leaders attempted to respond to the charges but to no avail. It is difficult to believe that the Nineteenth Amendment posed any real danger to white supremacy. The Constitution of 1901 had been successful in disfranchising black voters. In 1900 approximately 181,315 eligible black voters were registered, but that number declined to 3,742 in 1908 and continued to decrease. By 1919 the electorate was only one-half of what it had been in 1901, and the Democratic regime had long since gained control of politics.[50] Yet whites seemingly could not do enough to maintain white supremacy. The suffrage leaders themselves did not use the race issue; they did not attack black women, yet they could easily have done so. It was the antisuffragists and the men who raised the race issue and resorted to race baiting.

Despite the talk of the fear of blacks voting, it would appear that Alabama men (and some women) simply could not conceive of women voting. The real objection to woman suffrage was a perceived threat to gender roles. Suffrage challenged the accepted separation of the male sphere of the public world and the female sphere of the private world. Suffrage called into question all the traditional activities of women. It gave women the opportunity to act in politics; it recognized them as individuals within the family. It challenged the notion that women should subordinate their individual interests to those of the family. As citizens and voters, women would participate directly in society as individuals, not indirectly through their subordinate position as wives and mothers. Alabamians were not yet ready to recognize women as individuals with independent identities separate from the family.

10 ALABAMA WOMEN IN THE 1920s

lthough the Alabama legislature failed to ratify the Nineteenth Amendment, thirty-six other state legislatures voted in favor, making the requisite number for adding the amendment to the Constitution. At first, these ratifications came easily; those that had passed state suffrage amendments ratified first. Eleven came in the first month, while the next five months brought eleven more. The proponents of suffrage needed the support of thirty-six states, but the opponents had to hold only thirteen states to block ratification. By August 1920 thirty-five states had ratified and only one state, Tennessee, remained in which ratification seemed possible before the 1920 presidential election. North Carolina, Louisiana, and Mississippi voted against the measure before the Tennessee legislature took up the issue in the late summer of 1920. It took a Department of Justice ruling before the governor of Tennessee could call a special session of the legislature. After a wild ten days in Nashville, both houses of that legislature voted to ratify the amendment and the long struggle for suffrage was over. It had been seventy-two years since the women at the Seneca Falls Convention in 1848 demanded the right to vote. Now everywhere in the United States women had the legal right to vote. In the end ten states rejected the amendment and all but one of them was in the South.[1]

On September 4, 1920, the suffrage leaders in Birmingham held a victory parade that attracted 50,000 people. The city commission declared a holiday and the downtown stores closed for an hour in order to allow the employees to attend. The proclamation issued by the commission rejoiced that women had now been granted the right to vote and this group made it clear that they considered it a "notable step in the onward and upward progress of the nation." The proclamation concluded by saying that the commission urged the "womanhood of our community to assume the new burdens which enfranchisement entails by qualifying for active participation in the solution of municipal, state and national problems." The city commission was obviously looking to the next election when these active and civic-minded women would be able to vote.

Pattie Jacobs, carrying a large U.S. flag, led the first section of the parade, which consisted of the pioneer suffragist leaders. Members of the Alabama Equal Suffrage Association followed carrying banners We Have Registered and Have You Registered? Thirty-six cars representing the states that had ratified transported those women who did not want to march. Other automobiles carrying representatives of the women's clubs in the city followed. The women wore white dresses, white shoes, and white hats. Music was provided by the band from the Alabama Boys' Industrial School at East Lake. The pioneer leaders were the women who had the courage to admit publicly that they favored suffrage long before it was respectable to do so. In addition to Jacobs, these included Nellie K. Murdock, Martha L. Spencer, Elizabeth Johnston, Lillian Roden Bowron, Annie M. Robinson, Amelia Worthington Fisk, and Carrie M. Parke.[2] The celebration in Birmingham was so enthusiastic that it almost seemed that the state had ratified the amendment.

Even before the Nineteenth Amendment was ratified, the suffrage leaders disbanded the Alabama Equal Suffrage Association and created the Alabama League of Women Voters (ALWV) to take its place. This move by the women in the state followed similar action by the National American Woman Suffrage Association. As the day of victory approached, NAWSA began to lay plans for the next step after women had the vote. Clearly NAWSA would have fulfilled its purpose, yet an organization of two million women could not be allowed to disband. Carrie Chapman Catt outlined a plan of action as early as 1917. She proposed a nonpartisan League of Women Voters (LWV) that would unite the women of suffrage states in a central organization. The league was officially organized in March 1919 at NAWSA's Jubilee Convention, the fiftieth anniversary of the first grant of woman suffrage in Wyoming. The first congress of the league was held concurrently with the Victory Convention of NAWSA in February 1920.[3]

The advent of the vote did not unite the suffragists as the national leaders hoped it would. A heated debate began over the nonpartisan policy of the LWV, and for a time it was feared that the league would have to disband because of internal dissension. Catt wanted the league to work within the framework of the political parties, whereas Alice Paul and others wanted to create an independent political party of women. Since the idea of a third party based on gender frightened national leaders, a compromise was finally reached late in 1920. The goals of the LWV were first to instruct women in the tasks of citizenship so they could work more effectively within the existing political framework and, second, to mobilize public opinion behind reform programs.

The same confidence that permeated NAWSA took hold in the Alabama Equal Suffrage Association. AESA voted to disband at its convention in April 1920 and the same women then created the Alabama League of Women Voters. The leaders of the suffrage drive became the leaders of the league; they elected Lillian Roden Bowron to be the first president. Bowron was one of the organizers of the AESA and served as president of the Birmingham association in 1917. She was also active in several other organizations, serving on the boards of the YWCA, the first public kindergarten, and the Mercy Home. Other officers included Dixie Bibb Graves, Hattie Hooker Wilkins, Amelia Worthington Fisk, Luna E. Davie, Annie Joe Coates, Mollie Dowd, Lorraine B. Bush, Anne Bush Nesbitt, Mary Winslow Partridge, and Foribel B. Ohme. Despite the fact that she had been elected secretary of the national league, Pattie Jacobs found time to serve as legislative chair of the Alabama league.[4]

Before women could vote, however, the state legislature had to pass specific laws allowing them to register. The ALWV petitioned the governor to call a special session of the legislature to adopt the enabling legislation. Gov. Thomas E. Kilby complied and issued a special call for a session of the legislature to convene on September 14, 1920. The women had requested that the legislature take such action when it was in session in 1919, but the legislators had refused to do so. Hence a special session was needed. Pattie Jacobs, legislative chair of the league, attended the session to present the demands of the league and to see that the legislature adopted fair measures. It had been only a year since the same legislators had rejected the Nineteenth Amendment in a fierce struggle, but even the bitterest enemies of suffrage played the role of southern gentlemen and voted to adopt a bill that was entirely favorable to women. Alabama legislators, like legislators everywhere, were not at all sure what these new women voters were going to do. For a few years political leaders openly courted women's votes.[5]

The legislature adopted a bill that provided for the special registration of women until October 26 and exempted them from the payment of the poll tax until the following February 1921. Not all southern states acted to enable their women to vote in the November election. Georgia and Mississippi failed to call special sessions to enact the necessary laws to register women. In a letter to Governor Kilby, Pattie Jacobs declared, "I am more than ever thankful that I do not live in Georgia or Mississippi, whose governors allowed those women to be the only ones in the United States still deprived of the vote."[6]

The ALWV conducted an intensive campaign to encourage women to register, which turned out to be successful beyond all expectations. By the time of the November election 123,876 women had registered to vote in the state; 23,000 registered in Jefferson County alone. With the registration of women, more people voted than ever had before. The highest figure had been reached in 1900 with 154,764 voters, but in 1920 a record number of 241,080 voted. Evidence indicates that women cast approximately one-third of these votes. This is a remarkable achievement for a state in which opponents had claimed that Alabama women did not want to vote. Some women were so eager to register that they were waiting in line when the board of registrars opened. Volunteers were on hand to assist women in the registration. Many men accompanied their wives, daughters, and sisters to the registration office. Women inquired if they should register with their husband's name or their own name. For the first time women were identified by their own names and even listed as such when the newspaper printed the names of those who registered.[7]

On the first day that women were able to register in Birmingham, church bells and factory whistles sounded at noon to proclaim the glad tidings. Prominent suffrage leaders who registered that first day were Pattie Jacobs, Adele Goodwyn McNeel, Anne Bush Nesbitt, Lillian Roden Bowron, and Amelia Worthington Fisk. Approximately one hundred black women registered in Jefferson County, women who had enough education to pass the literacy test. The county at that time had 354 black male voters registered. Even the women who had opposed the amendment encouraged their members to register. The Southern Women's League for the Rejection of the Anthony Amendment said, "The time for debating the rights and wrongs of the amendment has passed and now it is time for the women to qualify as voters."

In addition to registering voters, ALWV embarked on another primary goal, which was to conduct citizenship schools in every congressional and county district. The purpose of these schools was to educate the women voters about politics, political parties, candidates, and issues. In September 1920, one month following the ratification of the amendment, Birmingham opened the first citizenship school in the state, followed shortly by schools in Montgomery and Mobile. The national league sent Mrs. T. T. Cotnam of Little Rock and Mrs G. V. R. Mechin of St. Louis to assist in conducting these schools. With the assistance of these women plus a great deal of local talent, the Alabama league held thirty-three citizenship schools before the November election. They also conducted innumerable single "voting demonstrations," using ballot boxes and sample ballots. The schools, which lasted for four or five days, included not only lessons in practical voting procedures, but also advanced lessons in political science. The topics studied included the structure of state, county, and city government in Alabama; the history of American government; and the League of Nations. In addition to running the citizenship schools, the league distributed an outline study-course on government prepared by the University of Alabama.[8]

The Alabama league spent its formative years trying to put together a cohesive state organization that would be an effective, nonpartisan political force. By the spring of 1921 the ALWV had organized a total of fifty-seven local leagues, which provided a good working base. Like the suffrage association before, the league continued to be interested in issues that affected women and children. Women continued to press for coguardianship of children for both mothers and fathers and an increase in the age of consent from fourteen to eighteen years. They supported protective labor legislation for women, an eight-hour day, prohibition of night work, and a minimum wage. They also favored prohibiting women from working in industry for six weeks before and after childbirth. In 1921 two important studies were conducted regarding working women. Alice Nelson Doyle compiled a *Compendium of Alabama Laws Relating to Women and Children,* which was published by the league. At the request of the league and the Alabama Federation of Women's Clubs, the newly created Women's Bureau of the U.S. Department of Labor surveyed the conditions of women's employment in the state. Despite these studies and recommendations, the legislature of Alabama failed to adopt the sort of protective legislation for women that most other states had done.[9]

The league women supported the newly established Department of Child Welfare and the activities of the director, Lorraine B. Bush. Bush asked the ALWV to assist in the establishment of advisory juvenile commissions and probation officers in every county. The legislature had adopted a law in 1915 creating such positions, but it had never been implemented. As a result of league action, several larger counties made an effort to comply with the law. The league saw its most important success when it persuaded the legislature to accept the Sheppard-Towner Act for maternity and infancy care, which was passed by the U.S. Congress in 1921. According to the provisions of this act, the federal government would provide matching funds to establish maternity and infant health care across the country. The state legislature appropriated its share of matching money to fund the budget of $45,000, creating twenty-one health units staffed with nurses across the state. For the first time in the history of the state, mothers and children could receive at least a minimum of health care. The legislature would never have accepted the federal government's offer if the ALWV had not lobbied for it.[10]

Like the suffrage associations, the league continued its interest in improving the educational system of the state. They continually pressed for higher salaries for public schoolteachers; they proposed teaching citizenship in the schools; and they desired to have women placed on school boards and boards of colleges and universities. The league further requested free textbooks for rural children, longer school terms, appropriations for vocational work in home economics, and the establishment of a home demonstration agent in each county. A handful of women were elected or appointed to school boards and the curriculum of some schools included citizenship and home economics, but the league had little success with the other proposals.[11]

The league, however, was concerned with new issues that had not previously arisen. Since women were now citizens and could vote, they believed that the rights of citizenship should extend to jury service. The league tried to persuade the legislature to allow women to serve on juries under certain conditions, but to no avail. Since by the 1920s movies were increasingly available and in the eyes of many were objectionable, the league wanted to regulate the motion picture shows. The league also dealt with national and international issues that had risen as a result of World War I; they favored a reduction of armaments and supported the United States joining the League of Nations.[12]

Another new issue of the twenties that was far more divisive was the Equal Rights Amendment, which the National Woman's Party proposed. The split between the women leaders continued even after the passage of the Nineteenth Amendment. Alice Paul of the NWP believed that suffrage was only a first step in granting women full legal and political rights. She proposed an ERA, which stated, "men and women shall have equal rights throughout the United States and every place subject to its jurisdiction." The NLWV did not favor the amendment because it would erode the gains of protective labor legislation, which were seen as a great victory for women. The league regarded women and men as equal in some respects, but they also felt that women needed certain special legislation to protect them as mothers. Once again differing views of feminism divided the women's movement.

In 1921 Paul and the NWP began a state-by-state campaign for equal rights bills, which included Alabama. Elsie Hill, temporary chair of the NWP, and Anita Pollitzer, national legislative secretary, held a meeting in Montgomery on October 24 to explain the proposal. The next day they presented the Bill of Rights for Women to the senate judiciary committee, which quickly quashed the bill by an adverse vote. Despite the rejection by the legislature, the ALWV became involved in the fight and a verbal war began in the state's newspapers. Speaking to a group of Montgomery women in November, Jacobs made it clear that the league was not opposed to the National Woman's Party, but it was opposed to the blanket law because of the danger to protective labor legislation. Paul was eventually successful in obtaining a hearing for the ERA in the U.S. Congress in 1923, but the amendment received little support; however, it continued to divide women during the decade of the 1920s.[13]

An innovation of this period was the creation of state legislative councils in which women's groups of diverse kinds joined together to work for legislation of interest to women. Under the leadership of the league and the Alabama Federation of Women's Clubs, the women of the state created the Legislative Council of Alabama Women in 1921. Nonpartisan in nature, the council was to promote legislation submitted by the constituent organizations and approved by the council. All state organizations of white women and all branches of national organizations having no state organizations were eligible for membership. Each organization was represented in the council by its president and another delegate. Committees were formed to work for specific legislation, and the council planned to maintain full-time lobbyists when the state legislature was in session.[14]

The major member organizations, in addition to the league and the Alabama Federation of Women's Clubs, were the WCTU, Business and Professional Women, the Parent-Teacher Association, and the American Association of University Women. The council also included several lesser-known groups: the Women's Trade Union League, National Woman's Party, and the Methodist Home Missionary Council. The legislative goals of the council were similar to those of the league with a few additions: the creation of a tuberculosis hospital, legislation requiring fathers to support their illegitimate children, and a request to the state to assume responsibility for the home for delinquent black girls that the Alabama Federation of Colored Women's Clubs established at Mt. Meigs. The legislative council was an excellent idea that could have been effective if the organizations represented had been active. However, it would appear that the burden of the work fell upon the league and the AFWC, neither of which had the resources or the personnel to monitor the actions of the legislature and lobby its members. In 1927 the league resigned from the council, which brought any effective work to an end.[15]

Not only did women lobby the legislators, but now they ran for office themselves. The opportunity for women candidates excited the league members. As early as January 1922 the Birmingham LWV tried to encourage Jefferson County women to run for the state legislature. Pattie Jacobs was mentioned as a "natural" in politics, but in the end she declined. A number of league women qualified to run for state and national office. Mrs. O. C. Maner, president of the Montgomery LWV, ran for the state house of representatives; Luna E. Davie, state LWV secretary from Montgomery and author of the newspaper column, ran for delegate to the state Democratic convention; Mrs. W. S. Edmundson, from Albany-Decatur, ran for the U.S. Congress from the Eighth District; and Hattie Hooker Wilkins of Selma ran for the state house. Wilkins was the only successful female candidate. Since she was a pioneer suffragist in Alabama, the league took great pride in her victory. Wilkins was a founding member of both the Alabama Equal Suffrage Association and the Alabama League of Women Voters. She was active in the AESA, serving on the board and also as secretary. Wilkins served only one term in the house and not until 1937 was another women elected to the legislature.[16]

The ALWV can claim one last victory during the 1920s—it forced the state to abolish its archaic practice of leasing convicts to private industry. By 1918 only Alabama and Florida still retained the convict lease system, which had been under attack for decades. As early as 1893 Julia Tutwiler described the system as one that combined all the evils of slavery without one of its ameliorating features, but even Tutwiler was unable even to modify, let alone abolish, the practice. Hastings H. Hart in the Russell Sage Foundation report of 1918 was sharply critical of the system. He pointed out that the state "does not and can not protect its prisoners from physical injury, accidental death, moral degeneracy, or even from murder." Hart recommended that the state abolish the practice of leasing prisoners for work in the coal mines, turpentine camps, or other private industries.[17]

In 1919 under the leadership of Gov. Thomas E. Kilby, the legislature voted to abolish the convict lease system in January 1923 and to build a new prison founded upon the principle of reformation of the prisoners. Kilby Prison was built and provisions were made for vocational training of the inmates. But Governor Kilby was not able to provide for all of the prisoners by the 1923 deadline and asked to have the deadline extended until 1924, at which time the new governor, William W. Brandon, would be faced with the issue. The 1923 legislature voted to continue the system no longer than 1927, leaving it to the governor to determine how and when the system would end. At this time Alabama was the only state still leasing its convicts out to private industry. The legislative council led by the league and AFWC was furious at this extension and vowed to fight any measure "which would make possible the continuation of the inhumane system which the women of Alabama have for many years earnestly striven to abolish."[18]

In the fight to abolish the system in 1923, the ALWV turned once again to Pattie Jacobs to chair a committee with the goal of organizing a citizens group. In June Jacobs paid a surprise visit to the convict camps at Banner and Flat Top in Jefferson County. She published a detailed report concerning the officials, the conditions of the buildings, the food, and the methods of punishment. Jacobs and the league recommended that the lease system be abolished and the whole prison system be taken out of politics. A month later the AFWC issued a similar recommendation. The Junior Chamber of Commerce of Birmingham joined with the league and the AFWC to secure the facts and place the issue before the people. By now the state was thoroughly aroused and virtually every newspaper supported the immediate abolition of the system. Once again the women of the league and the AFWC descended upon the legislature in July. The legislators told the women that if the revenue from the convict leasing were curtailed, the schools, charitable institutions, and child welfare would be the first to suffer. Jacobs recognized this argument as one of the oldest ways of escape. The ALWV believed that the legislature could be shown that other states maintained their schools and charities without the help of blood money. The motto of the campaign was "A matter of mercy instead of a mercenary matter." [19]

The mining companies maintained a powerful lobby in the state legislature and in the end they won. Both the senate and the house passed resolutions that they would not consider any further legislation on the subject of the convict lease system. The legislative session ended without taking any further action on the bill. Disappointed but not ready to give up, the ALWV kept its members interested in the issue by publishing weekly articles against the leasing system in Luna Davie's Woman Voter column. During the period from 1923 to 1927 public opinion against the system was aroused by the tragic murder of a leased convict and the subsequent beating of Attorney-General Maj. Harwell Davis by a mine owner. Finally in February 1927, after one of the most bitter battles ever fought in legislative halls, the state senate adopted the conference compromise report, which ended convict leasing on June 30, 1928. Convicts could be used for county public work, but could no longer be leased to private companies. As a tribute to the ALWV for its contribution to the campaign, the pen used to sign the bill into law by Gov. Bibb Graves was presented to the league in the name of the women of the state of Alabama. Like the WCTU and prohibition and the women's clubs and child labor, the women of the league forced the legislature to take action on an issue that they supported. [20]

Despite the success of the league in registering women voters in 1920, in pressuring the legislature to utilize the Sheppard-Towner Act, and in abolishing the convict lease system, the league was never as strong as the Alabama Equal Suffrage Association. This was true of leagues throughout the United States. NAWSA had two million members in 1920; the National League of Women Voters had only one-tenth that number. ALWV was led by a few women who had been active suffragists, but it was not successful in recruiting many new members to its causes. The league was strongest in the cities, especially in Birmingham, but it never reached the rural areas. It continued to conduct citizenship schools and to organize Get Out the Vote campaigns, but these were about the limit of their activities. Even the voter drive was not too successful, because the number of total voters declined from a high of 241,080 in 1920 to 166,593 in 1924. Lack of participation by women probably constituted a large portion of this decline; they may have been less interested in voting after the excitement of the first year and after they were required to pay the poll tax. As early as 1923 the national league sent representatives to Alabama to rejuvenate the state league. These representatives described the difficulties the state leaders had in holding the organization together. The same story appeared in numerous reports—a handful of women trying to maintain an entire state organization by themselves. The number of state leagues dwindled; the leaders could not find women to act as chairs of the various committees; letters went unanswered. By 1928 the ALWV was forced to disband.[21]

The women who were active in the league were the same women who had been leading the suffrage drive for more than a decade, and some were active members of women's clubs and the WCTU also. By the 1920s some of the early reformers had died or were too old to be very active. Others had developed different interests and had moved on to other endeavors. Pattie Jacobs, for example, was the first secretary of the NLWV in 1920 and in 1927 was elected vice-president. She also became Alabama's first National Democratic Committeewoman and the first woman on the National Democratic Executive Committee. These duties took her out of the state, but for a while she retained the job of legislative chair of the Alabama league. When the league had a big task such as fighting for the abolition of the convict lease system in 1923, it turned to Jacobs. But there was no one to take Jacobs's place when her interests took her elsewhere. The reform impulse of the Progressive period waned and by the early 1920s the issues of the previous decade had run their course. Prohibition, child labor, educational reforms, and prison reforms had more or less been resolved for the time being. The women of the 1920s moved on to other issues.[22]

By the end of the Progressive period in 1920 many middle-class Alabama women had undergone significant changes in roles, life-styles, values, and expectations. The dividing line between the public and private world was disappearing. Women could now participate in the public world in large numbers. As a consequence of their involvement in reform crusades, the women's club movement, and the campaign for woman suffrage, women could no longer be characterized as passive and dependent. They were not easily relegated to the private and domestic sphere. More than at any other time, women of the Progressive Era asserted themselves as willing, able, and rightful participants of the world.

This new role was a substantial change from the 1890s when the southern definition of the role of women was limited to that of the Southern Lady. The South had had a more rigid stereotyping of women than the rest of the country. In fact, the Southern Lady had been elevated to the position of a myth. According to this view women were supposed to be beautiful, gentle, efficient, morally superior, and at the same time ready to accept without question male superiority and authority. On political or public matters they were to be seen and not heard, while in the domestic or private sphere it was taken for granted that a woman would rule. The force of this cultural image of the Southern Lady was so strong that, according to historian Anne Firor Scott, southern women had to follow a more devious road to emancipation than women elsewhere. It was only after long apprenticeships in such ostensibly safe organizations as church societies and the WCTU that they began to venture into women's clubs and suffrage organizations.[23]

Alabama women had their first experiences in an organization run by women when they created their temperance unions in 1882. After these local unions united in 1884, they became interested in a wide range of social and economic issues and set out to better the world, all in the name of protecting the home. The WCTU waged the battle for temperance education, prison reform, and later total prohibition. These women established the Mercy Home as a refuge for homeless women and children. Martha L. Spencer made this her life's work, but it did not preclude her from active suffrage work. The Alabama women who worked in the WCTU had a totally different experience than they had ever had before. Temperance work had much to do with putting southern women into the mainstream of American life.

By the 1890s other women (and sometimes the same women) had formed literary clubs, which joined together in 1895 to create the Alabama Federation of Women's Clubs. The AFWC soon broadened its activities to include a long list of civic and community projects. Under the leadership of Elizabeth Johnston, the AFWC established the Alabama Boys' Industrial School, which was the first in the state. Lura Harris Craighead persuaded the club women to sponsor the Alabama School Improvement Association, which later became the Parent-Teacher Association of the state. The AFWC supported scholarships for women and Julia Tutwiler made it possible for them to attend the University of Alabama. Both the WCTU and the club women worked toward the abolition of child labor and the establishment of juvenile courts, with Nellie Kimball Murdock of the AFWC playing the leadership role.

Black women's clubs created the Alabama Federation of Colored Women's Clubs in 1899 and pursued similar goals to those of white women: education, self-improvement, and community service. Because black women had no other organizational structure through which to work, their women's clubs tackled many problems. Under the leadership of Margaret Murray Washington, they worked for temperance, improvement of jails and prisons, better schools, prevention of juvenile delinquency, and suffrage. But African-American women occupied a special sphere. They were united by a sense of racial pride, which gave them a distinct mission—the moral education of the race. They sought to uplift the entire race through such efforts as the mother's clubs. As a result of these various activities, both white and black women created a special place for themselves and thereby an avenue to public life and affairs.

Yet, at the same time, the enlargement of women's roles was closely tied to the fact that women were female. The argument for the expansion of women's sphere still derived its strength from the idea that women played a very special role in society because of their female morality, virtue, and ability to "keep house," whether at home or in the community. The activities of the women's clubs and the WCTU were all carried out in the name of the home and the family. Women had moved beyond the home, but they were still identified with it.

The woman suffrage movement was considered more radical than either the WCTU or the women's clubs because it challenged the doctrine of the two spheres. It demanded for women admission to citizenship and a connection with the social order not based on the family and their subordination within it. However, suffrage leaders played down the more radical aspects of suffrage and asked for the vote in order to achieve Progressive reforms that would protect the home. In fact, it was as a direct result of the desire to work for the abolition of child labor that Pattie Ruffner Jacobs, Nellie Kimball Murdock, and others organized the Alabama Equal Suffrage Association in 1912. Despite the different character of the suffrage drive, many of the same women could be found in all three organizations (for example, Martha L. Spencer and Elizabeth Johnston), yet neither the WCTU nor the AFWC supported suffrage in the early years. In 1915 the AESA unsuccessfully waged a campaign, led by Bossie O'Brien Hundley, to enfranchise women by an amendment to the state constitution. At this point the suffrage leaders shifted their policy and began to support the federal amendment that NAWSA was then pushing. However, even after Congress adopted the Nineteenth Amendment in 1919, the state legislature refused to ratify it.

In the course of the Progressive period, Alabama women moved through several stages in the evolution of their feminine consciousness. They first moved from the home into the WCTU and women's clubs in the 1880s and 1890s. They employed the traits of the lady to justify their departure from the home. They ended their confinement, took the ideology of the home with them, and began to influence the public realm. They became what can best be described as domestic feminists.[24] By the turn of the century, these Alabama women changed the direction of their interests. They became concerned with a wide range of Progressive reforms; they tackled a vast list of civic projects. They enlarged their sphere and moved to a second stage of domestic feminism, which can be defined as municipal housekeeping. But they still described their activities in terms of home and family.

At the same time club women began to occupy a larger public role, women who advocated suffrage also began to organize. Suffrage had never been a primary objective of club women. Such overt political participation was incompatible with their more cautious approach to obtaining influence through the invocation of women's traditional domestic qualities. The women who created the AESA, who waged campaigns to vote, and who lobbied the legislators had become public feminists. These suffragists were demanding direct entry in society as individuals, not indirect influence through their subordinate positions as wives and mothers. This view of women clashed with the traditional ideology of women's role. For this reason, the AFWC and the WCTU were originally opposed to suffrage.

However, the suffrage leaders shifted their arguments. They ceased to stress their view of women as atomistic individuals and instead stressed their roles as wives and mothers. With this approach, club women became convinced that suffrage could do no more harm to the family and home life than club work did. The paths of the club women and the suffragists then united in 1914 when the Alabama WCTU endorsed suffrage and in 1918 when the Alabama Federation of Women's Clubs voted to support suffrage. The traditions of domestic feminism and public feminism then merged in the fight for the suffrage.

Women's sphere had definitely expanded by 1920, but it was still a bounded space and thus continued to be segregated and limited in many ways. How to resolve this separation of female and male, private and public, domestic and political would prove to be an ongoing debate during the coming decades. However, many middle-class Alabama women had left the nineteenth century and were ready to step into the modern era.

NOTES

1. INTRODUCTION

1. Dewey W. Grantham, *Southern Progressivism: The Reconciliation of Progress and Tradition* (Knoxville: Univ. of Tennessee Press, 1983), xix.

2. Proceedings of the Woman's Christian Temperance Union of the State of Alabama, Jan. 22, 1884, Rare Book Room, University of Alabama Library, Tuscaloosa, Ala.; Report of the Alabama Woman's Christian Temperance Union, Report of the Thirty-first Annual Convention, Oct. 26–28, 1915 (Montgomery, Ala.: Paragon Press, 1915), Special Collections and Archives, Auburn University Libraries, Auburn, Ala.; see also James Benson Sellers, *The Prohibition Movement in Alabama, 1702 to 1943* (Chapel Hill: Univ. of North Carolina Press, 1943).

3. Lura Harris Craighead, *History of the Alabama Federation of Women's Clubs* (Montgomery, Ala.: Paragon Press, 1936), 1: 350 (hereafter cited as Craighead, *History of the AFWC*).

4. Josephine T. Washington, "The Influence of Club Work in Alabama," *National Association Notes* (July 1904): 14–17. This official publication of the National Association of Colored Women is deposited at the Tuskegee University Library, Tuskegee, Ala.

5. A. Elizabeth Taylor has written extensively on the suffrage drive in several southern states. Her works include: *The Woman Suffrage Movement in Tennes-*

see (New York: Bookman Associates, 1957); "The Woman Suffrage Movement in Texas," *Journal of Southern History* 17 (May 1951): 194–215; "The Woman Suffrage Movement in Arkansas," *Arkansas Historical Quarterly* 15 (Spring 1956): 17–52; "The Woman Suffrage Movement in Florida," *Florida Historical Quarterly* 36 (July 1957): 42–60; "The Woman Suffrage Movement in Mississippi, 1890–1920," *Journal of Mississippi History* 30 (Feb. 1968): 1–34; "The Woman Suffrage Movement in North Carolina, Part I," *North Carolina Historical Review* 38 (Jan. 1961): 45–62; "The Last Phase of the Woman Suffrage Movement in Georgia," *Georgia Historical Quarterly* 43 (March 1959): 11–28.

6. *Official Proceedings of the Constitutional Convention of the State of Alabama, May 21, 1901, to September 3, 1901* (Wetumpka, Ala.: Wetumpka Printing Company, 1940), 1: 464–71, 2: 1386–91, 3: 3812–81; Susan B. Anthony and Ida Husted Harper, eds., *The History of Woman Suffrage* (Indianapolis: Hollenbeck Press, 1902), 4: 465–69; Lee Norcross Allen, "The Woman Suffrage Movement in Alabama" (M.A. thesis, Alabama Polytechnic Institute, 1949), 1–16; Gillian Goodrich, "Romance and Reality: The Birmingham Suffragists 1892–1920," *Journal of the Birmingham Historical Society* 5 (Jan. 1978): 5–21.

7. Minutes of the Alabama Equal Suffrage Association, 1912–18, AESA Papers, Alabama Department of Archives and History, Montgomery, Ala.; Allen, "The Woman Suffrage Movement in Alabama," 17–161; Goodrich, "Romance and Reality," 5–21; John Irvin Lumpkin, "The Equal Suffrage Movement in Alabama, 1910–1920" (M.A. thesis, University of Alabama, 1949).

2. TEMPERANCE UNIONS, 1882–1915

1. Nancy Woloch, *Women and the American Experience* (New York: Alfred A. Knopf, 1984), 271–72.

2. Ruth Bordin, *Woman and Temperance: The Quest for Power and Liberty, 1873–1900* (Philadelphia: Temple Univ. Press, 1981), 3–14.

3. Ibid.

4. Ibid., 58.

5. Anne Firor Scott, "The 'New Woman' in the New South," *South Atlantic Quarterly* 65 (Autumn 1962): 477.

6. Bordin, *Woman and Temperance,* 58.

7. Ibid., 52, 76.

8. National Woman's Christian Temperance Union, *The Union Signal,*

Aug. 2, 1883, 5, on file in the National Woman's Christian Temperance Union Library, Evanston, Ill.

9. *Montgomery Advertiser,* Feb. 18, 1907.

10. *The Union Signal,* April 12, 1883, 12; Proceedings of the Woman's Christian Temperance Union of Alabama, Jan. 22, 1884; Sellers, *The Prohibition Movement in Alabama,* 53–54; Martha L. Spencer, "Sketch of the Alabama Woman's Christian Temperance Union," *Alabama White Ribbon* (published by the Alabama Woman's Christian Temperance Union), Dec. 1909, 4 (this monthly paper is deposited at the Alabama Department of Archives and History, Montgomery, Ala.).

11. *The Union Signal,* July 5, 1883, 4–5; Feb. 7, 1884, 12; Oct. 9, 1884, 10.

12. Minutes of the National Woman's Christian Temperance Union (hereafter cited as Minutes of the National WCTU), 1894, Report of the Corresponding Secretaries, 192–93, on file in the National Woman's Christian Temperance Union Library, Evanston, Ill.

13. Report of the Alabama Woman's Christian Temperance Union, Thirty-first Annual Convention, Oct. 26–28, 1915; Minutes of National WCTU, 1903, Report of the Corresponding Secretary, 133–34.

14. Bordin, *Woman and Temperance,* 37.

15. Proceedings of the Woman's Christian Temperance Union of Alabama, Jan. 22, 1884; Report of the Alabama Woman's Christian Temperance Union, Thirty-first Annual Convention, Oct. 26–28, 1915; Minutes of the National WCTU, 1906, Report of the Corresponding Secretary, 144.

16. Bordin, *Woman and Temperance,* 95–97.

17. Sellers, *The Prohibition Movement in Alabama,* 54.

18. Minutes of the National WCTU, 1891, Report of the Corresponding Secretary, 255–56.

19. *The Union Signal,* Dec. 3, 1885, 8.

20. Bordin, *Woman and Temperance,* 82–85.

21. Ibid.; Proceedings of the Woman's Christian Temperance Union of Alabama, Jan. 22, 1884; Carl V. Harris, *Political Power in Birmingham, 1871–1921* (Knoxville: Univ. of Tennessee Press, 1977), 189–96.

22. Minutes of the National WCTU, 1887, Report of the Corresponding Secretary, 324, and Report of the Juvenile Department, xxxvi; *The Union Signal,* Dec. 9, 1886, 11, and Nov. 24, 1887, 9.

23. Minutes of the National WCTU, 1890, Report of the Department of Colored Work, 218; Minutes of the National WCTU, 1896, Report of Colored Work, 184.

24. Minutes of the National WCTU, 1897, Report of Work among Colored People, 275; Minutes of the National WCTU, 1899, Report of Work among Colored People, 200; Minutes of the National WCTU, 1900, Report of Work among Colored People, 202; Minutes of the National WCTU, 1903, 12. Black women's clubs are fully discussed in chapter 4.

25. Sellers, *The Prohibition Movement in Alabama,* 55–56.

26. *Alabama White Ribbon,* July 1906, 1; April 1908, 3; May 1909, 3.

27. Sellers, *The Prohibition Movement in Alabama,* 56–57; Minutes of the National WCTU, 1886, Report of the Corresponding Secretary, ccxx–ccxxi; Minutes of the National WCTU, 1889, Report of the Corresponding Secretary.

28. Bordin, *Woman and Temperance,* 54.

29. Sellers, *The Prohibition Movement in Alabama,* 64; Minutes of the National WCTU, 1891, Report of the Corresponding Secretary, 255.

30. Sellers, *The Prohibition Movement in Alabama,* 64.

31. Bordin, *Woman and Temperance,* 53.

32. Thomas McAdory Owen, *History of Alabama and Dictionary of Alabama Biography* (Spartanburg, S.C.: Reprint Publishers, 1987), 4: 1965; Anne Gary Pannell and Dorothea E. Wyatt, *Julia S. Tutwiler and Social Progress in Alabama* (Tuscaloosa: Univ. of Alabama Press, 1961), 49–122.

33. Albert Burton Moore, *History of Alabama* (University, Ala.: University Supply Store, 1934), 814–15.

34. Minutes of the National WCTU, 1888, Report of the Department of Prison, Jail, Police, and Almshouse Work, 205–6.

35. Pannell and Wyatt, *Julia S. Tutwiler,* 106–19; Julia Strudwick Tutwiler, Educator, Friend of Humanity, Public Benefactor, Memorandum Printed by Friends, n.d., Alabama Department of Archives and History, Montgomery, Ala.; "Julia S. Tutwiler," *Alabama White Ribbon,* May 1916, 1.

36. Annual Report of the Mercy Home, Dec. 1906, 7, Mercy Home Papers, Department of Archives and Manuscripts, Birmingham Public Library, Birmingham, Ala.

37. Grantham, *Southern Progressivism,* 160–77; Edward S. LaMonte, "The Mercy Home and Private Charity in Early Birmingham," *Journal of the Birmingham Historical Society* 5 (Jan. 1978): 5–15.

38. LaMonte, "The Mercy Home," 5–15; Annual Report of the Mercy Home, Feb. 1, 1893, 2, 30; Minutes of the Second Meeting of the Board of Directors of the Mercy Home, Spring, 1892, Mercy Home Papers, Department of Archives and Manuscripts, Birmingham Public Library, Birmingham,

Ala.; Martha L. Spencer, "The Mercy Home," *Alabama White Ribbon,* April 1904, 1–2; Minutes of the National WCTU, 1892, Report of the Corresponding Secretary, 149. In addition to Spencer, Jefferies, and Murdock, the founding members of the Mercy Home were Mrs. A. N. Ballard, Mrs. W. M. Brooks, Mrs. T. N. Hamilton, Mrs. James F. Johnston, Mrs. L. F. Stratton, Mrs. William Redd, Mrs. W. J. Pierce, Mrs. John White, and Mrs. F. J. Tyler.

39. Minutes of the Board of Directors of the Mercy Home, Jan. 24, 1893; Annual Report of the Mercy Home, Dec. 1920, 12–13.

40. LaMonte, "The Mercy Home," 6–7.

41. Annual Report of the Mercy Home, Dec. 1895, 10; Minutes of the Board of Directors of the Mercy Home, Aug. 1, 1893, March 13, 1894.

42. Annual Report of the Mercy Home, Dec. 1900, 1; Annual Report of the Mercy Home, Dec. 1913, 29; "The Mercy Home Industrial Home for Girls, Birmingham, Alabama," *Alabama White Ribbon,* March 1909, 3.

43. Annual Report of the Mercy Home, Dec. 1914, 5.

44. Grantham, *Southern Progressivism,* 160–77.

45. Sellers, *The Prohibition Movement in Alabama,* 87, 94, 100; Minutes of the National WCTU, 1904, Report of the Corresponding Secretary, 130–31.

46. "Local Option Bill Passed Both Houses," *Alabama White Ribbon,* March 1907, 2; *Alabama White Ribbon,* July 1907, 2; *Montgomery Advertiser,* Feb. 7, 21, 26, 1907.

47. "The Prohibition Fight in Jefferson County," *Alabama White Ribbon,* Sept. 1907, 3; *Birmingham News,* Oct. 28, 1907.

48. Sellers, *The Prohibition Movement in Alabama,* 117; "A Great Victory," *Alabama White Ribbon,* Dec. 1907, 2; Minutes of the National WCTU, 1907, Report of Corresponding Secretary, 145; *Birmingham News,* Oct. 28, 1907.

49. Harris, *Political Power in Birmingham,* 194; *Birmingham News,* Oct. 29, 1907.

50. Sellers, *The Prohibition Movement in Alabama,* 120–21.

51. *Mobile Register,* Nov. 14, 17, 19, 1907; *Birmingham News,* Nov. 19, 1907.

52. *Mobile Register,* Nov. 20, 1907; Sellers, *The Prohibition Movement in Alabama,* 120–21; W. B. Crumpton, *A Story: How Alabama Became Dry* (Montgomery, Ala.: Paragon Press, 1925), 27–29.

53. Sellers, *The Prohibition Movement in Alabama,* 122; *Montgomery Advertiser,* Nov. 24, 1907.

54. Sellers, *The Prohibition Movement in Alabama,* 122–28, 135; *Montgomery Advertiser,* Aug. 19, 1909; *Birmingham News,* Aug. 19, 1909.

55. Sellers, *The Prohibition Movement in Alabama*, 135–37; *Alabama White Ribbon*, Aug. 1909, 1.

56. Sellers, *The Prohibition Movement in Alabama*, 146–48; Minutes of the National WCTU, 1911, Report of Corresponding Secretary, 125; *Birmingham News*, Nov. 30, 1909; *Montgomery Advertiser*, Nov. 30, 1909.

57. Sellers, *The Prohibition Movement in Alabama*, 149–75.

58. Ibid., 176–82.

59. Ibid., 183–89.

60. Belle Kearney, *A Slaveholder's Daughter* (Reprint, New York: Negro Universities Press, 1969), 118; Bordin, *Woman and Temperance*, 81; Anne Firor Scott, *The Southern Lady from Pedestal to Politics, 1830–1930* (Chicago: Univ. of Chicago Press, 1970), 135–63.

3. WHITE WOMEN'S CLUBS, 1890–1915

1. Woloch, *Women and the American Experience*, 289–90.

2. John Whiteclay Chambers II, *The Tyranny of Change: America in the Progressive Era, 1900–1917* (New York: St. Martin's Press, 1980), 86.

3. Jennie June Croly, *The History of the Woman's Club Movement in America* (New York: Henry G. Allen, 1898), 232–39.

4. Craighead, *History of the AFWC*, 1: 11–16. The clubs that organized the AFWC were the Highland Book Club, Cadmean Circle, Clionian Club (all from Birmingham), No Name Club (Montgomery), Progressive Culture Club (Decatur), and Thursday Literary Club (Selma).

5. Ibid., 24–25.

6. Ibid., 26.

7. Ibid., 150. Fear of public speaking was a common experience of women. See Theodora Penny Martin, *The Sound of Our Own Voices: Women's Study Clubs 1860–1910* (Boston: Beacon Press, 1987).

8. Craighead, *History of the AFWC*, 1: 177–78.

9. Ibid., 1: 93.

10. Ibid., 1: 105.

11. Ibid., 1: 182.

12. Ibid., 1: 350.

13. Karen J. Blair, *The Clubwoman as Feminist: True Womanhood Redefined, 1868–1914* (New York: Holmes and Meier Publishers, 1980), 117–19.

14. Blair, *The Clubwoman as Feminist*, 44; Ellen DuBois, "The Radical-

ism of the Woman Suffrage Movement: Notes Toward the Reconstruction of Nineteenth-Century Feminism," *Feminist Studies* 3 (Fall 1975): 63–71.

15. Craighead, *History of the AFWC,* 1: 165, 177, 410.

16. David M. Weakley, "History of Alabama Boys Industrial School," manuscript, Department of Archives and Manuscripts, Birmingham Public Library, Birmingham, Ala. Coming from the Tennessee Industrial School, Weakley served as superintendent and his wife as matron of the school from 1905 to 1948. By the 1930s their work was widely acclaimed throughout the state and by social workers. The University of Alabama granted Weakley an honorary degree in 1935.

17. Weakley, "History of Alabama Boys Industrial School," 277–83.

18. Ibid., 31–32, 284; Craighead, *History of the AFWC,* 1: 27.

19. Mary Johnston Avery, *She Heard With Her Heart* (Birmingham, Ala.: Birmingham Publishing Co., 1944), 60–67; Craighead, *History of the AFWC,* 1: 64. The founding members of the board in addition to Johnston were Alberta Williams Bush, Mrs. E. S. Fitzpatrick, Mrs. George B. Eager, Mrs. S. D. Cole, and Lura Harris Craighead.

20. Weakley, "History of the Alabama Boys Industrial School," 293–99; Craighead, *History of the AFWC,* 1: 384–85.

21. Craighead, *History of the AFWC,* 1: 101; Weakley, "History of Alabama Boys Industrial School," 113, 302–5; Hastings H. Hart, *Social Problems of Alabama* (New York: Russell Sage Foundation, 1918), 29. A copy of this study is deposited at the Alabama Department of Archives and History, Montgomery, Ala.

22. Weakley, "History of the Alabama Boys Industrial School," 320, 347, 353–54; Craighead, *History of the AFWC,* 1: 46.

23. Weakley, "History of the Alabama Boys Industrial School," 324–26. Other prominent women who served on the board include Adele Goodwyn McNeel, president of the board following Johnston; Marie Bankhead Owen, daughter of Sen. John H. Bankhead; Dixie Bibb Graves, wife of Gov. Bibb Graves; and Mary Clark Kilby, wife of Gov. Thomas E. Kilby.

24. Craighead, *History of the AFWC,* 1: 350.

25. Ibid., 1: 36–37.

26. Moore, *History of Alabama,* 543–61.

27. Ibid., 552–55.

28. Craighead, *History of the AFWC,* 1: 36–37, 53, 67.

29. Ibid., 67, 84–85; Mrs. A. T. Goodwyn, "What Women's Clubs Have Done for Education," and Mrs. J. D. Wyker, "What Women's Clubs Can

Do For Education," *Official Proceedings of the Alabama Educational Association,* 1899, copy on file in the Alabama Department of Archives and History, Montgomery, Ala.

30. Craighead, *History of the AFWC,* 1: 36.

31. Moore, *History of Alabama,* 728.

32. Ibid., 545–46.

33. Craighead, *History of the AFWC,* 1: 54, 67, 119, 132, 239, 250, 269.

34. Ibid., 1: 139.

35. Ibid., 1: 170–71, 193–94, 214–16, 254, 273. Fairhope is undoubtedly a unique situation because of the public spirit that existed in the town resulting from its origin as a utopian community built upon the beliefs of Henry George and his single-tax system.

36. Ibid., 1: 157–59.

37. Ibid., 1: 168–71, 193–94, 214–16.

38. Ibid., 1: 214–16; *Montgomery Advertiser,* Dec. 3, 1907.

39. Craighead, *History of the AFWC,* 1: 269; Moore, *History of Alabama,* 738.

40. Moore, *History of Alabama,* 739–42.

41. Craighead, *History of the AFWC,* 1: 117, 211, 239, 367–70; *Montgomery Advertiser,* Dec. 3, 1903. Women, however, were not appointed to school boards in even modest numbers until the 1920s.

42. Moore, *History of Alabama,* 738, 742; Hart, *Social Problems of Alabama,* 34–42.

43. Ralph M. Lyon, *A History of Livingston University, 1835–1963* (Livingston, Ala., 1976), 14–18; Pannell and Wyatt, *Julia S. Tutwiler,* 59–64. Today Alabama Normal School is Livingston State University.

44. Lyon, *A History of Livingston University,* 24; Lucille Griffith, *Alabama College 1896–1969* (Montevallo, Ala.: University of Montevallo, 1969), 3–19. Today the Alabama Girls' Industrial School is the University of Montevallo.

45. The University of Alabama was established in 1831 and Alabama A & M, the land-grant college for the state, was created in 1872. Today it is Auburn University.

46. James Benson Sellers, *History of the University of Alabama* (University, Ala.: Univ. of Alabama Press, 1953), 477–83.

47. Craighead, *History of the AFWC,* 1: 52.

48. Ibid., 1: 70, 232.

49. Ibid., 1: 334.

50. Ibid., 1: 151, 237, 331–33.

51. Petition of the Alabama Federation of Women's Clubs, Jan. 20, 1911, Alabama Department of Archives and History, Montgomery, Ala.

52. Craighead, *History of the AFWC*, 1: 299.

53. Ibid., 1: 365–66.

54. Ibid., 1: 17 (Mary LaFayette Robbins), 23 (Ella Gaines Parker Going), 31 (Anna Coor Pender Eager), 44 (Elizabeth Johnston Evans Johnston), 45 (Kate Hutcheson Morrissette), 46 (Lura Harris Craighead), 77 (Mrs. B. B. Ross), 77–78 (Clara Louise Berry Wyker), 90–91 (Conradine Skaggs McConaughy), 106 (Lillian Milner Orr), 135 (Lily Taylor Cochrane), 148 (Mabel Wiley Hutton Goode), 179 (Mrs. Joseph McLester), 201 (Mary Winn Gayle), 223 (Margaret Peterson Coleman), 262 (Mrs. John Herbert Phillips), 281 (Laura Montgomery Henderson), 313 (Lella Byrd Haley), 390 (Eleanor Gary Hooper). Most of these women were presidents of the AFWC. I also include Nellie Kimball Murdock in this group; biographical information on her can be found in chapter 5. I have used the women's own names whenever I knew them and tried to avoid calling them by their husbands' names.

4. BLACK WOMEN'S CLUBS, 1890–1920

1. Josephine B. Bruce, "The National Association of Colored Women's Clubs," *National Association Notes* (July 1904): 4–6; Paula Giddings, *When and Where I Enter: The Impact of Black Women on Race and Sex in America* (New York: William Morrow, 1984), 89–94; Mrs. Booker T. Washington, "Club Work among Negro Women," in *Progress of a Race*, ed. J. L. Nichols and William H. Crogman (Naperville, Ill.: J. L. Nichols, 1920), 177–79.

2. Gerda Lerner, ed., *Black Women in White America: A Documentary History* (New York: Pantheon Books, 1972), 436–37.

3. Woloch, *Women and the American Experience*, 292; Fannie Barrier Williams, "Club Movement among Negro Women," in *Progress of a Race*, edited by J. W. Gibson and W. H. Crogman (Miami, Fla.: Mnemosyne Publishing, 1969), 197–281.

4. Giddings, *When and Where I Enter*, 81–82.

5. Washington, "The Influence of Club Work in Alabama," 14–17.

6. Washington, "Club Work among Negro Women," 177–209; Mrs. Booker T. Washington, Synopsis of the Lecture on the Organizing of Women's

Clubs, June 2, 1910, and Report of the Tuskegee Woman's Club, Oct. 1909–
May 1910, Booker T. Washington Papers, 1909–10, box 982, Manuscript
Division, Library of Congress, Washington, D.C.; Lerner, *Black Women in
White America*, 443–44; Lena Cheeks Shehee, "Mrs. Margaret Murray Wash-
ington," *National Association Notes*, April 1928, 9; Cynthia Neverdon-Morton,
Afro-American Women of the South and the Advancement of the Race, 1895–1925
(Knoxville: Univ. of Tennessee Press, 1989), 132.

7. Quoted in Neverdon-Morton, *Afro-American Women of the South*, 133.

8. Mrs. Booker T. Washington, "The Tuskegee Woman's Club," *The Southern Workman* (Aug. 1920): 365.

9. Mrs. Booker T. Washington, "The Negro Home," Booker T. Washington Papers, containers 6–7, reel 6, Manuscript Division, Library of Congress,
Washington, D.C.

10. Neverdon-Morton, *Afro-American Women of the South*, 133; Emmett J.
Scott, "Mrs. Booker T. Washington's Part in Her Husband's Work," Booker T.
Washington Papers, containers 6–7, reel 6, Manuscript Division, Library of
Congress, Washington, D.C.

11. Washington, "The Tuskegee Woman's Club," 367; "Seventeenth Anniversary of Tuskegee Woman's Club," *Tuskegee Student*, June 14, 1913, on
file in Washington Collection, Tuskegee University Library, Tuskegee, Ala.;
Neverdon-Morton, *Afro-American Women of the South*, 134.

12. Washington, "The Tuskegee Woman's Club," 367–68.

13. Ibid., 365.

14. Ibid., 368.

15. Scott, "Mrs. Booker T. Washington's Part in Her Husband's Work";
Neverdon-Morton, *Afro-American Women of the South*, 123.

16. Scott, "Mrs. Booker T. Washington's Part in Her Husband's Work."

17. Mrs. Booker T. Washington, *Practical Help Leaflet No. 3*, Booker T.
Washington Papers, 1909–10, box 982, Manuscript Division, Library of Con-
gress, Washington, D.C.; Washington, "The Negro Home"; Lerner, *Black
Women in White America*, 455; Mrs. Booker T. Washington, "What the Negro
Woman is Doing for Herself," Montgomery *Colored Alabamian*, March 15,
1913, on file in Alabama Department of Archives and History, Montgomery,
Ala.

18. Scott, "Mrs. Booker T. Washington's Part in Her Husband's Work."

19. Ibid.; Washington, The Organizing of Women's Clubs; Washington,
"The Tuskegee Woman's Club," 366–67.

20. Toussaint L'Ouverture led a successful slave rebellion against the French on Santo Domingo in 1801; Frederick Douglass was the famous abolition leader and later active in the Republican party; Paul Lawrence Dunbar was a poet and novelist; and Blanche K. Bruce was a Reconstruction U.S. senator from Mississippi.

21. "The Mothers' Improvement Club," *Tuskegee Student*, Dec. 5, 1908; "Mothers' Club of the Children's House Ends Successful Year," *Tuskegee Student*, July 27, 1918. The *Tuskegee Student* was published weekly by the institute for the students and graduates.

22. Hart, *Social Problems of Alabama*, 39.

23. Mrs. Booker T. Washington, "Are We Making Good?" *Tuskegee Student*, Oct. 16, 1915; *Tuskegee Student*, March 1, 1919.

24. Montgomery *Colored Alabamian*, April 19, 1913.

25. Josephine T. Washington, "What Our Women in Alabama Have Done," *National Association Notes*, Feb. 1912, 10–13; "Minutes of the Alabama Federation of Colored Women's Clubs," July 1907, 8–9, July 1913, 3, 16, Alabama Federation of Colored Women's Clubs Papers, Washington Collection, Tuskegee University Library, Tuskegee, Ala.

26. Washington, "What Our Women in Alabama Have Done," 13; "Minutes of the Alabama Federation of Colored Women's Clubs," July 1913, 3, 16; "The Mt. Meigs reformatory," *Tuskegee Student*, Jan. 13, 1912, Feb. 10, 1912; Hart, *Social Problems of Alabama*, 31.

27. Josephine T. Washington, "Some Things Our Women Are Doing," *National Association Notes*, Nov. 1913, 17–18; *National Association Notes*, Jan.–March 1921, 9; "Minutes of the Alabama Federation of Colored Women's Clubs," July 1913, July 1916, July 1919, and June 1922.

28. Giddings, *When and Where I Enter*, 119–21. See also Rosalyn M. Terborg-Penn, "Afro-Americans in the Struggle for Woman Suffrage" (Ph.D. diss., Howard University, 1977).

29. Giddings, *When and Where I Enter*, 121–23; Miss N. H. Burroughs, "Black Women and Reform," *The Crisis* 10 (Aug. 1915): 187.

30. Washington, "What the Negro Woman is Doing for Herself"; Washington, "Club Work among Negro Women," 195.

31. Adele Logan Alexander, "How I Discovered My Grandmother," *Ms.* (Nov. 1983): 29–33; Giddings, *When and Where I Enter*, 121; Louis R. Harlan, ed., *The Booker T. Washington Papers* (Urbana, Ill.: Univ. of Illinois Press, 1972), 2: 230. Alexander suggests that her grandmother's life was plagued

with problems, including the strain of leading a "double life" in a racially hostile enviornment, which eventually overwhelmed her.

32. Adella Hunt Logan, "Woman Suffrage," *The Colored American Magazine* (Sept. 9, 1905): 487–89.

33. Adella Hunt Logan, "Colored Women as Voters," *The Crisis* 4 (Sept. 1912): 242–43.

34. "Mrs. Warren Logan Writes of the Doings Among Club Women around Tuskegee," Montgomery *Colored Alabamian,* April 10, 1915; "Minutes of the Alabama Federation of Colored Women's Clubs," July 1913, July 1919, and June 1922; *National Association Notes,* Sept. 1927, 6.

35. Giddings, *When and Where I Enter,* 95.

36. Ibid., 97.

37. Ibid., 100.

38. Darlene Clark Hine, "Rape and the Inner Lives of Southern Black Women: Thoughts on the Culture of Dissemblance," manuscript in possession of the author.

39. Washington, "What the Negro Woman is Doing for Herself."

5. CLUB WOMEN AND CHILD LABOR, 1903–1919

1. Craighead, *History of the AFWC,* 1: 246.

2. Hugh C. Bailey, *Edgar Gardner Murphy: Gentle Progressive* (Coral Gables, Fla.: Univ. of Miami Press, 1968), 65.

3. Ibid., 66.

4. Elizabeth H. Davidson, *Child Labor Legislation in the Southern Textile States* (Chapel Hill: Univ. of North Carolina Press, 1939), 22–24; Martha L. Spencer, "Sketch of the Alabama Woman's Christian Temperance Union, 1883–1909," *Alabama White Ribbon,* Dec. 1909, 4; Hugh C. Bailey, *Liberalism in the New South: Southern Social Reforms and the Progressive Movement* (Coral Gables, Fla.: Univ. of Miami Press, 1969), 162–63.

5. Irene M. Ashby, "The Fight Against Child Labor in Alabama," *American Federationist* 8 (1901): 150–57.

6. Bailey, *Edgar Gardner Murphy,* 67–68. See also Edgar Gardner Murphy, *Problems of the Present South* (New York: Macmillan, 1904).

7. Davidson, *Child Labor Legislation,* 27.

8. Bailey, *Edgar Gardner Murphy,* 68; Davidson, *Child Labor Legislation,* 30.

9. Ashby, "The Fight Against Child Labor in Alabama," 154.

10. Davidson, *Child Labor Legislation*, 31.

11. *Montgomery Advertiser*, Feb. 5, 7, 1901; Bailey, *Edgar Gardner Murphy*, 72–75; Davidson, *Child Labor Legislation*, 33–36.

12. Bailey, *Edgar Gardner Murphy*, 68–83; Davidson, *Child Labor Legislation*, 31–41.

13. Craighead, *History of the AFWC*, 1: 87–89.

14. Ibid., 1: 87–89, 109–111.

15. *Montgomery Advertiser*, Oct. 29, 30, Nov. 3, 10, 17, 28, Dec. 20, 1901.

16. Spencer, "Sketch of the Alabama Woman's Christian Temperance Union," 4.

17. *Huntsville Tribune*, Feb. 2, 1902.

18. Davidson, *Child Labor Legislation*, 42–44.

19. *Montgomery Advertiser*, Jan. 21, 28, Feb. 12, 13, 1903.

20. Craighead, *History of the AFWC*, 1: 106–7. Craighead had served as president of the AFWC between 1899 and 1901 and was an original member of the board of trustees of the Alabama Boys' Industrial School.

21. *Montgomery Advertiser*, Jan. 21, 28, 1903; Davidson, *Child Labor Legislation*, 48–49.

22. Bailey, *Edgar Gardner Murphy*, 84–85.

23. Craighead, *History of the AFWC*, 1: 108–9.

24. Davidson, *Child Labor Legislation*, 49–50; Bailey, *Edgar Gardner Murphy*, 84–85; Emory R. Johnson, ed., "Child Labor in Alabama," *Annals of the American Academy of Political Science* 21: 178–80; Martha L. Spencer, "Child Labor," *Alabama White Ribbon* (April 1907): 1.

25. *Birmingham News*, Feb. 11, 1903.

26. Davidson, *Child Labor Legislation*, 51.

27. Bailey, *Edgar Gardner Murphy*, 89–90.

28. Craighead, *History of the AFWC*, 1: 151, 175.

29. Moore, *History of Alabama*, 667–74; Allen Johnston Going, "The Governorship of B. B. Comer" (M.A. thesis, University of Alabama, 1940), 1–9.

30. Craighead, *History of the AFWC*, 1: 195–97.

31. Davidson, *Child Labor Legislation*, 218–23.

32. *Montgomery Advertiser*, Jan. 10, Feb. 8, 1907.

33. Going, "The Governorship of B. B. Comer," 81–82.

34. Ibid., 224–25; Craighead, *History of the AFWC*, 1: 196–97; "Child Labor in Alabama," *Alabama White Ribbon* (Sept. 1907): 2.

35. Alabama Federation of Women's Clubs, *Year Book*, 1910–11, 27, Alabama Department of Archives and History, Montgomery, Ala.

36. Davidson, *Child Labor Legislation,* 225.

37. "Historical Sketch of Alabama Clubwoman: Mrs. W. L. Murdock," Amaranth Club Papers, Department of Archives and Manuscripts, Birmingham Public Library, Birmingham, Ala.

38. *Birmingham News,* March 11, 1911; Allen, "The Woman Suffrage Movement in Alabama," 18–19.

39. Davidson, *Child Labor Legislation,* 225–28.

40. Ibid., 227.

41. Mrs. W. L. Murdock, "Conditions of Child Employing Industries in the South," *Child Labor Bulletin* 2 (May 1913–Feb. 1914): 125.

42. Davidson, *Child Labor Legislation,* 228–29.

43. Herschel H. Jones, *Child Labor in Alabama,* photographs by Lewis W. Hine (Birmingham, Ala.: Alabama Child Labor Committee, 1915). The Alabama Federation of Women's Clubs assisted in the publication of this pamphlet, a copy of which is deposited at the Alabama Department of Archives and History, Montgomery, Ala.

44. Davidson, *Child Labor Legislation,* 230–31.

45. *Montgomery Advertiser,* Jan. 12, 16, 17, 20, 25, 29, Feb. 21, 1915.

46. Mrs. W. L. Murdock, "Child Labor Reform in Alabama," *Child Labor Bulletin* 3 (May 1914–Feb. 1915): 83–84.

47. Craighead, *History of the AFWC,* 1: 370–71.

48. Davidson, *Child Labor Legislation,* 232–35.

49. Craighead, *History of the AFWC,* 1: 379–82.

50. Ibid., 417–20.

51. Ibid., 379–82.

52. Davidson, *Child Labor Legislation,* 235.

53. Murdock, "Child Labor Reform in Alabama," 83.

54. Davidson, *Child Labor Legislation,* 234–37.

55. Mrs. Joseph Bevard Jones, "The Alabama Federation and the Child Welfare Work," *Alabama Childhood* 1 (July–Sept. 1921): 34–38. This official bulletin of the Alabama Child Welfare Department is deposited at the Alabama Department of Archives and History, Montgomery, Ala.

56. Mrs. L. B. Bush, "A Decade of Progress in Alabama," *Journal of Social Forces* 2 (May 1924): 539–44.

6. THE SUFFRAGE ASSOCIATIONS OF THE 1890s

1. DuBois, "The Radicalism of the Woman Suffrage Movement," 63–71.

2. Ibid.

3. Woloch, *Women and the American Experience*, 325–27. See also Eleanor Flexner, *Century of Struggle: The Woman's Rights Movement in the United States* (Reprint; New York: Atheneum, 1973); Anne F. Scott and Andrew M. Scott, *One Half the People: The Fight for Woman Suffrage* (Philadelphia: J. B. Lippincott, 1975); and Ellen Carol DuBois, *Feminism and Suffrage: The Emergence of an Independent Women's Movement in America, 1848–1869* (Ithaca, N.Y.: Cornell Univ. Press, 1978).

4. Woloch, *Women and the American Experience*, 327–30.

5. Alan P. Grimes, *The Puritan Ethic and Woman Suffrage* (New York: Oxford Univ. Press, 1967), 27–77.

6. Woloch, *Women and the American Experience*, 333–34.

7. Marjorie Spruill Wheeler, "Southern Suffragists and the 'Negro Problem'" (paper presented at the First Southern Conference on Women's History, June 1988).

8. Aileen S. Kraditor, *The Ideas of the Woman Suffrage Movement, 1890–1920* (New York: Columbia Univ. Press, 1965), 163–218.

9. Ibid.

10. Ibid., 168–69; Anthony and Harper, eds., *The History of Woman Suffrage*, 4: 246; Giddings, *When and Where I Enter*, 123–24.

11. Giddings, *When and Where I Enter*, 123–24.

12. Sheldon Hackney, *Populism to Progressivism in Alabama* (Princeton: Princeton Univ. Press, 1969), 147.

13. Paul E. Fuller, *Laura Clay and the Woman's Rights Movement* (Lexington: Univ. Press of Kentucky, 1975), 53; J. Morgan Kousser, *The Shaping of Southern Politics: Suffrage Restriction and the Establishment of the One-Party South, 1880–1910* (New Haven: Yale Univ. Press, 1974), 130–38.

14. Fuller, *Laura Clay*, 56.

15. Ibid., 57–60; Anthony and Harper, eds., *The History of Woman Suffrage*, 4: 251.

16. Elizabeth Cady Stanton, Susan B. Anthony, Matilda Joslyn Gage, and Ida Husted Harper, eds., *History of Woman Suffrage* (Rochester, N.Y.: Susan B. Anthony, 1886), 3: 830; *Birmingham News*, Feb. 4, 1914.

17. Anthony and Harper, eds., *The History of Woman Suffrage*, 4: 465.

18. A Tribute to Mrs. Ellen Stephens Hildreth, given at the 1916 state

convention of the Alabama Equal Suffrage Association, AESA Papers, Alabama Department of Archives and History, Montgomery, Ala. In this same collection is a series of unidentified and undated newspaper articles about Hildreth. Her book published in 1891 was entitled *Mud Pies and How to Make Them; or Clay Modeling for the Home, Kindergarten and School.*

19. Anthony and Harper, eds., *The History of Woman Suffrage,* 4: 465; *Montgomery Advertiser,* June 16, 1901.

20. Anthony and Harper, eds., *The History of Woman Suffrage,* 4: 465; Allen, "The Woman Suffrage Movement in Alabama," 4–7.

21. Anthony and Harper, eds., *The History of Woman Suffrage,* 4: 465–66.

22. Ibid., 4: 475, 926, 583. Griffin also spoke to the Texas legislature on the subject of temperance instruction in the schools. One legislator who objected to her speaking said he did not intend that the short-haired women of Texas should take possession of the legislature. When Griffin was allowed to speak, she responded by saying, "I am not short-haired and God has so favored me that I am not even a Texan."

23. Ibid., 4: 680–81.

24. Ibid., 4: 466–68.

25. Wheeler, "Southern Suffragists and the 'Negro Problem.'"

26. Kousser, *The Shaping of Southern Politics,* 130–38.

27. Ibid., 165–71.

28. Ibid.

29. *Montgomery Advertiser,* June 11, 1901.

30. *Official Proceedings of the Constitutional Convention of the State of Alabama, 1901,* 1: 464–71; *Montgomery Advertiser,* June 11, 1901.

31. *Huntsville Republican,* June 15, 1901.

32. *Official Proceedings of the Constitutional Convention of the State of Alabama, 1901,* 3: 3816–20; Malcolm Cook McMillan, *Constitutional Development in Alabama, 1798–1901: A Study in Politics, the Negro, and Sectionalism* (Spartanburg, S.C.: Reprint Company, 1978), 278–79.

33. *Official Proceedings of the Constitutional Convention of the State of Alabama, 1901,* 3: 3824–28, 3888.

34. Ibid., 3: 3856–73.

35. Ibid., 3: 3824–28, 3856–70.

36. *Montgomery Advertiser,* Nov. 20, 1901; Ida Husted Harper, ed., *The History of Woman Suffrage* (New York: J. J. Little and Ives Company, 1922), 6: 1.

7. RE-CREATION OF THE SUFFRAGE ASSOCIATIONS, 1910–1914

1. Harper, ed., *The History of Woman Suffrage,* 6: 2.

2. "Miss Gordon Talks On Suffragism" and "Equal Suffrage League Organized," unidentified newspaper clippings, Pattie Ruffner Jacobs Papers, Scrapbook 1, Department of Archives and Manuscripts, Birmingham Public Library, Birmingham, Ala. Jacobs's two-volume scrapbook, "The Woman Suffrage Movement in Alabama, Birmingham and the Nation," covers the years 1911–14 (hereafter cited as Jacobs Scrapbook 1 or 2).

3. Harper, ed., *History of Woman Suffrage,* 6: 2–3; "Suffrage Leaders Elect Officers," unidentified clipping, Jacobs Scrapbook 2.

4. Minutes of the Alabama Equal Suffrage Association, Oct. 9, 1912, Alabama Equal Suffrage Association Papers, Alabama Department of Archives and History, Montgomery, Ala. (hereafter cited as Minutes of the AESA); *Birmingham Ledger,* Oct. 10, 1912.

5. "Call To Organize Alabama Equal Suffrage Association," unidentified newspaper clipping, Jacobs Scrapbook 1.

6. Letter from Pattie Ruffner Jacobs to Mrs. Stubbs, Jan. 3, 1914, National American Woman Suffrage Association Papers, Manuscript Division, Library of Congress, Washington, D.C.; *Birmingham News,* July 13, 27, 1913.

7. Biographical Note, Introduction to the Pattie Ruffner Jacobs Papers, Department of Archives and Manuscripts, Birmingham Public Library, Birmingham, Ala.; J. Wayne Flynt and Marlene Hunt Rikard, "Pattie Ruffner Jacobs: Alabama Suffragist" (paper presented at the First Southern Conference on Women's History, June 1988); Marie Stokes Jemison, "Ladies Become Voters," *Southern Exposure* 3 (Spring 1979): 48–59.

8. Biographical Note, Introduction to the Pattie Ruffner Jacobs Papers; Flynt and Rikard, "Pattie Ruffner Jacobs: Alabama Suffragist."

9. "Mrs. Jacobs Speaks at Tennessee Convention," unidentified newspaper clipping, Sept. 1914, Jacobs Scrapbook 2; *Birmingham News,* July 27, 1913.

10. "Suffragists Poll Four to One at the State Fair," unidentified newspaper clipping, Jacobs Scrapbook 2; Mrs. Oscar R. Hundley, "Woman Suffrage at the Alabama State Fair," *Birmingham Magazine* (Jan. 1916), 20–21.

11. "Equal Suffrage League Will Investigate the Rules of School Board," *Birmingham Ledger,* Oct. 19, 1912; "Statement Issued by Dr. Phillips," *Birmingham Age-Herald,* Nov. 6, 1912; "Suffragists Win: Miss Worthington Back at

School," *Birmingham Ledger,* Nov. 6, 1912; "Reply to Phillips Statement Made by a Suffragette," unidentified newspaper clipping, Nov. 11, 1912, Jacobs Scrapbook 2; *Birmingham News,* Feb. 5, 1914. Amelia Worthington continued to be a very active member of the AESA serving as secretary and later editor of the newsletter. When suffrage was won, she worked for the League of Women Voters in Alabama. She later moved to Massachusetts where she became the executive field director of the Massachusetts Planned Parenthood Association. An oral interview with Amelia Worthington Fisk made in June 1975 recounting these events and her later life can be found at the Schlesinger Library, Radcliffe College, Cambridge, Mass.

12. "Local Suffragettes Want Member on School Board," unidentified newspaper clipping, Jacobs Scrapbook 2.

13. *Montgomery Times,* unidentified newspaper clipping, Jacobs Scrapbook 2.

14. "When Women Really Win," unidentified clipping, Jacobs Scrapbook 2.

15. "Headquarters of Equal Suffragists Opened Yesterday," *Birmingham Age-Herald,* June 8, 1913.

16. "Miss Sparks Speaks," unidentified newspaper clipping, Jacobs Scrapbook 2; *Woman's Journal,* July 11, 1914; AESA Fortnightly Bulletin of Suffrage News, Nov. 1, 1917.

17. Minutes of the AESA, First Annual Convention, Selma, Jan. 29, 1913; Minutes of the AESA, Second Annual Convention, Huntsville, Feb. 4, 1914, and Minutes of the AESA, Third Annual Convention, Tuscaloosa, Feb. 2, 1915.

18. "Heflin Against Woman Suffrage," unidentified newspaper clipping, Jacobs Scrapbook 2.

19. "Mrs. Jacobs has Answer to Heflin on Suffrage Issue," unidentified newspaper clipping, Feb. 16, 1913, Jacobs Scrapbook 2.

20. Harper, ed., *History of Woman Suffrage,* 5: 463.

21. *Woman's Journal,* Boston, Dec. 6, 1913. See also other clippings in Jacobs Scrapbook 1.

22. "Southern Women Are Not Moons," "Dixie Women Demand Vote," "Women of the South Demand the Ballot," unidentified newspaper clippings, Jacobs Scrapbook 1; *Birmingham News,* Dec. 6, 1913.

23. *Birmingham News,* Dec. 6, 1913; Harper, ed., *History of Woman Suffrage,* 5: 395.

24. Flexner, *Century of Struggle,* 237–39, 248–61.

25. Scott and Scott, *One Half the People,* 31–33; Minutes of the AESA, Jan. 29, 1913.

26. Scott and Scott, *One Half the People,* 31–33; see also Christine A. Lunardini, *From Equal Suffrage to Equal Rights: Alice Paul and the National Woman's Party, 1910–1928* (New York: New York Univ. Press, 1986).

27. Kraditor, *The Ideas of the Woman Suffrage Movement,* 174–79; Minutes of the AESA, March 11, 1914.

8. CAMPAIGN FOR A STATE AMENDMENT, 1914–1915

1. Minutes of the AESA, Feb. 4–5, 1914; "Suffrage Convention to be Held in Huntsville," *Birmingham News,* Jan. 25, 1914.

2. "Alabama Equal Suffrage Association Convenes in Annual Session," *Huntsville Mercury-Banner,* Feb. 4, 1914.

3. Minutes of the AESA, Feb. 4–5, 1914; *Huntsville Mercury-Banner,* Feb. 4, 1914; "1915 Legislature Will Be Asked To Give Women Vote," *Birmingham News,* Feb. 6, 1914.

4. Minutes of the AESA, Feb. 6, 1914; *Birmingham News,* Feb. 4, 1914.

5. "Alabama Women To Ask Full Suffrage 1915 Legislature," *Birmingham Ledger,* Dec. 19, 1913; *Huntsville Mercury-Banner,* Feb. 5, 1914.

6. Letter from Pattie Jacobs to Mrs. Stubbs, Jan. 13, 1914, National American Woman Suffrage Association Papers, Manuscript Division, Library of Congress, Washington, D.C.

7. "Women of Great Prominence Will Make Visit to Birmingham in March," *Birmingham News,* Feb. 15, 1914; "Official Program is Announced for Suffrage Meeting," "Jane Addams Will Visit Local Mines," *Birmingham News,* March 1, 1914.

8. "Visitors are Given Suffrage Greeting When They Arrive," *Birmingham News,* March 9, 1914.

9. *Birmingham News,* March 9, 1914; Mrs. Oscar R. Hundley, "Woman Suffrage and the Alabama Legislature," *Birmingham Magazine* (Oct. 1915): 28–29, 52–54.

10. "Head of Movement to Win votes for Women in Alabama," unidentified newspaper clipping, Jacobs Scrapbook 1.

11. "Suffragists Will Fight Underwood; To Invade South," *Birmingham Age-Herald,* Feb. 21, 1914.

12. "What Do The Men of Alabama Think of This?" *Montgomery Advertiser,* Feb. 22, 1914.

13. "No Politics in Visit of National Suffrage Board," *Birmingham Ledger,* Feb. 28, 1914. Underwood won the election and began his career for the Senate, and the suffragists lost one of their few supporters in Congress. In 1919 Underwood voted against the Nineteenth Amendment.

14. "Petitions Signed Urging Cause Of Equal Suffrage," *Birmingham News,* March 1, 1914.

15. "Party Men Think Woman Suffrage Is To Become Issue," *Birmingham Age-Herald,* July 4, 1914.

16. "Not by Federal Enactment," *Birmingham Ledger,* March 21, 1914.

17. " 'Suffrage First' Slogan of Alabama Woman Suffragists," unidentified newspaper clipping, Dec. 5, 1914, Jacobs Scrapbook 2; "South To Work To Win Alabama," *Woman's Journal,* Dec. 12, 1914.

18. "Woman Suffrage," *Birmingham News,* June 7, 1914; Minutes of the AESA, Nov. 23, 1914, Jan. 9, Feb. 4, 1915.

19. Minutes of the AESA, March 10, 1915; "Woman Suffrage," *Birmingham News,* June 7, 1914; *Birmingham Age-Herald,* Aug. 10, 1915.

20. Letter from Jacobs to Stubbs, Jan. 13, 1914.

21. Bossie O'Brien Hundley Scrapbook, 1914–15, Department of Archives and Manuscripts, Birmingham Public Library, Birmingham, Ala. (hereafter cited as Hundley Scrapbook); Hundley, "Woman Suffrage and the Alabama Legislature," 28.

22. "Mrs. Jacobs' Talk Draws 49 To The Suffrage Fold," *Mobile Register,* Jan. 23, 1914; "Suffrage Speaker Charms Audience With Logic and Her Personality," *Anniston Star,* May 21, 1914; "Mrs. Oscar R. Hundley Leaves Today On a Cross State Trip in a 'Hudson Six' In Interest of Woman Suffrage," *Birmingham Age-Herald,* May 5, 1914; Minutes of the AESA, Feb. 2, 1915.

23. "Mrs. Pattie Ruffner Jacobs, A Southern Woman with a Message," unidentified newspaper clipping, Dec. 21, 1914, Jacobs Scrapbook 2.

24. "Woman Suffrage After All Tends to the Making of the Home, Says Mrs. Jacobs," *Montgomery Advertiser,* Nov. 20, 1914.

25. William H. Chafe in his path-breaking book, *The American Woman: Her Changing Social, Economic, and Political Roles, 1920–1970* (London: Oxford Univ. Press, 1972), wrote of the narrowing of the vision of the twentieth century leaders. Nancy F. Cott in *The Grounding of Modern Feminism* (New Haven: Yale Univ. Press, 1987) develops the theme of this paradox that laid the ground for modern-day feminism.

26. "Pretty, Brainy Suffragette Surprises Those Looking for Woman With Hatchet," "Suffrage Speaker Charms Audience With Logic and Her Personality," unidentified newspaper clipping, Jacobs Scrapbook 2.

27. "Local Woman Paid Tribute by Leslie's Magazine," *Birmingham News,* May 19, 1914; "Suffragists No Less Ardent In Their Home Life Than In Devotion to the Cause," *Birmingham News,* June 6, 1914.

28. *Birmingham Age-Herald,* Jan. 17, 1915.

29. *Birmingham Age-Herald,* Jan. 22, 1915; Hundley, "Woman Suffrage and the Alabama Legislature," 29.

30. *Birmingham Age-Herald,* Jan. 29, 1915; Hundley, "Woman Suffrage and the Alabama Legislature," 28–29, 52; Jemison, "Ladies Become Voters," 55.

31. Hundley, "Woman Suffrage and the Alabama Legislature," 52.

32. *Montgomery Advertiser,* Feb. 6, 1915; *Birmingham Age-Herald,* Feb. 7, 14, 1915.

33. Bossie O'Brien Hundley, "Brief in Behalf of Pending Bills and Constitutional Amendments Seeking to Confer The Rights of Suffrage Upon the Women of Alabama," Birmingham, Ala., May 1, 1915, NAWSA Papers, Manuscript Division, Library of Congress, Washington, D.C.

34. "Equal Suffrage Given First Real Baptism of Fire," "Woman Suffrage Wins Skirmish in Upper House," unidentified newspaper clippings, Hundley Scrapbook.

35. "Woman Suffrage Loses By Welch's Vote in Committee," "Suffragists Have Just Begun The Fight, Says Mrs. B. O'Brien Hundley," Aug. 6, 1915, unidentified newspaper clipping, Hundley Scrapbook.

36. Ibid.

37. "Woman Suffrage Gaining Ground in Legislature," "Suffrage Bill Taken Off Adverse Calendar," unidentified newspaper clippings, Hundley Scrapbook.

38. "Thousands Attend Wetumpka 'Cue,'" unidentified newspaper clipping, August 12, 1915, Hundley Scrapbook.

39. Unidentified newspaper clippings, Hundley Scrapbook.

40. "A Protest Against Woman's Suffrage in Alabama," Alabama Equal Suffrage Association Papers, Alabama Department of Archives and History, Montgomery, Ala..

41. Alabama Equal Suffrage Association, "Reply to the Anonymous 'Protest Against Woman's Suffrage in Alabama,'" Alabama Equal Suffrage Association Papers, Alabama Department of Archives and History, Montgomery, Ala.; Hundley, "Woman Suffrage and the Alabama Legislature," 53; Jemison, "Ladies Become Voters," 56.

42. "Green Sees Light and Turns Back on Woman Suffrage in Alabama," *Birmingham Age-Herald,* Aug. 25, 1915; Hundley, "Woman Suffrage and the Alabama Legislature," 52.

43. *Journal of the House of Representatives of the State of Alabama, Session of 1915,* 2: 2962–64; "Suffragists Are Encouraged Over State Situation," *Birmingham News,* Aug. 26. 1915.

44. "Woman Suffrage Proposals Will Lose Overwhelmingly in Next Legislature, According to Poll by the Age-Herald," *Birmingham Age-Herald,* Oct. 4, 1914.

9. FINAL YEARS OF THE SUFFRAGE DRIVE, 1916–1919

1. Scott and Scott, *One Half the People,* 33–36; Flexner, *Century of Struggle,* 262–75.

2. Harper, ed., *History of Woman Suffrage,* 6: 4–5. This article was written by Pattie Ruffner Jacobs.

3. Harper, ed., *History of Woman Suffrage,* 6: 463.

4. Minutes of the AESA, Oct. 9, 1915, Jan. 15, Feb. 9, 1916; Kraditor, *The Ideas of the Woman Suffrage Movement,* 163–218. Kate Gordon was so opposed to federal action that she actually worked against the ratification of the Nineteenth Amendment after it was passed by Congress in 1919.

5. Minutes of the AESA, Feb. 9–11, 1916, May 7, 1918; Letter from William C. Radcliffe to Carrie Chapman Catt, Jan. 1, 1916, reproduced in the National American Woman Suffrage Association (NAWSA) *Headquarters News Letter,* Jan. 15, 1916, Manuscript Division, Library of Congress, Washington, D.C.

6. Minutes of the AESA, Feb. 9–11, 1916; Minutes of the AESA, President's Report, Feb. 12, 1917.

7. Minutes of the AESA, President's Report, Feb. 12, 1917.

8. Minutes of the AESA, Feb. 9–11, 1916; Minutes of the AESA, President's Report, Feb. 12, 1917; NAWSA *Headquarters News Letter,* April 1916.

9. Minutes of the AESA, Report of the Organization Committee, Feb. 12, 1917; AESA Suffrage School, Alabama Equal Suffrage Association Papers, Alabama Department of Archives and History, Montgomery, Ala.; National League of Women Voters, *The Woman Citizen,* April 1917, Manuscript Division, Library of Congress, Washington, D.C.; *Birmingham News,* Feb. 14, 16, 17, 1917.

10. Report of Editor of Suffrage Bulletin, Feb. 11 to March 4, March 4 to July 28, July 28 to Dec. 9, 1916; and Annual Report of the Editor of the Alabama Suffrage Bulletin, Feb. 11, 1916 to Feb. 2, 1917, Alabama Equal Suffrage Association Papers, Alabama Department of Archives and History, Montgomery, Ala..

11. Minutes of the AESA, July 28, 1916, Fall/Winter 1916–17, Feb. 12–13, 1917.

12. Minutes of the AESA, Feb. 12, Oct. 17, 1917; *The Woman Citizen,* Sept. 22, 1917.

13. Scott and Scott, *One Half the People,* 40–41; Minutes of the AESA, President's Report, Feb. 12, 1917.

14. "Alabama Enters the Federal Suffrage Campaign," *The Suffragist,* May 26, 1917, National Woman's Party Papers, reel 43, 1917, Manuscript Division, Library of Congress, Washington, D.C.; *Birmingham News,* May 13, 20, 1917.

15. *Birmingham News,* May 18, 20, July 1, 1917.

16. Minutes of the AESA, Oct. 17, 1917, Jan. 19, 1918. Other members of the committee appointed by the NWP were Mrs. J. L. Hannon, Mrs. T. L. Hill, Mrs. Pauline Gillam, and Miss Etoile White.

17. Suffrage Resolution Adopted by the Alabama Educational Association, Alabama Equal Suffrage Association Papers, Alabama Department of Archives and History, Montgomery, Ala.; AESA Fortnightly Bulletin of Suffrage News, June 1, Aug. 1, 1917.

18. Scott and Scott, *One Half the People,* 40–41.

19. Harper, ed., *History of Woman Suffrage,* 6: 5; Amelia Worthington, Concerning the Birmingham Equal Suffrage Association, Department of Archives and Manuscripts, Birmingham Public Library, Birmingham, Ala.; AESA Fortnightly Bulletin of Suffrage News, June 15, 1917; *Birmingham News,* March 18, 1917.

20. *Birmingham News,* May 26, 27, 1917; AESA Fortnightly Bulletin of Suffrage News, June 15, 1917.

21. AESA Fortnightly Bulletin of Suffrage News, July 1, Aug. 15, 1917; Worthington, Concerning the Birmingham Equal Suffrage Association; Minutes of the AESA, June 9, 1917; *The Woman Citizen,* Aug. 25, Sept. 8. 1917; Hart, *Social Problems of Alabama,* 19–21; *Birmingham News,* Aug. 15, 1917.

22. AESA Fortnightly Bulletin of Suffrage News, Aug. 15, Sept. 1, Oct. 1, 1917; *The Woman Citizen,* Aug. 25, Sept. 8, Oct. 13, Oct. 20, Dec. 21, 1917.

23. Oscar W. Underwood, "Woman Suffrage," speech in the Senate of the

United States, June 3, 1919, Alabama Department of Archives and History, Montgomery, Ala.; Scott and Scott, *One Half the People*, 41–45.

24. Mrs. Frank Leslie gave a legacy of more than $1 million to the NAWSA in 1917, which was used for a variety of purposes.

25. Harper, ed., *History of Woman Suffrage*, 6: 5–6; Minutes of the AESA, June 9, Oct. 17, 1917; *The Woman Citizen*, Dec. 21, 1918.

26. Oscar W. Underwood to Floyd S. Kincey, June 21, 1919, in Oscar W. Underwood Collection, Southern Historical Collection, University of North Carolina Library, Chapel Hill, N.C.

27. Evans C. Johnson, *Oscar W. Underwood: A Political Biography* (Baton Rouge, La.: Louisiana State Univ. Press, 1980), 279.

28. Minutes of the AESA, Jan. 19, May 7–8, 1918.

29. Minutes of the AESA, Jan. 19, March 18, May 7–9, 1918; *The Woman Citizen*, Dec. 21, 1918.

30. Harper, ed., *History of Woman Suffrage*, 6: 6–7.

31. Ibid., 6: 7–8; "Obligation Owed to Women," *Birmingham Age-Herald*, May 27, 1919; "Ex-Gov. Comer Believes Alabama Legislature Should Ratify Suffrage," *Birmingham Age-Herald*, May 30, 1919; "Women And The Republic," *Mobile Register*, June 5, 1919; "Alabama Should Ratify Suffrage Amendment," *Birmingham Ledger*, June 5, 1919; "Why Suffrage Amendment Will Be Ratified," *Montgomery Journal*, June 10, 1919; Dr. Crumpton's Questionnaire to the Alabama Solons, Alabama Equal Suffrage Association Papers, Alabama Department of Archives and History, Montgomery, Ala.

32. Flexner, *Century of Struggle*, 295–96.

33. *The Woman's Protest*, March 1916, National Association Opposed to Woman Suffrage Papers, Manuscripts Division, Library of Congress, Washington, D.C.; *Selma Times*, Feb. 12, 1916.

34. Marie Bankhead Owen's opposition to suffrage appears to be contradictory to her life-style. She was a strong woman who had a career as the society editor of the *Montgomery Advertiser* and later followed her husband as the archivist of the state archives. But despite her nontraditional actions, she held traditional beliefs about the role and position of women.

35. Harper, ed., *History of Women Suffrage*, 6: 7–9; "Women's Campaign Opposing Suffrage Act Opens Friday," June 22, 1919, "Anti-Ratification League Its Slogan For State Campaign," June 24, 1919, "Lister Hill Eloquently Appeals For State Rights In Opposing Ratification," June 24, 1919, "Legislators Urged To Defeat Susan B. Anthony Amendment," June 25, 1919, "Anti-

Ratification League Of City Has Splendid Meeting," July 3, 1919, "Suffrage Amendment Is Attacked," July 12, 1919, unidentified newspaper clippings, Alabama Woman's Anti-Ratification League Scrapbook, 1919–20, Alabama Department of Archives and History, Montgomery, Ala. (hereafter cited as the Anti-Ratification Scrapbook).

36. "Women's Campaign Opposing Suffrage Act opens Friday," June 22, 1919, unidentified newspaper clipping, Anti-Ratification Scrapbook.

37. "Legislators Urged To Defeat Susan B. Anthony Amendment," June 25, 1919, unidentified newspaper clipping, Anti-Ratification Scrapbook.

38. "Lister Hill Eloquently Appeals For State Rights In Opposing Ratification," June 24, 1919, unidentified newspaper clipping, Anti-Ratification Scrapbook; "The Anti-Ratification League," *Montgomery Advertiser*, June 25, 1919; "Who Will Vote?" *Montgomery Advertiser*, June 9, 1919.

39. "Suffrage Amendment Is Attacked," July 12, 1919, unidentified newspaper clipping, Anti-Ratification Scrapbook.

40. "The Anti-Ratification League," *Montgomery Advertiser*, June 25, 1919.

41. "Suffrage Amendment Is Attacked," July 12, 1919, unidentified newspaper clipping, Anti-Ratification Scrapbook; "Lister Hill Eloquently Appeals for State Rights in Opposing Ratification," June 24, 1919, unidentified newspaper clipping, Anti-Ratification Scrapbook.

42. "Chief Justice Alabama Supreme Court Urges Woman Suffrage," *Huntsville Daily News*, July 25, 1919; "Enfranchisment of Negro Women In Big Numbers Absurd Idea," *Montgomery Advertiser*, June 7, 1919.

43. "Why Suffrage Amendment Will Be Ratified," *Montgomery Journal*, June 10, 1919; "Anti-Suffragists Try To Evade the Issue," *Birmingham Age-Herald*, June 6, 1919.

44. "Alabama Should Ratify Suffrage Amendment," *Birmingham Ledger*, June 5, 1919; "Anti-Suffragists Try To Evade the Issue," *Birmingham Age-Herald*, June 6, 1919.

45. Harper, ed., *History of Woman Suffrage*, 6: 7; "The Leader of the Democratic Party Speaks," *Huntsville Daily News*, July 25, 1919.

46. Harper, ed., *History of Woman Suffrage*, 6: 8; "Secretary of Navy Daniels Urges the Ratification of the Suffrage Amendment," "Patterson Says Votes for Women Very Important," unidentified newspapers clippings, AESA Papers, Alabama Department of Archives and History, Montgomery, Ala.

47. *Journal of the House of Representatives of the State of Alabama, Session of 1919*, 1: 846–47; *Mobile Register*, July 17, 1919.

48. *Journal of the House of Representatives of the State of Alabama Session of 1919*, 1: 846–47; "Gentlemen of the Legislature of Alabama," unidentified newspaper clipping, Anti-Ratification Scrapbook.

49. *Journal of the Senate of the State of Alabama, Session of 1919*, 1: 836–39; *Journal of the House of Representatives of the State of Alabama, Session of 1919*, 2: 2275–77; Harper, ed., *History of Woman Suffrage*, 6: 8–9.

50. McMillan, *Constitutional Development in Alabama*, 352–55.

10. ALABAMA WOMEN IN THE 1920S

1. Scott and Scott, *One Half the People*, 45–46. The states that rejected the amendment were Alabama, Delaware, Florida, Georgia, Louisiana, Maryland, Mississippi, North Carolina, South Carolina, and Virginia. The southern states that voted for the amendment were Arkansas, Kentucky, Texas, and Tennessee.

2. "Women Voters Make Ready for Victory Parade to be Held in City on Saturday," *Birmingham Age-Herald*, Sept. 2, 1920; *Birmingham News*, Sept. 4, 1920; *The Woman Citizen*, Oct. 2, 1920, 487.

3. Mary Swenson Miller, "Lobbyist for the People: The League of Women Voters of Alabama, 1920–1975" (M.A. thesis, Auburn University, 1978), 14–17.

4. *The Woman Citizen*, Oct. 30, 1920, 618, April 9, 1921, 1158; Miller, "Lobbyist for the People," 17–18. See also assorted newspaper clippings in a scrapbook compiled by Mrs. A. J. Bowron, Birmingham, Ala., 1919–20, which is deposited in the Department of Archives and Manuscripts at the Birmingham Public Library, Birmingham, Ala. (hereafter cited as Bowron Scrapbook).

5. *The Woman Citizen*, Oct. 30, 1920, 618; Miller, "Lobbyist for the People," 22–23. Jacobs anticipated the power of women's votes when she published a list of the U.S. senators and representatives from Alabama as well as the state legislators with their officially recorded vote on suffrage. This list was widely publicized and the men became aware of the possible political consequences.

6. Pattie R. Jacobs to Governor Thomas Kilby, Nov. 7, 1920, folder 91A, Alabama League of Women Voters Papers, Special Collections and Archives, Auburn University Library, Auburn, Ala.

7. *The Woman Citizen*, Nov. 6, 1920, 646; "Alabama's Women Register to Vote for the First Time in History of South," *Birmingham Age-Herald*, Aug. 28,

1920; "23,000 Women Qualify for Participation in the General Election," unidentified newspaper clipping, Bowron Scrapbook; McMillan, *Constitutional Development in Alabama*, 355.

8. *The Woman Citizen*, Oct. 30, 1920, 618, and April 9, 1921, 1158; Miller, "Lobbyist for the People," 25–27.

9. Resolutions Adopted by the Alabama League of Women Voters in Session in Montgomery, April 1920, Bowron Scrapbook; Resolutions Adopted by the ALWV, First Annual Convention, Birmingham, April 25–26, 1921, Bowron Scrapbook; Miller, "Lobbyist for the People," 36–37; Alice Nelson Doyle, *Compendium of Alabama Laws Relating to Women and Children* (Alabama League of Women Voters, 1921); Women's Bureau, U.S. Department of Labor, *Women in Alabama Industries* (Washington: Government Printing Office, 1924). Doyle, a lawyer herself, was secretary to the Alabama Supreme Court judges and acted as the league's lawyer.

10. Miller, "Lobbyist for the People," 29, 38; Alabama League of Women Voters, *News Bulletin*, Feb. 26, 1923, series 2, box 8, National League of Women Voters Records, Manuscript Division, Library of Congress, Washington, D.C.; "The Woman Voter," *Montgomery Journal*, Feb. 25, 1923.

11. Miller, "Lobbyist for the People," 37.

12. Resolutions of the ALWV, 1920 and 1921, National League of Women Voters Records, Manuscript Division, Library of Congress, Washington, D.C.

13. *Montgomery Journal*, Oct. 23, 25, 28, Nov. 8, Nov. 13, Dec. 18, 1921; Miller, "Lobbyist for the People," 29–31.

14. "The Woman Voter," *Montgomery Journal*, Nov. 27, 1921; "The Legislative Council of Alabama Women," series 2, box 701, NLWV Records, Manuscript Division, Library of Congress, Washington, D.C.; Mildred White Wells, *History of the Alabama Federation of Women's Clubs* (Montgomery: Paragon Press, 1968), 2: 89.

15. "Legislative Council of Alabama," series 2, box 701, NLWV Records; Mollie Dowd to Miss Harris, March 12, 1927, series 2, box 74, NLWV Records, Manuscripts Division, Library of Congress, Washington, D.C.; Miller, "Lobbyist for the People," 35, 61; Anne Firor Scott, "After Suffrage: Southern Women in the Twenties," *Journal of Southern History* 30 (Aug. 1964): 303.

16. "The Woman in Politics," *Montgomery Journal*, Aug. 20, 1922; *Birmingham Age-Herald*, Jan. 22, 1922; Miller, "Lobbyist for the People," 46; "Selma Woman Blazed Trail for Women in State Politics," unidentified newspaper clipping, Marie Jemison Stokes Papers, Department of Archives and Manuscripts, Birmingham Public Library, Birmingham, Ala.

17. Hart, *Social Problems of Alabama*, 43–71.

18. "Alabama Women and Convict Leasing," *The Woman Citizen*, June 19, 1923, 19; Moore, *History of Alabama*, 816; "The Woman Voter," *Montgomery Journal*, Jan. 10, and Jan. 21, 1923.

19. "Alabama Women and Convict Leasing," 19; *Birmingham Age-Herald*, June 3, 1923; Miller, "Lobbyist for the People," 40–41.

20. Moore, *History of Alabama*, 816; *Montgomery Journal*, July 18, July 20, Aug. 3, Sept. 13, 1923; Miller, "Lobbyist for the People," 41–42.

21. Chafe, *The American Woman*, 25–47; Report of Eleanor Laird, NLWV, Jan. 4–8, 1923, Montgomery, Ala., NLWV Records, 1922–24, series 2, box 15; "Alabama Get Out the Vote," NLWV Records, 1924–26, series 2, box 46; "Alabama League of Women Voters," Bowron Scrapbook. The ALWV was not reorganized until 1950.

22. Flynt and Rikard, "Pattie Ruffner Jacobs: Alabama Suffragist," 14; Biographical Note, Introduction to the Pattie Ruffner Jacobs Papers, Department of Archives and Manuscripts, Birmingham Public Library, Birmingham, Ala.

23. Scott, *The Southern Lady from Pedestal to Politics*, 4–21, 135–63.

24. Daniel Scott Smith, "Family Limitation, Sexual Control, and Domestic Feminism in Victorian America," *Feminist Studies* 1 (Winter–Spring 1972): 40–57. Smith first used the phrase to describe a growing autonomy that he perceived nineteenth-century women developing within the home, most notably by limiting sexual intercourse with their husbands, but Smith's phrase has wider application.

BIBLIOGRAPHY

MANUSCRIPT COLLECTIONS

Alabama Department of Archives and History, Montgomery, Alabama

Alabama Child Welfare Department
  Alabama Childhood, 1921–25
Alabama Equal Suffrage Association Papers
  Minutes, 1912–18
  Correspondence
Alabama Federation of Women's Clubs
  Year Book, 1910–11
Alabama Woman's Anti-Ratification League Scrapbook, 1919–20
Alabama Woman's Christian Temperance Union Papers
  Alabama White Ribbon, 1903–20
  Records of Annual Meetings, 1884 and 1915
  Scrapbook
Birmingham Equal Suffrage Association Papers
Ellen Stephens Hildreth Scrapbook
Montgomery *Colored Alabamian*, 1913–15
Southern Women's League for the Rejection of the Anthony Amendment
  Papers

Special Collections and Archives, Auburn University Library, Auburn, Alabama

Alabama League of Women Voters Papers
Auburn Equal Suffrage Association Papers
Alabama Woman's Christian Temperance Union
    Report of the Thirty-first Annual Convention, 1915

Department of Archives and Manuscripts, Birmingham Public Library, Birmingham, Alabama

"History of the Alabama Boys Industrial School," manuscript by David M.
    Weakley
Alabama Woman's Anti-Ratification League Papers
Amaranth Club Papers
Birmingham Equal Suffrage Association Papers
Mrs. A. J. Bowron Scrapbook
Carrie Chapman Catt Papers
Bossie O'Brien Hundley Scrapbook, 1914–15
Pattie Ruffner Jacobs Papers
League of Women Voters of Greater Birmingham Papers
Marie Jemison Stokes Papers
Mercy Home Papers
    Annual Reports, 1892–1920
    Minutes of the Board of Directors, 1892–1920

Manuscripts Division, Library of Congress, Washington, D.C.

Booker T. Washington Papers
Congressional Union for Woman Suffrage Papers
    The Suffragist, 1914–19
National American Woman Suffrage Association Papers
    Headquarters News Letter, 1916–17
    The Woman's Journal and Suffrage News, 1914–18
    Correspondence

National Association Opposed to Woman Suffrage Papers
  The Woman's Protest
National League of Women Voters Records
  The Woman Citizen, 1917–25
  Correspondence, 1919–28
Mary Church Terrell Papers
Madeline McDowell Breckenridge Papers
Nannie Helen Burroughs Papers
National Woman's Party Papers
  The Suffragist, 1914–19
  Correspondence 1914–23
Southern States Woman Suffrage Conference Papers
  New Southern Citizen, 1915–17
Women's Joint Congressional Committee Papers

National Woman's Christian Temperance Union Library, Evanston, Illinois

  National Woman's Christian Temperance Union Papers
    Minutes of Annual Meetings, 1884–1920
    The Union Signal, 1890–1920

Schlesinger Library, Radcliffe College, Cambridge, Massachusetts

  Amelia Worthington Fisk, Oral Interview, June 1975
  Sue Shelton White Papers
  Nellie Nugent Sommerville Papers

Washington Collection, Tuskegee University Library, Tuskegee, Alabama

  Alabama Federation of Colored Women's Clubs Papers
    Records of Annual Meetings, 1907, 1913, 1916, 1919, 1922, 1926
  Adella Hunt Logan Papers
  Margaret Murray Washington Papers

National Association of Colored Women Papers
Records of Annual Meetings, 1908, 1914, 1916
National Association Notes, 1904–20
Tuskegee Student, 1908–20

Rare Book Room, University of Alabama Library, Tuscaloosa,
Alabama

Proceedings of the Woman's Christian Temperance Union of the State of
Alabama, 1884

Southern Historical Collection, University of North Carolina Library,
Chapel Hill, North Carolina

Edgar Gardner Murphy Papers
Oscar W. Underwood Papers

UNPUBLISHED THESES, DISSERTATIONS, AND PAPERS

Allen, Lee Norcross. "The Woman Suffrage Movement in Alabama." M.A.
thesis, Alabama Polytechnic Institute, 1949.
Bigelow, Martha Carolyn Mitchell. "Birmingham: Biography of a City of the
New South." Ph.D. diss., University of Chicago, 1946.
Camhi, Jane Jerome. "Women against Women: American Antisuffragism
1880–1920." Ph.D. diss., Tufts University, 1973.
Flynt, J. Wayne, and Marlene Hunt Rikard. "Pattie Ruffner Jacobs: Alabama
Suffragist." Paper delivered at the First Southern Conference on Women's
History, June 1988.
Going, Allen Johnston. "The Governorship of B. B. Comer." M.A. thesis,
University of Alabama, 1940.
Hamilton, Tullia Brown. "The National Association of Colored Women, 1896–
1920." Ph.D. diss., Emory University, 1978.
Harris, David Alan. "Racists and Reformers: A Study of Progressivism in
Alabama, 1896–1911." Ph.D. diss., University of North Carolina, 1967.

Hine, Darlene Clark. "Rape and the Inner Lives of Southern Black Women: Thoughts on the Culture of Dissemblance." Manuscript in possession of the author.

Jackson, Emma Louisa Meyer. "Petticoat Politics: Political Activism among Texas Women in the 1920s." Ph.D. diss., University of Texas, 1980.

Jenkins, Maude T. "The History of the Black Women's Club Movement in America." Ph.D. diss., Columbia Teacher's College, 1984.

Lerner, Elinor. "Immigrant and Working Class Involvement in the New York City Woman Suffrage Movement, 1905–1917: A Study in Progressive Era Politics." Ph.D. diss., University of California, Berkeley, 1981.

Lipscomb, Susan Dowdell. "The History of the Prohibition Movement in the State of Alabama." M.A. thesis, Alabama Polytechnic Institute, 1931.

Lumpkin, John Irvin. "The Equal Suffrage Movement in Alabama, 1910–1920." M.A. thesis, University of Alabama, 1949.

Miller, Mary Swenson. "Lobbyist for the People: The League of Women Voters of Alabama, 1920–1975." M.A. thesis, Auburn University, 1978.

Morrison, Glenda E. "Women's Participation in the 1928 Presidential Campaign." Ph.D. diss., University of Kansas, 1978.

Rausch, Eileen R. " 'Let Ohio Women Vote:' The Years to Victory, 1900–1920." Ph.D. diss., University of Notre Dame, 1984.

Spiers, Patricia L. "The Woman Suffrage Movement in New Orleans." M.A. thesis, Southern Louisiana College, 1965.

Terborg-Penn, Rosalyn M. "Afro-Americans in the Struggle for Woman Suffrage." Ph.D. diss., Howard University, 1977.

Wheeler, Marjorie Spruill. "Southern Suffragists and the 'Negro Problem.' " Paper presented at the First Southern Conference on Women's History, June 1988.

ORGANIZATIONAL PUBLICATIONS AND RECORDS

Alabama Educational Association. *Official Proceedings*, 1899

Journal of the House of Representatives of the State of Alabama, 1915 and 1919.

Journal of the Senate of the State of Alabama, 1915 and 1919

Official Proceedings of the Constitutional Convention of the State of Alabama, May 21, 1901, to September 3, 1901. 3 vols. Wetumpka, Ala.: Wetumpka Printing Company, 1940.

Women's Bureau, U.S. Department of Labor. *Women in Alabama Industries*. Washington, D.C.: Government Printing Office, 1924.

NEWSPAPERS AND MAGAZINES

Anniston Star, May 21, 1914
Birmingham Age-Herald, 1912–23
Birmingham Ledger, 1912–19
Birmingham Magazine, Oct. 1915, Jan. 1916
Birmingham News, 1903–17
The Crisis, May 1911, June 1912, Sept. 1912, Aug. 1915
Huntsville Daily News, July 25, 1919
Huntsville Mercury-Banner, Feb. 4, 5, 1914
Huntsville Republican, June 15, 1901
Huntsville Tribune, Feb. 2, 1902
Journal of the Birmingham Historical Society, Jan. 1961, Jan. 1978, July 1980
Mobile Register, Nov. 1907, Jan. 23, 1914, June–July 1919
Montgomery Advertiser, 1901–19
Montgomery Journal, 1919–23
Selma Times, Feb. 12, 1916

BOOKS

Avery, Mary Johnston. *She Heard With Her Heart*. Birmingham, Ala.: Birmingham Publishing Co., 1944.
Bailey, Hugh C. *Edgar Gardner Murphy: Gentle Progressive*. Coral Gables, Fla.: Univ. of Miami Press, 1968.
——— . *Liberalism in the New South: Southern Social Reformers and the Progressive Movement*. Coral Gables, Fla.: Univ. of Miami Press, 1969.
Beeton, Beverly. *Women Vote in the West: The Woman Suffrage Movement 1869–1986*. New York: Garland Publishing, 1986.
Blair, Karen J. *The Clubwoman as Feminist: True Womanhood Redefined, 1868–1914*. New York: Holmes and Meier Publishers, 1980.
Bordin, Ruth. *Woman and Temperance: The Quest for Power and Liberty, 1873–1900*. Philadelphia: Temple Univ. Press, 1981.

Boucher, Ann. *Alabama Women: Roles and Rebels*. Troy, Ala.: Troy State Univ. Press, 1978.

Buechler, Steven M. *The Transformation of the Woman Suffrage Movement: The Case of Illinois, 1850–1920*. New Brunswick, N.J.: Rutgers Univ. Press, 1986.

Catt, Carrie Chapman, and Nettie Rogers Shuler. *Woman Suffrage and Politics: The Inner Story of the Suffrage Movement*. Seattle: Univ. of Washington Press, 1923.

Chafe, William H. *The American Woman: Her Changing Social, Economic, and Political Roles, 1920–1970*. London: Oxford Univ. Press, 1972.

Chambers, John Whiteclay, II. *The Tyranny of Change: America in the Progressive Era, 1900–1917*. New York: St. Martin's Press, 1980.

Clark, Willis G. *History of Education in Alabama 1702–1889*. Washington, D.C.: Government Printing Office, 1889.

Clarke, Ida Clyde. *American Women and the World War*. New York: D. Appleton and Co., 1918.

——— . *Women of Today*. New York: Women of Today Press, 1928.

Clinton, Catherine. *The Other Civil War: American Women in the Nineteenth Century*. New York: Hill and Wang, 1984.

Clopper, Edward N. *Child Welfare in Alabama*. New York: National Child Labor Committee, 1918.

Cooper, Anna Julia. *A Voice from the South*. 1892. Reprint. New York: Negro Universities Press, 1969.

Cott, Nancy F. *The Grounding of Modern Feminism*. New Haven: Yale Univ. Press, 1987.

Craighead, Lura Harris. *History of the Alabama Federation of Women's Clubs*. Vol. 1, *1895–1918*. Montgomery, Ala.: Paragon Press, 1936.

Croly, Jennie June. *The History of the Woman's Club Movement in America*. New York: Henry G. Allen, 1898.

Crumpton, W. B. *A Story: How Alabama Became Dry*. Montgomery, Ala.: Paragon Press, 1925.

Dabney, Virginius. *Liberalism in the South*. Chapel Hill: Univ. of North Carolina Press, 1932.

Davidson, Elizabeth H. *Child Labor Legislation in the Southern Textile States*. Chapel Hill: Univ. of North Carolina Press, 1939.

Davis, Allen F. *Spearheads for Reform: The Social Settlement and the Progressive Movement*. New York: Oxford Univ. Press, 1967.

Doyle, Alice Nelson. *Compendium of Alabama Laws Relating to Women and Chil-*

dren. Alabama League of Women Voters, 1921.

DuBois, Ellen Carol. *Feminism and Suffrage: The Emergence of an Independent Women's Movement in America, 1848–1869*. Ithaca, N.Y.: Cornell Univ. Press, 1978.

Epstein, Barbara Leslie. *The Politics of Domesticity: Women Evangelism, and Temperance in Nineteenth Century America*. Middletown, Conn.: Wesleyan Univ. Press, 1981.

Felton, Rebecca Latimer. *Country Life in Georgia*. Atlanta: Index Printing Co., 1919.

Flexner, Eleanor. *Century of Struggle: The Woman's Rights Movement in the United States*. Reprint. New York: Atheneum, 1973.

Fuller, Paul E. *Laura Clay and the Woman's Rights Movement*. Lexington: Univ. of Kentucky Press, 1975.

Gibson, J. W., and W. H. Crogman. *Progress of a Race*. Reprint. Miami, Fla.: Mnemosyne Publishing, 1969.

Giddings, Paula. *When and Where I Enter: The Impact of Black Women on Race and Sex in America*. New York: William Morrow, 1984.

Going, Allen Johnston. *Bourbon Democracy in Alabama, 1874–1890*. University, Ala.: Univ. of Alabama Press, 1951.

Gordon, Elizabeth Putnam. *Women Torch-Bearers: The Story of the Woman's Christian Temperance Union*. Evanston, Ill.: WCTU Publishing House, 1924.

Gordon, Felice D. *After Winning: The Legacy of the New Jersey Suffragists, 1920–1947*. New Brunswick, N.J.: Rutgers Univ. Press, 1986.

Grantham, Dewey W. *Southern Progressivism: The Reconciliation of Progress and Tradition*. Knoxville: Univ. of Tennessee Press, 1983.

Griffith, Lucille. *Alabama College 1896–1969*. Montevallo, Ala.: Univ. of Montevallo, 1969.

Grimes, Alan P. *The Puritan Ethic and Woman Suffrage*. New York: Oxford Univ. Press, 1967.

Hackney, Sheldon. *Populism to Progressivism in Alabama*. Princeton: Princeton Univ. Press, 1969.

Hall, Jacquelyn Dowd, et al. *Like a Family: The Making of a Southern Cotton Mill World*. Chapel Hill: Univ. of North Carolina Press, 1987.

Hammond, L. H. *Southern Women and Racial Adjustment*. The Trustees of the John S. Slater Fund, Occasional Papers, no. 19. 1917.

Harlan, Louis R., ed. *The Booker T. Washington Papers*. Urbana, Ill.: Univ. of Illinois Press, 1972.

Harris, Carl V. *Political Power in Birmingham, 1871–1921*. Knoxville: Univ. of

Tennessee Press, 1977.

Hart, Hastings H. *Social Problems of Alabama*. New York: Russell Sage Foundation, 1918.

Hartley, Sharon, and Rosalyn Terborg-Penn. *The Afro-American Woman: Struggles and Images*. Port Washington, N.Y.: Kennikat Press, 1978.

Haskin, Sara Estelle. *Women and Missions*. Nashville, Tenn.: Publishing House of the M. E. Church, South, 1920.

Hawks, Joanne V., and Shelia L. Skemp, eds. *Sex, Race and the Role of Women in the South*. Jackson: Univ. of Mississippi Press, 1983.

Irwin, Inez Haynes. *The Story of the Woman's Party*. New York: Harcourt Brace, 1921.

Johnson, Evans C. *Oscar W. Underwood: A Political Biography*. Baton Rouge, La.: Louisiana State Univ. Press, 1980.

Jones, Herschel H. *Child Labor in Alabama*. Photographs by Lewis W. Hine. Birmingham, Ala.: Alabama Child Labor Committee, 1915.

Kearney, Belle. *A Slaveholder's Daughter*. Reprint. New York: Negro Universities Press, 1969.

Kirby, Jack Temple. *Darkness at the Dawning: Race and Reform in the Progressive South*. Philadephia: J.B. Lippincott, 1972.

Kousser, J. Morgan. *The Shaping of Southern Politics: Suffrage Restriction and the Establishment of the One-Party South, 1880–1910*. New Haven: Yale Univ. Press, 1974.

Kraditor, Aileen S. *The Ideas of the Woman Suffrage Movement, 1890–1920*. New York: Columbia Univ. Press, 1965.

———. *Up from the Pedestal: Selected Writings in the History of American Feminism*. Chicago: Quadrangle Books, 1968.

Lemons, J. Stanley. *The Woman Citizen: Social Feminism in the 1920s*. Urbana, Ill.: Univ. of Illinois Press, 1973.

Lerner, Gerda, ed. *Black Women in White America: A Documentary History*. New York: Pantheon Books, 1972.

Loewenberg, Bert James, and Ruth Bogin. *Black Women in Nineteenth-Century American Life*. University Park, Penn.: Pennsylvania State Univ. Press, 1976.

Lyon, Ralph M. *A History of Livingston University, 1835–1963*. Livingston, Ala., 1976.

Lunardini, Christine A. *From Equal Suffrage to Equal Rights: Alice Paul and the National Woman's Party, 1910–1928*. New York: New York Univ. Press, 1986.

McMillan, Malcolm Cook. *Constitutional Development in Alabama, 1798–1901:*

A Study in Politics, the Negro, and Sectionalism. Spartanburg, S.C.: Reprint Company, 1978.

Martin, Theodora Penny. *The Sound of Our Own Voices: Women's Study Clubs 1860–1910.* Boston: Beacon Press, 1987.

Martin, William Joseph. *Has the State a Soul? A Discussion of the Present Methods of Employing Convicts.* N.p., 1922.

Mason, Lucy Randolph. *Standards for Workers in Southern Industry.* N.p.: National Consumers' League, 1931.

Moore, Albert Burton. *History of Alabama.* University, Ala.: University Supply Store, 1934.

Morgan, David. *Suffragists and Democrats.* East Lansing, Mich.: Michigan State Univ. Press, 1972.

Murphy, Edgar Gardner. *Problems of the Present South.* New York: Macmillan, 1904.

Neverdon-Morton, Cynthia. *Afro-American Women of the South and the Advancement of the Race, 1895–1925.* Knoxville: Univ. of Tennessee Press, 1989.

Nichols, Carole. *Votes and More for Women: Suffrage and After in Connecticut.* New York: Haworth Press, 1983.

Nichols, J. L., and William H. Crogman, eds. *Progress of a Race.* Naperville, Ill.: J.L. Nichols and Co., 1920.

Owen, Thomas McAdory. *History of Alabama and Dictionary of Alabama Biography.* Spartanburg, S.C.: Reprint Company, 1987.

Pannell, Anne Gary, and Dorothea E. Wyatt. *Julia S. Tutwiler and Social Progress in Alabama.* Tuscaloosa: Univ. of Alabama Press, 1961.

Paulson, Ross Evans. *Women's Suffrage and Prohibition: A Comparative Study in Equality and Social Control.* Glenview, Ill.: Scott, Foresman and Co., 1973.

Robbins, Mary LaFayette. *Alabama Women in Literature.* Selma: Selma Printing Co., 1895.

Scott, Anne Firor. *The Southern Lady from Pedestal to Politics, 1830–1930.* Chicago: Univ. of Chicago Press, 1970.

Scott, Anne F., and Andrew M. Scott. *One Half the People: The Fight for Woman Suffrage.* Philadelphia: J.B. Lippincott, 1975.

Sellers, James Benson. *History of the University of Alabama.* University, Ala.: Univ. of Alabama Press, 1953

———. *The Prohibition Movement in Alabama, 1702 to 1943.* Chapel Hill: Univ. of North Carolina Press, 1943.

Stanton, Elizabeth Cady, Susan B. Anthony, Matilda Joslyn Gage, and Ida

Husted Harper, eds. *History of Woman Suffrage.* 6 vols. Various publishers, 1881–1922.

Summersell, Charles Grayson. *Alabama History for Schools.* Montgomery: Viewpoint Publications, 1970.

Talmadge, John E. *Rebecca Latimer Felton: Nine Stormy Decades.* Athens, Ga.: Univ. of Georgia Press, 1960.

Tatum, Noreen Dunn. *A Crown of Service: A Story of Women's Work in the Methodist Episcopal Church, South, from 1878–1940.* Nashville: Parthenon Press, 1960.

Taylor, A. Elizabeth. *The Woman Suffrage Movement in Tennessee.* New York: Bookman Associates, 1957.

Tindall, George Brown. *The Emergence of the New South, 1913–1945.* Baton Rouge: Louisiana State Univ. Press, 1967.

Tyler, Helen E. *Where Prayer and Purpose Meet: 1874—The WCTU Story— 1949.* Evanston, Ill.: Signal Press, 1949.

Wells, Mildred White. *History of the Alabama Federation of Women's Clubs.* Vol. 2, *1917–1968.* Montgomery, Ala.: Paragon Press, 1968.

Willard, Frances E. *Woman and Temperance.* Reprint. New York: Arno Press, 1972.

Woloch, Nancy. *Women and the American Experience.* New York: Alfred A. Knopf, 1984.

Woodward, C. Vann. *The Origins of the New South, 1877–1913.* Baton Rouge: Louisiana State Univ. Press, 1951.

ARTICLES

Alexander, Adele Logan. "How I Discovered My Grandmother." *Ms.* (Nov. 1983): 29–33.

———. "Private Consequences of a Public Controversy: Grandmother, Grandfather, W.E.B. Du Bois and Booker T. Washington." *The Crisis* 90 (Feb. 1983): 8–11.

Ashby, Irene M. "The Fight Against Child Labor in Alabama." *American Federationist* 8 (1901): 150–57.

Blocker, Jack S. "Separate Paths: Suffragists and the Women's Temperance Crusade." *Signs* 10 (Spring 1985): 460–76.

Brownell, Blaine A. "Birmingham, Alabama: New South City in the 1920s." *Journal of Southern History* 38 (Feb. 1972): 21–48.

Bush, Mrs. L. B. "A Decade of Progress in Alabama." *Journal of Social Forces* 2 (May 1924): 539–45.

Carver, Joan S. "First League of Women Voters in Florida: Its Troubled History." *Florida Historical Quarterly* 63 (April 1985): 383–405.

Cott, Nancy F. "Feminist Politics in the 1920s: The National Woman's Party." *Journal of American History* 71 (June 1984): 43–68.

Delpar, Helen. "Coeds and the 'Lords of Creation': Women Students at the University of Alabama, 1893–1930." *Alabama Review* 42 (October 1989): 292–312.

DuBois, Ellen. "The Radicalism of the Woman Suffrage Movement: Notes Toward the Reconstruction of Nineteenth-Century Feminism." *Feminist Studies* 3 (Fall 1975): 63–71.

———. "Working Women, Class Relations, and Suffrage Militance: Harriot Stanton Blatch and the New York Woman Suffrage Movement, 1894–1909." *Journal of American History* 74 (June 1987): 34–58.

Du Bois, W. E. B. "Votes for Women: A Symposium of Leading Thinkers of Colored America." *The Crisis* 8 (Aug. 1914): 176–92.

Freedman, Estelle B. "The New Woman: Changing Views of Women in the 1920s." *Journal of American History* 61 (Sept. 1974): 372–93.

Goodrich, Gillian. "Romance and Reality: The Birmingham Suffragists 1892–1920." *Journal of the Birmingham Historical Society* 5 (Jan. 1978): 5–20.

Goodwyn, Mrs. A. T. "What Women's Clubs Have Done for Education." *Proceedings of the Alabama Educational Association* 3 (1899): 31–33.

Hundley, Mrs. Oscar R.. "Woman Suffrage and the Alabama Legislature." *Birmingham Magazine* (Oct. 1915): 28–29, 52–54.

———. "Woman Suffrage at the Alabama State Fair." *Birmingham Magazine* (Jan. 1916): 20–21.

———. "Woman Suffrage." *Birmingham Magazine* (Feb. 1916): 23–24.

Jemison, Marie Stokes. "Ladies Become Voters." *Southern Exposure* 3 (Spring 1979): 48–59.

Johnson, Kenneth R. "Kate Gordon and the Woman-Suffrage Movement in the South." *Journal of Southern History* 38 (Aug. 1972): 365–92.

Jones, Mrs. Joseph Bevard. "The Alabama Federation and the Child Welfare Work." *Alabama Childhood* 1 (July–Sept. 1921): 34–38.

LaMonte, Edward S. "The Mercy Home and Private Charity in Early Birmingham." *Journal of the Birmingham Historical Society* 5 (Jan. 1978): 5–15.

Logan, Adella Hunt. "Colored Women as Voters." *The Crisis* 4 (Sept. 1912): 242–43.

——. "Woman Suffrage." *The Colored American Magazine* (Sept. 9, 1905): 487–89.

Morrissette, Kate Hutcheson. "Traveling Libraries in Alabama." *Sewanee Review* 7 (July 19, 1898): 345–48.

Murdock, Mrs. W. L. "Child Labor Reform in Alabama." *Child Labor Bulletin* 3 (May 1914–Feb. 1915): 82–84.

——. "Conditions of Child Employing Industries in the South." *Child Labor Bulletin* 2 (May 1913–Feb. 1914): 124–28.

Pickens, William. "The Woman Voter Hits the Color Line." *The Nation* 3 (Oct. 6, 1920): 372–73.

Rainer, Olivia. "The Early History of Music Clubs of Troy, Alabama." *Alabama Historical Quarterly* 24 (Spring 1962): 68–96.

Scott, Anne Firor. "After Suffrage: Southern Women in the Twenties." *Journal of Southern History* 30 (Aug. 1964): 298–318.

——. "The 'New Woman' in the New South." *South Atlantic Quarterly* 65 (Autumn 1962): 473–83.

Smith, Daniel Scott. "Family Limitation, Sexual Control, and Domestic Feminism in Victorian America." *Feminist Studies* 1 (Winter–Spring 1972): 40–57.

Strom, Sharon Hartman. "Leadership and Tactics in the American Woman Suffrage Movement." *Journal of American History* 62 (Sept. 1975): 296–315.

Swenson, Mary E. "To Uplift a State and Nation: The Formative Years of the Alabama League of Women Voters, 1920–1921." *Alabama Historical Quarterly* 37 (Summer 1975): 115–35.

Taylor, A. Elizabeth. "The Woman Suffrage Movement in Arkansas." *Arkansas Historical Quarterly* 15 (Spring 1956): 17–52.

——. "The Woman Suffrage Movement in Florida." *Florida Historical Quarterly* 36 (July 1957): 42–60.

——. "The Last Phase of the Woman Suffrage Movement in Georgia." *Georgia Historical Quarterly* 43 (March 1959): 11–28.

——. "The Woman Suffrage Movement in Mississippi, 1890–1920." *Journal of Mississippi History* 30 (Feb. 1968): 1–34.

——. "The Woman Suffrage Movement in North Carolina, Part I." *North Carolina Historical Review* 38 (Jan. 1961): 45–62.

——. "The Woman Suffrage Movement in Texas." *Journal of Southern History* 17 (May 1951): 194–215.

Terrell, Mary Church. "What Role is the Educated Negro Women to Play in the Uplifting of Her Race." In *Twentieth Century Negro Literature*, ed. D. W. Clup. Reprint. Miami, Fla.: Mnemosyne Publishing, 1969.

Washington, Mrs. Booker T. "Club Work among Negro Women." In *Progress of a Race,* ed. J. L. Nichols and William H. Crogman, 177–209. Naperville, Ill.: J. L. Nichols, 1920.

———. "The Tuskegee Woman's Club." *The Southern Workman* (Aug. 1920): 365–69.

Williams, Fannie Barrier. "The Club Movement among Colored Women of America." In *A New Negro for a New Century,* by Booker T. Washington, 107–281. Reprint. Miami, Fla.: Mnemosyne Publishing, 1969.

———. "Club Movement among Negro Women." In *Progress of a Race,* ed. J. W. Gibson and W. H. Crogman, 197–281. Reprint. Miami, Fla.: Mnemosyne Publishing, 1969.

Worthman, Paul B. "Working Class Mobility in Birmingham, Alabama, 1880–1914." In *Anonymous Americans: Exploration in Nineteenth-Century Social History,* ed. Tamara K. Hareven, 172–213. Englewood Cliffs, N.J.: Prentice-Hall, 1971.

Wyker, Mrs. J. D. "What Women's Clubs Can Do for Education." *Proceedings of the Alabama Educational Association* 3 (1899): 34–37.

INDEX

Ruffin, Josephine St. Pierre, 70, 72
Russell Sage Foundation, 51, 54, 60, 83, 213

St. John's Episcopal Church, 95
Sayre Secret Ballot Act, 129
Scott, Anne Firor, 13, 216
Second Mississippi Plan, 123
Sellers, James B., 17
Selma, 7, 14, 19, 21, 35, 43, 45, 60, 72, 135, 136, 137, 171, 178, 180, 195, 212
Selma Times, 140
Seneca Falls Convention, 119, 204
Severance, Caroline, 42
Shafroth, John, 188
Shaw, Anna Howard, 124, 136, 143, 149, 155, 158, 160, 167, 171, 174, 186
Sheppard-Towner Act, 209–10, 214
Sibert, Marietta, 22
Snell, Mrs. H. H., 160
Sorosis, 42
Southern Association of College Women, 68
Southern States Woman Suffrage Conference, 151, 177, 184
Spencer, Martha L., 1, 10, 15, 26, 30, 94, 205, 217–18
Stanton, Elizabeth Cady, 120, 150, 187
Stone, Lucy, 120, 122, 150
Suffrage, 6, 9, 16, 17–18, 43, 48; black women, 83–88
Swift, Wiley H., 115

Talladega College, 19
Taylor, Alberta Chapman, 126, 153
Temperance education, 16, 20–21, 76
Terrell, Mary Church, 70, 71
Thigpen, Mrs. Charles, 196
Thomas, E. Perry, 195–97

Thurman, Lucy, 20
Thursday Literary Club, 43
Trax, Lola C., 179–80
Treaty of Versailles, 188
Tuscaloosa, 10, 14, 15, 23, 72, 99, 138, 152, 180, 188
Tuscaloosa Times, 140
Tuskegee, 7, 69, 72, 74
Tuskegee Institute, 70, 72, 74, 75, 78, 80, 81
Tuskegee Mother's Club, 77–80
Tuskegee Negro Conference, 77
Tuskegee Woman's Club, 72, 74, 75, 77, 85
Tutwiler, Henry, 23
Tutwiler, Julia S., 10, 23–25, 42, 61, 62, 64, 96, 128, 167, 213, 217
Tyson, John R., 195, 197

Underwood, Oscar W., 157, 158, 181, 188–89
United Daughters of the Confederacy, 68, 167, 185
University of Alabama, 42, 48, 53, 62, 63, 64, 217
University scholarships for women, 62–65

Verbena, 118, 125, 126
Voice from the South, 71

Washington, Booker T., 7, 20, 70, 72, 77
Washington, Josephine, 82
Washington, Margaret Murry, 1, 20, 69–70, 72–74, 76, 77, 81, 82, 85, 90, 217
Weakley, David M., 51
Weakley, S. D., 201
Weisel, Annie K., 33
Wetumpka, 20, 76